EARLY CHILDHOOD PROGRAMS

AND THE PUBLIC SCHOOLS:

BETWEEN PROMISE AND PRACTICE

EARLY CHILDHOOD PROGRAMS AND THE PUBLIC SCHOOLS

Between Promise and Practice

ANNE MITCHELL
Bank Street College of Education

MICHELLE SELIGSON
FERN MARX
Wellesley College Center for Research on Women

Auburn House
New York · Westport, CT · London

Library of Congress Cataloging-in-Publication Data

Mitchell, Anne (Anne W.)
  Early childhood programs and the public schools: between promise
and practice / Anne Mitchell, Michelle Seligson, Fern Marx.
    p. cm.
  Bibliography: p.
  Includes index.
  ISBN 0-86569-193-2
  1. Socially handicapped children—Education (Preschool)—United
States. 2. School facilities—Extended use—United States.
3. Child care services—United States. I. Seligson, Michelle,
1941-   II. Marx, Fern. III. Title.
LC4091.M57 1989
371.96'7—dc19   89-31076

Library of Congress Catalog Card Number: 89-31076
ISBN: 0-86569-193-2

First published in 1989

Auburn House, 88 Post Road West, Westport, CT 06881
An imprint of Greenwood Publishing Group, Inc.

Printed in the United States of America

The paper used in this book complies with the
Permanent Paper Standard issued by the National
Information Standards Organization (Z39.48-1984).

10 9 8 7 6 5 4 3 2

This book is dedicated to all of America's children—everyone of whom deserves the best beginning we can possibly give. It is also dedicated to our own children—Amelia, Jon, Sally, David, Rani, and Michael—and to the staffs of all the early childhood programs that cared for and educated them. With the help of our families and these dedicated professionals we have learned a great deal; without them our work would not have been possible.

ACKNOWLEDGMENTS

The Public School Early Childhood Study was an ambitious undertaking that at times threatened to overtake us! Describing the universe of early childhood programs in relation to the public schools meant examining not only the new state-legislated prekindergarten programs but also their predecessors—Head Start, Special Education, Chapter I, parent education, publicly funded child care—the entire array of separate and largely uncoordinated programs for children under the age of five. As we began to work together as a team, in two different locations and under two different institutional umbrellas, we came to understand that collaborating can produce an exciting synergy of ideas and that it can also be very tough work. The rewards and challenges of collaboration were as real for our team of researchers and writers as they were for the early childhood programs we studied. While gathering and analyzing data with teams in two different locations was difficult, writing a book together with four hundred miles between us was not easy, either! Nonetheless, we think this study has met (and perhaps even exceeded) our high expectations. We thank each other, and acknowledge both the joy and the difficulty we experienced. And we thank our respective families and friends for their forbearance and support.

When we initially raised the idea of the Public School Early Childhood Study in 1984, it was Barbara Finberg, Vice President of the Carnegie Corporation of New York, who first welcomed the idea and opened the dialogue that led to the development of a grant proposal. Vivien Stewart, Gloria Brown, and Sheila Smith at Carnegie, along with Pru Brown, Edward Meade, and Shelby Miller at the Ford Foundation, helped and challenged us as we wrestled with formulating the study's methods and goals.

At Bank Street Jim Levine, Bob Granger, and Jane Knitzer were valued colleagues, especially at the early design stage. We thank Jim, too, for his consultation on publishing the manuscript.

Throughout the study and in the writing of this book, Janice Molnar contributed her incredible energy and intellectual rigor, and, in addition to authoring the Program for Children and History chapters, contributed in depth to many other sections of the manuscript. Kathy Modigliani's chapter on teachers reflects her concern about the relationship between the quality of programs and the dignity and professionalism of those who work in them.

Several members of the study's Advisory Council contributed their thinking to sections of the manuscript. We would like to thank especially Gwen Morgan, Norton Grubb, and Deborah Phillips, who also gave us the apt phrase, "between promise and practice." Colleagues working on complementary early childhood policy projects were also resources to us, especially Tom Schultz of the National Association of State Boards of Education and Larry Schweinhart of High/Scope.

Sharon Lynn Kagan reviewed the first draft of the manuscript and offered thoughtful comment throughout. Paddy Yost and Jeff Fisher, our New York editing team, contributed structure and smoothness to this book; they deserve a standing ovation for their deep, careful, and speedy review of each chapter of the manuscript. Liz Westfall at Bank Street contributed her unflagging enthusiasm and good spirits to the production of the manuscript (and provided administrative support throughout the study).

March 1989

A. M., M. S., AND F. M.

CONTENTS

CHAPTER 3
Administration of Early Childhood Programs   63

CHAPTER 4
Financing Early Childhood Programs   82

INTRODUCTION

Parents, business leaders, child and family advocates, educators, public officials, and the media are all deeply concerned about two major trends: our failure to educate the ever-increasing numbers of disadvantaged children, and the growing need for child care fueled by dramatic changes in family life. Ignoring either of these trends poses dire consequences for the future of society. In nearly every call to action on these issues, high-quality early childhood programs are noted as part of the solution. It is becoming widely known that quality early childhood programs can have strong and lasting positive effects on later school and life success for young children—especially for disadvantaged three- and four-year-olds. Young children, especially those most vulnerable because of such factors as poverty, must receive services meeting the highest standards if they are to have productive lives. As noted by the Committee for Economic Development:[1]

This nation cannot continue to compete and prosper in the global arena when more than one-fifth of our children live in poverty and a third grow up in ignorance. And if the nation cannot compete, it cannot lead. If we continue to squander the talents of millions of our children, America will become a nation of limited human potential. It would be tragic if we allowed this to happen. America must become the land of opportunity—for every child.

All parents want their children to have a good educational start; nowadays, most parents also want and need high-quality child care. As this nation begins to grapple with developing a large-scale response to these intertwined needs, community institutions of all sorts will have to mobilize to shoulder their share of the responsibility for making high-quality early childhood programs widely available and readily accessible. Public schools are increasingly viewed as a major partner in that effort. However, as a nation, we are far from agreeing on the best route to providing early childhood services, whether with regard to a specific approach, scope, resources needed, or where the locus of control should reside. As researchers interested in how American institutions take up the challenge of serving young children and their families, we are concerned about the process and quality of these efforts, and about how decision makers define their task.

Early Childhood Programs and the Public Schools: Between Promise and Practice is addressed to those who make policy or participate in the current public discussion about the future of services for young children and their families: federal and state legislators, state commissioners of Social Services and Education, policy planners, education and advocacy organizations, and elected officials and public school administrators who must make decisions about the future role of the schools.

Our spotlight in this book is on the public schools and their involvement in programs that provide some portion of the care and education of children under the age of five. The book is about early childhood services generally with major emphasis on the public schools as providers of early childhood programs. It is based on our collective experience in the early childhood world and on our analysis of the results of a three-year research project known as the *Public School Early Childhood Study*. The study was initiated in 1985 by Bank Street College of Education in New York and the Wellesley College Center for Research on Women in Massachusetts, and was funded by the Carnegie Corporation of New York and the Ford Foundation. The study explored the public school system—state and local—as a provider of programs for young children within the broader early childhood community. It focused on the policies and practices of local public school districts and examined the role of the states in legislating, managing, regulating, and funding early childhood services generally—with particular attention to those delivered by public schools through both long-established and more recent initiatives.

The Forces That Led to the Study (and This Book)

We designed the Public School Early Childhood Study to capture state policy across the spectrum of early childhood services—prekindergarten programs, child care, part-day and full-day services, Head Start, and others. To illuminate some of the trends and tensions that are affecting the process of reaching consensus on a national early childhood agenda, we recorded the activity of a large sample of school districts operating such programs and looked closely at the practices of a small number of public school district-operated early childhood programs.

One of the trends that we perceive as particularly significant is the continuing misperception of early childhood education and child care as discrete services. A look at the prekindergarten legislation developed in states during the past decade shows clearly that the new state-funded prekindergarten programs are almost universally part-day, part-year programs, with few accommodations to working families through extended services, such as before- and after-school child care. Yet, during the same period, child care has moved steadily higher on the agenda for serious policy attention. Many states have taken steps to improve their child care infrastructure: increased support of child care resource and referral services, expansion of direct child care services, increased funding for child care (in the face of serious federal funding cuts). From a number of sources, we understood that policymakers did not generally perceive child care programs as educational opportunities for young children. (Nor did they recognize the child care function that so-called "educational" programs fulfill.) Since, until recently, child care has been treated primarily as a social welfare program, the assumptions made by policymakers were understandable. We wanted to help eliminate this perceived dichotomy and to ensure that it did not continue to influence the programs and policies that states enacted in the future.

A second important trend is the growing concern with the quality of all programs for young children—whether in public schools or other settings. Concerns come from diverging sources. Some developmental psychologists and other early childhood experts have voiced concern about unrealistic expectations both of children's performance and of the promised long-range gains resulting from their participation in early childhood programs—whatever their auspice. The tendency for some teachers and parents to demand earlier reading and writing is pushing children too hard and too soon, denying them the opportunity for healthy development through play, and perhaps permanently damaging their disposition toward learning. Particularly in regard to public schools, the concern is often expressed in terms of the curriculum (or content) of an early childhood program: Should the curriculum be academic, or cognitive, or developmental? Broadly developmental or more narrowly intellectual? Focused on school readiness or child development? Tensions exist between the theoretical purity of promoting healthy child development and the extreme variation among practices that are all said to be based on child development.

A third trend is the increasing focus on the public schools as the locus for stepped-up efforts to increase the access of disadvantaged preschoolers to early education opportunities. Prior to the study, little information was available on the extent of public school involvement in early childhood education. We knew from our earlier research and experience that public schools were certainly more involved in before- and after-school child care for school-aged children than in early childhood education for prekindergartners. But we also knew that some school districts had been providing programs to children younger than five for many years: The Philadelphia School District has had several types of child care and nursery school programs for more than 40 years; California has had significant state involvement in the early childhood field since World War II; and New York's experimental prekindergarten programs have been a fixture of public schools in many of the state's communities since 1966.

The Forces That Moved Early Childhood Higher on the Policy Agenda

Over the past five years, the federal government, with the exception of continuing the Head Start program, has not played the major role in early childhood policy. Most of the policy action was, and probably will continue to be, primarily on the state level.

For many states during this period, the education reform movement provided a ready vehicle to carry state policymakers' growing interest in early childhood programs, an interest that has been fed by increased attention to the *positive findings of longitudinal studies* of early childhood programs. The most well-known of these is, of course, the High/Scope Foundation's Perry Preschool Program. The media attention given to the release of "Changed Lives"[2] spurred a number of mayors, governors, and legislators to read at least the executive summary. The positive results of Head Start evaluation research, evaluations of older state prekindergarten programs, and the clearly positive findings from the Consortium for Longitudinal Studies (of which the Perry Preschool was one of 12 programs) have not had such widespread media attention, although their findings are equally compelling and have contributed to the rising interest in early childhood programs.[3]

As the focus of *education reform* moved from the secondary school to the elementary school in the shift from outcomes to inputs, states (driven in part by the compelling evidence of the effectiveness of prekindergarten programs) began to create state-funded, public school-based prekindergarten programs. South Carolina, Texas, and Illinois were among the first of this wave, although some states already had similar programs in place (notably those in New York and California, which were created in the mid-1960s along with Head Start). Although the primary motivation for this wave of new programs for young children was concern for children's school readiness and school success in the context of the states' education reform agenda, another force was also at work: *dramatic increases in the labor force participation of mothers.*

The statistics *are* dramatic: 100 percent increases since 1970; three-quarters of mothers with school-age children work; two-thirds of mothers with preschoolers work; over half of all mothers of infants are back in the labor force within a year of the birth of their child.[4] While dramatic statistics make great legislative rhetoric, the concern for child care in the creation of state-funded prekindergarten programs in the 1980s appeared to be mainly rhetorical in that only four of the newest state-legislated programs (in Massachusetts, Vermont, New Jersey, and Florida) clearly permit services to extend to the full working day. Even in these states, very few full-working-day programs have been funded. *No* state prekindergarten efforts deal with direct services to children as young as infants.

In 1979, seven states funded prekindergarten programs in their public schools and four contributed state funds to Head Start. Currently 32 states are involved—3 with statewide parent education programs, 12 contributing to Head Start, and 27 funding a total of 33 prekindergarten programs. Most of the expansion in prekindergarten programs occurred between 1985 and 1987 (the peak years of education reform). The rate of expansion moved in sync with the tempo of education reform and has now definitely slowed. Most of the more populous states now have programs, as do the states where the largest numbers of poor children reside (New York, California, Illinois, Texas, Florida). A few new states may join the ranks with new programs, as Iowa and Colorado did late in 1988; a few other states with existing programs may create new ones, as New Jersey recently did. But education reform, as the vehicle for creating prekindergarten programs, is running out of steam as the focus of education reform efforts shift to restructuring.[5]

Thus concern about young children and their need for services became a hallmark of the mid-1980s that manifested itself in state policies and programs of early childhood education. State financing alone will never be able to meet the need if *all* children are to have access to good early childhood programs. Although questions remain about what share of the financial burden should appropriately be borne by parents themselves and by the various public sources—federal, state, county, and city—some level of support from each will probably be needed. It is clear by now that some public role in the care and education of children—earlier than at traditional school entry—has become a social and economic necessity.

The Early Childhood Community as an "Ecosystem"

Our particular approach emphasizes the fact that early childhood programs have as many images as there are lenses through which to examine them. Programs can be seen as preventing later school failure and ensuring a better chance at success for children as adults, especially for children at greater risk because of poverty, racism, and other factors. They can be seen as employment-related child care for parents working or seeking work, a view increasingly articulated in the welfare reform agenda. They can be seen as an opportunity to provide parents with parent education and training.

We see early childhood programs—and early childhood policy-making—as encompassing all these aspects. Neither the public schools nor any single other agency must provide all of these services; to make all necessary services available to their consumers, however, schools and other agencies in a community must learn how to make links with each other. This all-encompassing model, our particular lens on the subject, resembles the ecological model of Urie Bronfenbrenner, who has written of the family as a unit inseparable from the community in which it exists. Programs that work together in a community might be said to form a web or network; its threads can be so woven as to make all services stronger and more readily available to the families who need them.

In a strict sense, there is no early childhood system, that is, no planned system. But, from an ecological perspective, there is an early childhood "ecosystem" of sorts that has evolved over time. It is the early childhood community which consists of all the child care services and nursery schools operated under public, private, or religious auspices, whatever they are called—playschool, child care center, early learning center, prekindergarten, early childhood center, preschool, Head Start, child care, child development center, family child care home. The name of a program or where it is housed are *not* indications of a particular program's quality so much as they are clues to its present purpose (for example, nursery school means part-day, while child care center implies longer hours) or historical origins (for example, day nursery implies origins in the day nursery movement of the early part of the century). Figure I–1 depicts the major providers of early childhood services as a community.

The essential elements of any ecosystem are its many interrelated parts (or subsystems) and their dynamic relationship to each other, or their interdependence. If one part changes, the others necessarily change in response. Given that this early childhood ecosystem exists, we were interested not only in counting and describing public school prekindergarten programs but, more importantly, in examining the effects these programs would have in the ecosystem of the early childhood community. Throughout this book, the terms *early childhood community*, *early childhood ecosystem*, and *early childhood system* are used interchangeably.

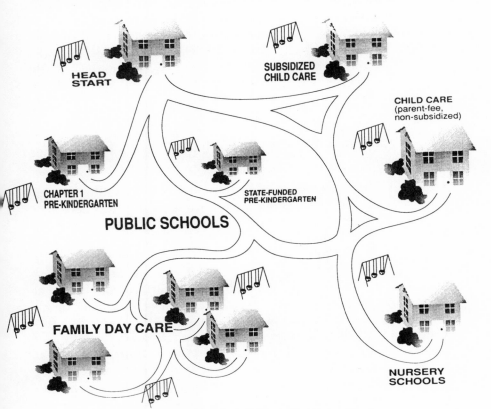

Figure I-1 The Early Childhood Community

Regardless of nomenclature, all early childhood programs serve young children and, in general, are more alike than they are different from one another. The following statements apply to all such programs and serve to illuminate the degree to which they are similar:

- All programs for young children have the potential to provide both education and care. Families seeking services for their children tend to look to a program to provide aspects of both.
- Although some programs may emphasize one of these aspects (care or education) more than the other, good programs will be able to measure up to recognized standards and criteria in each, regardless of particular emphasis. Programs may differ by name, stated goal, hours of operation, and scope of service (part-day, full-school-day, full-working-day), but they should not differ qualitatively, that is, in staff qualifications, staff–child ratios, developmentally appropriate curriculum, and parent involvement.
- Good programs for young children serve the child *and* the child's family. At the very least, the diverse cultural, economic, and social characteristics of families in America should be considered when programs are planned; ideally, there should be program components that speak directly to family concerns—components that create an environment receptive to parent input and responsive to the varied needs of families, whether for child care, parent education, or a host of other services.

Because our perspective is on the entire early childhood community ecosystem, we wanted to use terminology in this book that would clearly embrace the range of programs within that ecosystem. Thus we elected to use *early childhood programs* and *prekindergarten programs* as the best general descriptors of a wide array of programs for children. (In this book, both *early childhood* and *prekindergarten* refer to children from birth to age five, that is, younger than kindergarten entry age.) The programs themselves use different names, but whatever they are called— Pomona's *Children's Centers* in California, Chicago's *Child/Parent Center*, Affton-Lindbergh's *Early Childhood Education* in St. Louis, or Palm Beach County's *Chapter I/Migrant Program*—they are all *early childhood programs* serving *prekindergarten children*—programs for children between birth and age five before they enter kindergarten.

Exploring the Promise of Public Schools as Providers of Early Childhood Services

There is promise in the entrance of schools into the early childhood arena. In many communities they have the best facilities available, and we have found that when public school programs reflect adequate support, financing, and knowledge of good practice in early childhood development, they are excellent providers. A national poll conducted in 1987 by the Gallup organization found that most Americans think that schools should do more for young children and families. Parents would like more responsive schools, and we know that in those school districts and schools where school boards, superintendents, and principals have promoted before- and after-school programs, prekindergarten programs or parent education and other family support services, parents' attitudes about the schools are positive.

The essential early childhood policy question is: How to expand the supply of, improve quality in, and increase access to early childhood programs for all children—but especially for those who are disadvantaged? We were well aware that the components of the existing early childhood system—the child care centers, family child care homes, nursery schools, and other formal and informal services—are simply not enough in number or sufficiently rich in resources to do the work of educating and caring for all young children. Public schools offer attractive features as a solution to the pressing demand for an increased supply of affordable, accessible, quality early childhood programs. We agreed that public schools are a logical locus for more services for young children, but we also recognized certain problems with the public schools. For example, public schools have a stable funding base of public tax dollars; public school is free. The potential for *expansion* through expanding the public school's tax base to include prekindergarten services holds out the promise of affordable programs. But in some communities formerly secure school funding has become much less certain as bond issues fail to pass and may be insufficient even to cover current programs, let alone new ones. The potential for *increased accessibility* is clear—the public school system is a permanent fixture of our society. There are public school buildings in every community. But in many communities—particularly urban areas which are home to many disadvantaged children—school buildings are already overcrowded, leaving no room for new programs. The promise of *improvements in quality* is more elusive. Public school teachers are professional educators (who enjoy much higher societal status than child care workers), but few public school teachers are trained in early childhood education and fewer in child development.

As the public school system is turned to as the solution to yet another societal problem, we also wondered what school administrators and elected school officials thought—and whether the schools were either interested in, or prepared for, an expanded role. We knew that some school administrators are eager to enter this new arena, while others want to stay focused on K–12 education. The promise of public schools is clear notwithstanding the potential problems. Looking at current practices and the current role of schools offers some answers to questions about the ability of the public school system to play an expanded role in the early childhood community.

The Practice of Early Childhood Education in Public Schools

We wanted to know how many schools were involved in the provision of early childhood programs. We also wanted to learn about the nature of the involvement: What kinds of programs are schools providing? Who teaches in them? What age groups are served? Are school programs comprehensive, like Head Start, offering a variety of educational, health, and social services to children and families? Are schools providing full-working-day coverage so that parents who work outside the home can use them for a significant part of their child care arrangements?

Currently, there are barriers on the practice side to the schools' achieving their promise. Too many public school programs use standardized approaches that leave little room for spontaneity. Outdoor play is not an integral part of all programs, as it should be. Many prekindergarten classrooms end the school day at midday, leaving some families to make additional—and often difficult—arrangements. School assistance in the form of full-working-day programs, extended day services, or transportation to community services would help create continuity in the child's daily experience—and would certainly help parents.

And what about the quality of early childhood programs, especially school-based programs? The National Association for the Education of Young Children has developed standards for developmentally appropriate practice and for the development of legislation on early childhood programs. We wanted to learn more about the quality of current public school early childhood programs in relation to these criteria. Are school-based programs more cognitively oriented than their counterparts in the community? Do they reflect the consensus on best practice with regard to staff–child ratios, teacher qualifications, parent involvement, child-directed activity, and the importance of play?

We were interested in the implications of increased public school involvement in a field in which programs have traditionally been located in many other community settings—churches, synagogues, private nursery schools and child care centers, and family child care homes, the last of which currently serve more than half of the children enrolled in out-of-home child care nationally. Does public school provision of early childhood programs represent competition with other community providers? What is the nature of collaboration among schools and other community agencies serving young children and their families? Do parents prefer public school programs to those offered under other auspices?

Because most of the current policy action on early childhood has come from the states via governors and legislatures, we wanted to learn more about the development of these state initiatives, which have resulted in many new state-funded programs for young children. Would states decrease funding for child care programs while increasing funding for public prekindergarten programs? Because many of these state initiatives were "top-down" rather than "bottom-up" efforts fueled by grassroots pressures, we wondered if and how the top-down initiatives reflected local needs and the concerns of parents and others.

In this book, we develop these questions and some of their answers. Themes have emerged from our research that we think will help to illuminate the public dialogue taking place about the future provision of services to young children and their families. Public schools are by now clearly a part of the early childhood "ecosystem." Schools can and do offer high-quality prekindergarten programs—and also programs that are mediocre. In this way, they resemble other programs in the early childhood community and also share with them the need for aggressive and immediate public policy directed at improving quality and expanding access for more children.

Our goal is to help bring the promise and the practice closer together, showing by example the ways in which some programs and policies have achieved that and how they have done so. In conducting the study, analyzing the findings, and writing this book, we have had to confront some of our own stereotypes about the capacity of the public school to change, to extend its boundaries, and to embrace an expanded definition of education. The stereotypes are familiar: A public school is part of a rigid, immutable bureaucracy that cares more about paperwork than about children; public school curricula are overly academic and narrow; public schools are not capable of offering children a developmentally appropriate experience; public schools are unresponsive to families and communities. We have come to believe that there are many positive signs that schools and other community organizations will indeed rise to the challenge of making the most of America's resources to serve young children and families.

What Might the Future Bring?

What could programs for young children look like in the future? In our focus on the public schools as a relatively new partner in the provision of early childhood programs, five themes that informed the study have emerged as qualities we hope will characterize future early childhood programs whether in public schools or elsewhere: high quality, equity of access, responsiveness to families, comprehensiveness, and collaboration.

Quality

The study's working definition of quality derives from research findings on best practice with regard to group size, ratios, and staff training. Curriculum, parent involvement, and continuity are additional features of quality. Well-trained teachers will use a planned classroom approach—a curriculum rooted in a clearly articulated philosophy with a basis in child development and learning theory. Site visits to 13 programs disclosed a variety of approaches to quality in school-based programs, from child-centered approaches to highly structured, skills-mastery curricula. In *all* programs the quality of leadership was *directly related* to program quality.

Equity

The goal of early childhood public policy should be to offer services to all children whose families want them. This universality of access does not mean that the schools must provide all the early childhood services in a community. Some have argued that public schools must be prepared to assume the full burden of offering access to good care and education to all children; that this expectation is unrealistic becomes clear when it is seen in the light of local school district decision making, the pattern of state funding policy, the growing market of private entrepreneurship, and the diversity of parental choice. Rather, a system—built on the foundation of the existing early childhood community—of multiple providers of service supported by multiple funding sources is more likely than a unitary system to meet the range of needs of multiple populations and to ensure the desired multiple outcomes (improved economic and social conditions of families, reduction of the use of costly intervention programs for adolescents, improved quality of childhood life and better school performance, among others).

Currently, about two-thirds of the states with prekindergarten legislation target their programs to at-risk children. The majority of nontargeted programs are in the states with permissive legislation funding prekindergarten as other public schooling is funded, using state education reimbursement formulas. In some districts in which the school is operating programs independent of state legislation or in its absence, only parents who can pay for services have access to them. None of these methods presently ensures access to all children.

Responsiveness to Families

Parent involvement is essential in early childhood programs. The accumulated wisdom of the early childhood profession strongly supports this. Parent involvement is a key element in Head Start programs, and was a mandatory component of Chapter I programs until recently. Evaluations of New York State's prekindergarten program and others that participated in the Consortium for Longitudinal Studies showed that children whose parents were more involved in the program made significantly greater gains and that these parents had higher expectations for their children's educational and vocational attainment.

Parents are clearly affected positively by involvement in good early childhood programs. Parents have needs for information and support as parents as well as other adult needs—fellowship with other adults or education for themselves—that may be only indirectly related to parenting but may be critical to the survival of the family. Adequately supporting one's family—through paid work or the pursuit of training—is essential to parental self-esteem.

School-based programs generally are supplying only a portion of the need for child care. Some working parents use part-day programs as part of self-constructed child care packages. Others choose to work split shifts so that they can use a free, half-day public school program as child care. Yet others use relatives, friends, or neighbors to pick up and care for their child after school. Responsiveness to child care needs is certainly not common in public school programs, and other indicators of family respon-siveness, such as a longer school year, transportation, and flexible scheduling of parent conferences, are not widely available either.

Comprehensive and Collaboration

Today's early childhood programs and the institutions that sponsor them must be prepared to address the child *and* the family. Shortsighted policy that ignores family issues—especially of at-risk children and their families—such as the need for health, nutrition, and social services, will not, in the end, provide maximum benefit to the child. Achieving comprehensiveness (identifying and making available these necessary additional services) is a function of the extent to which institutions are able to coordinate and collaborate at both the state and local levels.

If these themes can be transformed into reality in all early childhood programs throughout the ecosystem, we will have taken a giant step toward making America once again the land of oppor-tunity—for every child (*and* family).

Organization of This Book

This book is organized in 11 chapters. Where appropriate, each chapter concludes with specific recommendations on policy and practice. Chapter 1 presents the historical context of public school involvement in early childhood programs and provides a lens for understanding the thrust of current activities. This chapter shows the parallel and interwoven development of kindergarten, nursery schools, and child care; delineates the involvement of the public schools in the provision of services during the Depression and World War II years; and moves through the 1960s to 1980 to show the growth and subsequent decline of federal policy support of early childhood programs and the emergence of the role of the states under the Reagan administration.

Chapter 2 is a presentation of facts and findings from the Public School Early Childhood Study. Typologies drawn from the State Survey and the District Survey are the organizational framework for presenting the data, which include the type of state prekinder-garten enactments, funding streams, eligibility of children, coor-dination mechanisms, program components (curriculum, compre-hensive services), regulations, and staffing. Three different prekindergarten program types are profiled in detail. This chapter includes ten tables that guide readers through this overview of the study's major findings.

Chapter 3 focuses on administration of early childhood programs at the state and district level, including the administrative locus of state-funded prekindergarten programs and the forms of district administration. The forces influencing administrative choices and the merits of each are discussed. Chapter 4 addresses issues related to the financing of prekindergarten programs at the state and school district level. It discusses the different funding streams and financing mechanisms supporting these programs and contrasts the financing system employed to support programs depending on the age—under or over five—of the children served.

Chapter 5 is about regulations and guidelines—often a critical factor in setting program standards and ensuring quality, but also often a cause of confusion, as policymakers strive for a common language and providers attempt to sort out what regulations apply to which domain. Chapter 6 deals with the eligibility of children and families for the services offered by the public schools. It addresses questions about universality of access and equity in the distribution of resources that are raised by the establishment of income-based eligibility criteria. The pros and cons of universal versus targeted approaches are presented.

Chapter 7 addresses the need for greater coordination across domains (among state agencies funding various programs; between the child care sector and the schools; among state and local agencies that serve the same children). It presents examples of coordination and collaboration that have made linkages possible between and among domains at both the state and local level, and it describes specific legislative and administrative mandates and other mechanisms that facilitate cooperation. Chapter 8 discusses personnel and other issues related to the proper staffing of early childhood programs, such as staff qualifications, appropriate training and experience, comparisons between school and child care teacher credentialing, pay equity issues, recruitment, retention, and job satisfaction.

Chapter 9 covers the program for children themselves, in terms of curriculum and components. It discusses how well the public school programs appear to meet the acknowledged criteria for quality in early childhood programs and what criteria the state may mandate in legislation and subsequent program standards and guidelines. At the local level, it discusses program philosophies, curricula, staffing patterns and group structure, and "vertical" and "horizontal" continuity—that is, the programmatic consistency between different stages of a child's educational experience and the flow between the early childhood program and any other programs the children attend daily in the same location or outside it.

Chapter 10 attends to a central question underlying much of the book: being responsive to families. It covers a wide range of methods by which policymakers, school administrators, and elected officials may create family-oriented programs and policies and begin to change attitudes about the role of the schools vis-à-vis children whose parents do not resemble those of the past. An expanded conception of parent participation is presented which encompasses and extends the traditional model beyond direct involvement in the child's education to include parents' needs both as parents and as adults. Chapter 11, called "The Future: Where Do We Go from Here?" concludes the book with a best-case scenario for the future.

Endnotes

1. Committee for Economic Development (1987). *Children in need.* New York: Author.
2. Berrueta-Clement, J.R., L.J. Schweinhart, W.S. Barnett, A.S. Epstein, and D.P. Weikart (1984). Changed lives: Effects of the Perry Preschool Program on youths through age 19. *Monographs of the High/Scope Educational Research Foundation 8.*
3. Berrueta-Clement et al. (1984).

   McKey, R.H., B.J. Barrett, L. Condelli, H. Ganson, C. McConkey, and M.C. Plantz (1985). *The impact of Head Start on children, families and communities. Final report of the Head Start Evaluation, Synthesis and Utilization Project* (Stock No. 017-092-00098-7). Washington, D.C.: U.S. Government Printing Office.

   Hubbell, R. (1983). *A review of Head Start research since 1970. Head Start Evaluation Synthesis and Utilization Project* (DHHS-OHDS-83-31184). Washington, D.C.: U.S. Government Printing Office, Administration for Children, Youth and Families.

   The University of the State of New York (1982). *Final Report: Evaluation of the New York State experimental prekindergarten program.* Albany, N.Y.: The University of the State of New York, The State Education Department, Division of ESC Education Planning and Development.

   Lazar, I., and R.B. Darlington (1978). *Lasting effects after preschool: A report of the Consortium for Longitudinal Studies.* (DHEW Publication No. [(OHDS)] 79-30178). Washington, D.C.: U.S. Government Printing Office.
4. U.S. Department of Labor, Bureau of Labor Statistics (August 1988). *Labor force statistics derived from current population survey, 1948–1987.* Bulletin No. 2307. Washington, D.C.: U.S. Government Printing Office.

5. Restructuring might include some prekindergarten-related efforts, such as the early childhood units for children aged 4 through 8, that the National Association of State Boards of Education recommends be instituted within elementary schools. For more details, see National Association of State Boards of Education (1988). *Right from the start*. The Report of the NASBE Task Force on Early Childhood Education. Alexandria, Va.: Author.

Chapter 1

THE HISTORICAL CONTEXT

The history of public school involvement in prekindergarten programs is a unique strand—at times distinctly parallel, at times directly interwoven—within the broader fabric that is the history of early childhood programs and policies in this country. This chapter does not attempt to present that history in full. The tale, though relatively short (spanning but 150 years), is not an easy one to tell. Often times, one decade's beliefs and practices contradict those of the next. Individual voices rise and fall in concert with the wider flow of social events and trends, including immigration, industrialization, private philanthropy, philosophy, psychology, politics, and war. A key theme of the story, however, is social reform and its impact on programs for children. It is social reform that was the prime instigator of public school involvement in early childhood education in the last two decades of the nineteenth century. A variation of that same theme is driving the interest in public school support of prekindergarten programs today.

Nineteenth-Century Influences

If the history of public school involvement in early childhood programs were to be summed up in just one word, that word would be *kindergarten*. In the second quarter of the nineteenth century, three European approaches to the care and education of young children were introduced in the United States: infant schools from Great Britain, the *creches* from France, and the *kleinkinderbeschaftingungsansalt* (small-children-occupational-institute, mercifully shortened to *kindergarten*) from Germany.

Note: This chapter was authored principally by Janice Molnar.

(Nursery schools are essentially an American invention which did not make an appearance until almost three-quarters of a century later.)

When characterizing the evolution of these programs, historical observers frequently draw a line of demarcation, with nursery school–kindergarten/education on one side and day nurseries (modeled after the French creche and the predecessors of today's "day care centers")/social welfare on the other. However, with the exception of nursery schools (which, with brief exceptions during the Depression and World War II, have maintained their middle-class educational focus from their beginnings in 1915 to the present day), the lines are actually much muddier. Although primarily considered welfare-focused, day nurseries have had an educational element of varying intensity throughout their history, most recently as articulated in the National Association for the Education of Young Children (NAEYC) Guidelines for Developmentally Appropriate Practice. Although growing out of an educational philosophy, it was the drive—rooted in welfare and social reform—to educate and culturally assimilate the poor urban immigrant that extended kindergarten's influence and ultimately its expansion into the public schools. According to the editor of *Century Magazine*, writing in 1903, it was kindergarten that provided "our earliest opportunity to catch the little Russian, the little Italian, the little German, Pole, Syrian, and the rest and begin to make good American citizens of them."[1]

The history of early childhood education in the United States is generally believed to have begun in Boston. The Boston Infant School, established in 1828, is considered the country's first day care center. Accepting children between the ages of 18 months and 4 years, the school was open for 9 hours (13 hours in the summer months). Its purpose was twofold: to enable mothers to work and to enable their children to "be removed from the unhappy association of want and vice, and be placed under better influences."[2] A central theme of the infant schools was "the mind of the child and the education of all children."[3] An emphasis on the importance of the early years (before age six) was combined with a desire to infuse "these experiments on the infant mind" into the larger educational system.

Unfortunately, it was the French creche, not the British infant school, that became the model for the day nursery, the grandparent of today's system. Established in Paris in 1844 for the children of working mothers, the first American creche opened in New York City in 1854. Affiliated with New York Hospital, the nursery for the children of poor women was primarily geared toward hygienic custodial care. Upon arrival in the morning, the day's first activity for the children, who ranged in ages from six weeks to six years, was to be bathed and then dressed in hospital clothes. "Education," as it existed, consisted of training in household tasks, manners, and orderliness.

Day nurseries expanded throughout the nineteenth century, especially during the 1880s and 1890s, as waves of European immigrants and migrants from the American countryside overwhelmed urban tenement houses and ghetto neighborhoods. In addition to serving its primary purpose of caring for children, most day nurseries attempted to serve mothers as well, through parent education (in homemaking skills and physical care of children) and employment services (usually in domestic help). Supported largely by the private philanthropy and on-site volunteer work of upper-class women, day nurseries reached 175 in number by 1898, the same year the National Federation of Day Nurseries was created.[4]

At about the time the first day nurseries were beginning, the earliest kindergartens were being established. Transplanted to America by German immigrants in the 1840s, the first kindergarten for English-speaking children opened in Boston in 1860. What distinguished the kindergarten from other programs for children was its educational philosophy. Designed by Friedrich Froebel, kindergarten was rooted in fundamental beliefs about the nature of childhood as an uncorrupted embodiment of God's reason.[5] The kindergarten curriculum (which consisted of 6 "gifts," or geometric forms to be used in prescribed manipulations, and 4 "occupations," which enabled children to create their own forms through various craft-like activities)[6] was intended to "cultivate the divine essence of the child and discern his deeper, inner good nature."[7] Tuition was high ($50 a term,[8] compared with parents' fees of 10 cents per day in the day nurseries[9]), and the program was geared to the children of educated, well-to-do families.

This was not the case for long, however. In 1870, the Boston school board opened an experimental kindergarten in one of its public schools. It lasted for several years, until "the city could not afford to extend the system."[10] A second public kindergarten was opened in Brighton, Massachusetts, in 1873 but was closed the following year when Brighton was annexed to Boston.

St. Louis

A turning point for the expansion of kindergarten was its adoption by the St. Louis public schools, beginning with the opening of a single experimental classroom in 1873 and followed by rapid

growth. A mere seven years later there was a district-wide enrollment of 77,828 children between the ages of four and six.[11] Such
growth would undoubtedly not have occurred had not a visionary
superintendent stumbled upon a substitute teacher experimenting
with the kindergarten technique.[12] The superintendent, William
Torrey Harris, later United States Commissioner of Education, was
a Hegelian philosopher disturbed by inequities in educational
opportunity for children living in the factory and levee districts of
St. Louis. Children of factory workers frequently had only three
years of school, entering at age seven and leaving to go to work by
age ten. At first, Harris hoped to address the problem by lowering
the legal age for public education to include children under six.
However, upon being exposed to kindergarten methods and sub-
sequently meeting Susan Blow, a substitute teacher in the district
and the daughter of a prominent St. Louis family, Harris successfully recommended that the board open a kindergarten on an
experimental basis.

Expansion was not automatic, however. Resistance existed on
numerous levels, several with a ring familiar to today's debates
about the role of public schools in prekindergarten education. As
reported in the *Saint Louis Annual Report of 1874*, and as summarized by Michael Shapiro,[13] issues were wide-ranging: a general
resistance to educational innovation; fears of an attempt to Ger-
manize the schools; attitudes concerning the respective roles of
the family and school in early education; beliefs by conservatives
that the kindergarten was too lenient, by liberals that it was too
restrictive; a sense that the program was an expensive "educational
frill" that would strain an already overcrowded district; fears by
primary teachers that the kindergarten would make the child
"intractable" and unfit for the primary school; doubts that appropriately trained teachers could be found; concerns that young
children could not maintain regular attendance. Harris and Blow
successfully responded to these issues (to cut costs, for example,
they used trained volunteers instead of paid teachers), and the
program—and its reputation—grew. Blow actually conducted
classes in a kindergarten "classroom" exhibited at the Philadelphia
Centennial Exposition of 1876; apparently it was one of the most
successful exhibits at the fair.[14] Nevertheless, kindergarten was
initially slow in spreading to other public school systems.

The Free Kindergarten Crusade

Ironically, large-scale expansion of kindergarten into the public
schools was preceded by a period of weakening boundaries be-

tween kindergarten and day nurseries. Following a four-year depression (1873–1877), a philanthropic movement arose to create
free kindergartens for poor children. Part of the impetus—for the
expansion of day nurseries in this period, as well—was the debate
around "child-saving" solutions. Both the day nursery and the
kindergarten came to be seen as preferred alternatives over re-
moval of children from their homes and placement into rural
homes or institutions. *Kindergartners*, as the advocates and teachers of kindergarten were called, "saw themselves as activists in
broad social reform"[15] and broadened their mission, with almost
religious fervor, to include the provision of food, clothing, and
parent education, along with the education of children. Teachers
were to spend afternoons (the kindergarten program was conducted in half-day morning sessions) visiting children's homes or
inviting mothers to the classroom for lectures on health, hygiene,
nutrition, and child care. "What happened in the classrooms was
supposed to be transferred to the home and neighborhood. . . .
Through the child, the family could be reached, and through that,
the society."[16] During the 1880s more than one thousand free
kindergartens (supported by donations from wealthy philanthropists as well as by subscriptions from the middle class) were
established. Also during this period, kindergartens were incorporated into the emerging settlement houses; in fact, a kindergarten
program was often one of the first social services to be offered.

It was the success of the free kindergarten movement that led to
large-scale public school adoption of kindergartens. By 1890 there
were simply too many children, teachers, and schools and insufficient financial and organizational resources to sustain them. Kindergarten enrollment had jumped from 31,117 to 143,720 during
the 1880s, a quadrupling in just one decade. "If the social-settle-
ment kindergarten was effective in the neighborhood, free kindergartners reasoned, why not simply extend its services throughout
the city?"[17] At first, kindergartners asked only for unused classroom
space.[18] However, by the 1890s middle-class subscribers and private philanthropists were unwilling to continue supporting the
kindergartens, and more than just space was needed.

In response, free kindergarten associations organized. As described by Shapiro:[19]

> *In most larger cities, the campaign for public school kindergartens
> followed a predictable pattern. . . . First, there was exposure of the
> corruption and inefficiency of the public-school program [for older
> children] in the press. Second, free kindergartners, in alliance with
> municipal reformers and the press, pointed out the sharp contrast
> between the ideals of the free kindergartens and the reality of the*

public schools. . . . Third, publicity often forced municipal govern-
ments to convene special commissions to investigate the conditions
of public schools, free kindergartens, and other urban child-saving
agencies.

In short, the kindergarten seemed like "a panacea for urban public
education." Although public school adoption was a slower process
in the smaller cities, by 1898 there were over 4,300 kindergartens
in almost 200 cities nationwide; 16 cities even boasted a special
supervisor of kindergartens.[20]

With public school adoption of kindergarten, however, came
changes. In particular, the early twentieth-century techniques of
centralized management resulted in the elimination of certain core
components of the kindergarten program. For instance, neighborhood-based differences, which admittedly were related to variations in program quality, entrance criteria, and the like, were
abandoned in favor of standardized procedures. The autonomy of
the kindergarten director was curtailed. Charitable work (community education, home visits, social welfare) was eliminated. As cost-
cutting measures, assistant teachers were removed, home visits
were cut, and a double-session was instituted. Faced with a potential shortage of qualified teachers, special training requirements
for kindergarten teachers were waived. The locus of control
switched from women to men. Last and hardly least, the classroom
teacher's authority was diminished; all curricula were subject to
the approval of a department supervisor, usually a primary educator, and the final approval of the principal. Resulting discontent
probably made the ground fertile for the educational progressivism
of the early twentieth century. But growing divisiveness within the
kindergarten movement between the Froebelians and the new
Progressives led to fundamental disagreements over things as basic
as the "proper relation of work and play in the kindergarten."
Endless arguments ensued. By 1915 the kindergarten movement,
as a major educational reform effort, was in disarray. The result
was an increasing emphasis on the kindergarten curriculum by
Progressives influenced by the philosophy of John Dewey. Those
who argued for the role of kindergarten as a major way to reform
society as a whole no longer dominated the debate over early
childhood education.

A New Century

By the turn of the century, over half of all kindergartens were
operated by public schools,[21] an extraordinary transformation in a

mere quarter century. But half were not. This other half had a diverse array of sponsors, including German language schools, churches and religious groups (kindergartens were even established by missionaries proselytizing in less developed countries), temperance groups, labor unions, private businesses, and settlement houses. As Bernard Spodek has observed:[22]

> *This variety of sponsors caused some confusion between the idea of the kindergarten as an educational institution and the concept of the creche or day nursery, which served a child-caring function. . . . As kindergartens became diversified, their practices often reflected the purposes of the sponsors. Church-related kindergartens taught religious precepts, while settlement house kindergartens were concerned with meeting broad social needs. Confusion between education and philanthropy was evident.*

At the same time, changes were occurring in other programs for children. Day nurseries began a period of decline, due largely to changes in societal perceptions of poverty, the appropriate maternal role, and the role of government in social welfare. A societal (especially philanthropic) notion of the "deserving" versus "undeserving" poor was gradually articulated, based on two complementary sets of ideas: first, that individuals—not institutions (as the settlement houses believed)—were responsible for their destitute conditions; and, second, that unrestricted access to day nurseries would result in more mothers seeking employment, which in turn would lead to diminished parental responsibility and depressed male wages. Thus day nurseries developed admissions criteria which discouraged a mother from going to work unless she was either a "destitute widow" or a "woman with a sick husband."[23] These admissions policies resulted in increased stigmatization of the day nurseries, as they served ever larger proportions of "undeserving poor." The fate for the day nurseries was sealed in 1911 with the passage of mothers' pension legislation (the forerunner of today's Aid to Families with Dependent Children) in two states. By 1919, 39 states were offering modest public stipends to mothers for staying at home with their children.[24]

Paradoxically, at the very same time that mothers' pension legislation was rolling through the states, so were compulsory school laws. Compulsory school attendance was seen as a response to a growing need for an educated work force in an industrial society. First passed in 1910, all states had compulsory attendance laws by 1918.[25] The first ripple effect on public school involvement in early childhood programs was small but significant. Los Angeles and Gary, Indiana, opened up the nation's first public school

nurseries shortly after passage of their states' compulsory attendance laws, largely because older siblings were no longer available
to care for their younger brothers and sisters.

It was also during this period that nursery schools came into
being. First organized by a group of faculty wives at the University
of Chicago in 1915 to "offer an opportunity for wholesome play for
their children, to give the mothers certain hours of leisure from
child care and to try the social cooperation of mothers in child
care,"[26] nursery schools quickly became popular throughout the
United States. Although geared to the middle and upper classes,
they "were more like current day-care centers than like current
nursery schools."[27] A 1928 survey showed that 60 percent ran all-
day programs (8:30 to 4:30) and enrolled children as young as 18
months of age.

In their early years nursery schools were important because of
their impact on the professionalization of early childhood staff.
Many nursery schools were affiliated with university-based research centers that were at the cutting edge of the new "child-
study" movement. Stimulated by the observational research of
Clark University president G. Stanley Hall, the child-study movement redefined the traditional view of children (especially as
represented by the Froebelians) and their appropriate education.
They steered away from a focus on the intellect to one on the
emotions, away from the use of geometric objects symbolizing
abstract ideas to concrete activities connected to everyday life. The
university centers included teacher training along with their research functions. Beginning in the 1920s, day nurseries were used
as training sites for future nursery school teachers. Gradually,
nursery school thinking and methods (in some cases, even teachers) were incorporated into the day nurseries.

The Great Depression

It was, however, the Great Depression that caused a significant
intermingling of all these existing modes of early childhood programs—nursery schools, kindergartens, and day nurseries. Victims
of mass unemployment in the 1930s included large numbers of
early childhood teachers. Lazerson reports the results of a 1934
survey of 700 cities indicating that, in contrast to average overall
layoffs of 5 percent among teaching staff, kindergarten teachers
were cut back by 19 percent between 1930 and 1933. Many cities
eliminated kindergartens altogether.[28] Nursery school and day
nursery teachers faced similarly grim prospects.

In 1933 the federal government stepped in via the Federal

Emergency Relief Administration (later the Works Progress Administration [WPA]) with money to create nursery schools. Its purpose was not so much to provide education or child care, as to provide jobs for teachers, nurses, and other unemployed educational staff (even including clerical workers, cooks, and janitors). Funds bypassed the usual federal and state bureaucracies and went directly to local school districts. Within a year 3,000 schools were operating, enrolling 65,000 children and employing 7,500 teachers and other workers.[29]

As the first significant federal contribution to early childhood programs,[30] the WPA effort of the 1930s has obvious political importance. From an educational point of view, moreover, the federal effort is noteworthy for its integrated programmatic approach. Although the WPA-funded early childhood programs were called "nursery schools," they were in fact full-day, five-day-per-week, year-round multiservice centers that offered health and nutritional care, parent education, preservice and inservice training for staff, as well as education and care for children. And, in spite of these very traditionally nonschool activities, most of the WPA programs were located in schools. The result was an interesting amalgam of elements from day nurseries, nursery schools, and kindergartens that was truly greater than the sum of its parts. In addition, because of the economic impact of the Depression, the nursery schools often enrolled children from many social classes, rather than just youngsters from poor families. (The eligibility requirement for the program was income-based, but with Depression-level incomes, many families qualified.)

World War II

Even before a political decision could be made about the long-term, post-Depression future of the WPA programs, World War II intervened and created its own political exigency. This time it was the child care component that, due to the incredible need for female labor force participation, was most in demand. The Community Facilities (Lanham) Act, passed in 1941, made federal dollars available to establish day care centers in "war-impacted areas." With the abolition of the WPA in 1942, many Lanham Act centers simply moved into the spaces left by the WPA programs. The majority were thus located in public schools. The integrated programming of the Depression-era nursery schools was basically continued in the Lanham centers. This time around, though, the income-eligibility criteria were dropped; a sliding fee scale was instituted instead. But, as with the WPA programs, the distinction between education and welfare was eliminated. And programmatically, it has been said that by 1942 the educational and developmental philosophies of the nursery school and day nursery (day care center) were indistinguishable;[31] only half-day, all-day distinctions remained. And, as for the public schools? They seemed to be solely a provider of space, not educational ideology. Although it is estimated that Lanham Act centers may have met only 40 percent of the wartime need for child care, up to a million and a half children in 47 states were served.[32]

The Postwar Years

The postwar years saw a return to the earlier mythology that women belong at home caring for their children. Despite opposition, Lanham Act centers were closed by February 1946. Only California and New York State continued support (with local matching of funds) of child care programs that had been operational during the war. California, moreover, has the distinction of having maintained to the present day its Children's Centers (as California's wartime nurseries came to be called) in the public schools, with the state Department of Education having administrative responsibilities. The centers are administered by the state education agency even while requiring a welfare-like means test to determine eligibility.

Nationally, the day care picture in the 1950s was bleak. Although the myth proclaimed that mothers were at home, the reality was different. In 1950 three times as many mothers were in the work force as during the prewar years. By 1959 five times as many mothers were working as in 1940, with day care facilities available for only 2.4 percent of their children.[33]

Kindergartens, in contrast, enjoyed expansion. In 1901–1902 approximately 5 percent of all four- to six-year-olds were enrolled in kindergarten; by 1925 the number had increased to 12 percent. It was the postwar years that saw the biggest increases: from one-third of all five-year-olds in 1949, to 54 percent in 1962, and to an incredible 98 percent by 1966.[34] It was in the public schools that much of that growth spurt occurred. Whereas in 1949 the public schools had space for not quite 30 percent of the five-year-old age cohort (29.2 percent were enrolled in public school kindergartens, 4.3 percent in nonpublic school programs), that percentage increased to almost half by 1962 and two-thirds by the mid-1960s.[35]

One More War

In maintaining continuity with its earlier forays into support of early childhood programs in times of national emergency, the

federal government declared yet another war in the early 1960s—
the War on Poverty. Revisiting nineteenth-century ideals of social
reform through education, programs of the 1960s derived from a
deficit model that saw the child as a vehicle for changing the
family. Money was available through multiple funding streams,
some going only to the schools, some bypassing them. In 1962 the
Social Security Act was amended to include funds for day care.
Five years later came the addition of Titles IV-A and IV-B, an
uncapped source (with a required 25 percent state match) for day
care for low-income families. Added in the same year, Title IV-C
provided day care funding for welfare mothers who needed additional training or education in order to obtain employment. In
1965 Title VII of the Housing and Urban Development Act provided support (in the form of direct funding as well as technical
assistance) for day care centers. The Model Cities legislation of
1966 included day care as a fundable demonstration program.

In 1972, the federal Revenue Sharing Act capped the amount of
Social Security Act funds (Titles IV-A and IV-B) available for child
care programs. Fortunately, in 1974 Title XX—perhaps the most
broad-reaching of the social services amendments—was added to
the Social Security Act, replacing child care funding previously
done via Title IV-A. Funding specifically targeted to schools was
made available with the passage of the Elementary and Secondary
Education Act (ESEA) in 1965. And, of course, probably the main
legacy of the era, Head Start, was created in 1964.

This federal push, dramatic as it was, was targeted to low-
income children and their families—specifically, to enable their
mothers to work (or gain the necessary skills to work). Thus it was
legislation geared more to parental employment than to child
development. Head Start was the exception, albeit an important
one, not the rule. Those funds directed to schools (ESEA funds,
for example) were also targeted to low-income students, who were
also low-achieving.

As noted earlier, it was in this period that kindergarten was
becoming close to universal. In contrast to the (predominantly
half-day) compensatory education programs, for which "need" had
to be established and which included a social services component,
the (also half-day) kindergarten and nursery school were becoming
normative for the middle class. They generally did not include
extra services and did not restrict eligibility (if they were located
in the public schools). However, the fact that kindergarten and
nursery school programs lacked a social services component was
not necessarily a reflection of a different set of "needs" than existed
for low-income families who were eligible for day care services.

Many middle-class families used—and still use—half-day "educational" programs as a partial day care arrangement.

Comprehensive Child Development Legislation

At the federal level, the 1970s brought several aborted attempts at
legislating comprehensive child care initiatives. The Comprehensive Child Development Program Act was vetoed by President
Nixon in 1971. This piece of legislation would have created a
nationally coordinated network of child development programs
offering a wide range of educational, social, and medical services.
Eligibility would have cut across income levels and would not have
been tied to maternal employment. In his veto message, the
President highlighted the "fiscal irresponsibility, administrative
unworkability, and family-weakening implications" of the bill.[36]

Both themes—coordinated, comprehensive approaches on the
one hand, and "family-weakening implications," on the other—
were revisited in 1974 and 1975, when Congress attempted to pass
the Child and Family Services Act. This legislation would have
made $1.85 billion available for planning, developing, establishing
(including training and technical assistance), maintaining, and
operating a wide variety of child and family service programs,
including part- or full-day, center- or home-based programs; social
services; health care including pre- and postnatal; medical and
developmental screening; food and nutrition services; and "programs designed to extend child and family service gains (particularly parent participation) into kindergarten and early primary
grades."[37] Priority was to go to "those preschool children and
families with the greatest need in a manner designed to strengthen
family life and to insure direct participation of the parents of the
children served . . . through a partnership of parents, state, and
local government and the federal government."[38] Under this act,
sponsors of programs could have included local education agencies
in addition to other public and private nonprofit agencies. The act
also would have created a federal Child and Family Services
Coordinating Council whose purpose would have been to coordinate resources and services. Unfortunately, H.R. 2966 was the
victim of a vicious smear campaign initiated by an anonymous flyer
originally distributed in Indiana. Reminiscent of the themes noted
by President Nixon in his veto of the Comprehensive Child Development Program Act in 1971, opposition to the Child and Family
Services Act of 1975 consisted of fears over the certain "breakdown
in family order, increase in delinquency and a Godless Russian/

Chinese type regimentation of young minds."[39] The bill never made it through Congress.

The final attempt during the 1970s was the Child Care Act of 1979, which proposed to direct funding to the states to assist working parents in purchasing child care. The bill was withdrawn by Senator Cranston prior to a vote.

Late in the next decade, another attempt was made at passing comprehensive child care legislation. The Act for Better Child Care (ABC) was introduced in Congress in late 1987. Designed by a broad coalition of national organizations and child advocates, the bill proposed the provision of $2.5 billion (in the first year) to assist low- and middle-income families in purchasing child care and to make various improvements in the infrastructure of the child care system. Public schools were clearly included as one of many eligible service providers. Although not passed in 1988, ABC generated considerable support and was reintroduced in 1989, joined by numerous other child care bills including the Child Development and Education Act introduced by Representative Augustus Hawkins, which proposes a major role for public schools.

The Role of Public Schools

The 1971 and 1975 bills generated intense controversy over the potential role of the public schools. In 1974 the American Federation of Teachers (AFT), which had lobbied forcefully for the Comprehensive Child Development Act of 1971, proclaimed that the first educational priority of the nation should be universal early childhood education. This stand was refined a year later, when as part of its lobbying effort for the Child and Family Services Act of 1975, the AFT recommended that public schools be designated the primary sponsors, "allowing other public and nonprofit organizations to assume responsibility if a school system is unwilling or unable to accept it."[40] AFT president Albert Shanker was direct in linking this far-reaching recommendation to the "operational feasibility created by empty classrooms and a surplus of employable, trained teachers"[41]—both the result of a shrinking school-age population. The AFT also argued that the public schools had stronger professional standards than the child care system in addition to a well-established bureaucracy, thus eliminating the need to construct a new bureaucracy for early childhood education. Many "interpreted this argument as a self-serving attempt to put unemployed teachers back to work."[42] The call for public school involvement in prekindergarten education was not a new one. Originally, kindergartens did serve children younger than age five (as young as 22 months in Boston in the 1880s); only gradually was the entry age raised to eliminate children younger than five.[43] Perhaps the first clear call for opening public school doors as a matter of course to children below kindergarten entry age was voiced in 1945 by the Education Policies Committee of the National Education Association (NEA), which recommended that "schooling be extended to three- and four-year-olds, closely integrated with the rest of the program of public education, especially to educate children whose parents are not able by circumstances, nature, or training to give them the values inherent in a carefully directed program."[44] Twenty years later, the NEA amended its position—both narrowing the age range and broadening its definition of eligibility—to recommend that all children, at the age of four, should have access to a public school program at public expense.

The Role of the States

Not until the 1980s did the states take on a role of importance in support of early childhood programs—both in and out of the public schools. In large measure, state support has been due to federal legislation that has transferred responsibility for funding a multitude of programs from the federal to state and local levels. Child care funding through Title XX, for example, was transferred into the Social Services Block Grant, an act which essentially did two things. It increased the level of states' decision-making power over the allocation of funds to a whole variety of social services, including child care. It also increased the level of competition among the funded (or fundable) programs by reducing the overall level of funding. A national survey conducted by the Children's Defense Fund in 1988 revealed that, as a result of 1981 cuts, 23 states were serving fewer children with Title XX (now Social Services Block Grant) dollars than in 1981.[45]

Discounting state funds in the form of mandated federal matching dollars, the 1980s have seen state support for early childhood programs, especially for programs in the public schools, increase tremendously. Spurred by the promise of education reform, one state after another has pledged its commitment to early childhood education. State financial support has been a long time coming, however, even though two idiosyncratic states provided funds for early childhood programs at the turn of the century. In 1901 Maryland donated $3,000 to support two day nurseries in Baltimore.[46] In 1903 New Jersey became the first state to permit funds for prekindergarten programs.

Other than Maryland's and New Jersey's isolated efforts, and the commitments made by California and by New York to continue support for day care facilities after federal funds disappeared at the close of World War II, the states took no further action until compensatory education was rediscovered in the 1960s. That decade saw both California and New York create a new funding stream for public school preschool programs, modeled in many ways after Head Start. They were joined by Pennsylvania, West Virginia, and Washington, D.C. Maryland rejoined the roster in 1979, and from that point to this dozens of states have jumped on the education reform bandwagon.

Issues for the Present

As the interest in public school involvement in prekindergarten programs grows, some of the issues raised in earlier debates over public school involvement in kindergarten are being revived. Marvin Lazerson rightly cautions that "historical analogies are at best tenuous and dangerous." However, after an analysis of some of the parallels between kindergartens at the turn of the century and preschools today, he admits that the parallels are "incredibly striking."[47] Some of the issues that make the parallels so striking are those having to do with articulation between kindergarten and the primary grades, universal versus targeted programs, and the role of education as a panacea for solving social problems.

Articulation

In a 1982 article Bernard Spodek introduced his concerns about the downward extension of the primary grades into kindergarten, by quoting from the 1908 yearbook of the National Society for the Scientific Study of Education:[48]

> *In passing from the kindergarten to the primary school, there is a break. Do what you will to soften the change, to modify the break, it still remains a break. Three general methods of dealing with the difficulty have been employed: (1) To provide a connecting class to take the child out of his kindergarten habits and introduce him to those of the primary school: in the words of some teachers, "to make him over." (2) To modify the kindergarten and make it more nearly resemble the primary schools. (3) To modify the primary school to make it more nearly resemble the kindergarten. To these might be added a fourth: To do a little bit of each.*

The turn of the century saw intense debate between kindergarten and primary teachers. Kindergarten teachers argued that kindergarten techniques should be extended upward into the primary grades. The primary teachers responded that kindergarten children were not as willing to conform to the structured regimen of the primary grades, evidence that (in Marvin Lazerson's words) "schools should remain schools and should not become play houses."[49] Both groups lost some ground in this argument. As a result of pressures from kindergarten teachers, storytelling, recess, rest periods, and arts and crafts were introduced into the primary grades. However, after 1900 the new dual emphases on testing and reading readiness inevitably led to a certain loss of spontaneity in the kindergarten. An early childhood educator in the early 1930s is quoted as saying:[50]

> *In order to survive [in the public schools], we could not tell of the work we were doing with the families or with parents; we must try to prove as soon as possible that the children who had attended kindergarten could progress so much faster in the first grade. Consequently, we lost our splendid birthright of family welfare work and knowing the child in his home, and we began to work for very elementary forms of the three R's.*

That process has accelerated over the years until today, when the use of standardized testing and of commercially produced reading and math series (justified as necessary to ensure continuity of learning through the elementary grades) is the norm rather than the exception.

Universal Versus Targeted Programs

Although the original ideology of the kindergarten was its universality, when they moved into the public schools at the turn of the century, kindergartens were considered the special province of the poor. A Massachusetts superintendent, writing in 1897, voiced the opinion that "the kindergarten should be established not for the benefit of those children who come from homes of culture and refinement; but on the contrary, it should receive those children that have had little, if any, good home-training."[51] The issue of targeting—then and now—conflicts with notions about universality of the public school system (a generally held conception since the 1820s in the northern states), an issue as yet unresolved with respect to prekindergarten programs.

Education as a Solution to a Social Problem

In a pessimistic essay written in 1970, Marvin Lazerson criticizes those who see prekindergarten education *alone* as leading to major social change and in so doing are able to avoid the larger, more complex political issues that also demand action. "Education is a lot cheaper than new housing and new jobs."[52]

The point is not to lessen support for early childhood education but to acknowledge that it cannot stand alone. Children also need self-sufficient, competent parents and stable, safe neighborhoods. The naive optimism of the early free kindergartners is frequently echoed by those present-day advocates for expanded public support of early education, who see the strength and power of early childhood education as a panacea that it never was and never can be. Early childhood education must be one part of a larger social strategy—a series of interconnected efforts—to improve housing, improve health care, and expand job opportunities, if it is to deliver on its promises.

The push for public school involvement in early childhood education began in a climate of social reform. In large measure, it is rooted there today.

Endnotes

1. Lazerson, M. (1970). Social reform and early-childhood education. *Urban Education* 5:84–202, 89.
2. *Constitution and By-Laws of the Infant School Society*. Boston, (n.p.). Quoted in M.O. Steinfels (1973). *Who's minding the children: The history and politics of day care in America*. New York: Simon and Schuster, p. 36.
3. Fein, G.G., and A. Clarke-Stewart (1973). *Day care in context*. New York: John Wiley & Sons, p. 13.
4. Kerr, V. (1973). One step forward—two steps back: Child care's long American history. In P. Roby (Ed.), *Child care—Who cares?* New York: Basic Books, Inc., pp. 157–169.
5. Shapiro, M.S. (1983). *Child's garden: The kindergarten movement from Froebel to Dewey*. University Park, Pa.: The Pennsylvania State University Press, p. 20.
6. For a succinct description of Froebels "gifts" and "occupations" see B. Spodek (1982). The kindergarten: A retrospective and contemporary view. In L.G. Katz (Ed.), *Current topics in early childhood education*. Volume IV. Norwood, N.J.: Ablex Publishing Corporation, pp. 173–191.
7. Shapiro (1983), pp. 21–22.
8. Lazerson (1970), p. 89.
9. Kerr (1973), p. 159.
10. Blow, S.E. (1900). Kindergarten education. In N.M. Butler (Ed.), *Monographs on education in the United States*, p. 37. Prepared for the United States Commission to the Paris Exposition of 1900.
11. Ibid., p. 38.
12. For a complete account, see Shapiro, M.S. (1983).

13. Shapiro (1983), p. 55.
14. Ibid., pp. 55–56.
15. Lazerson (1970), p. 90.
16. Ibid., p. 91.
17. Shapiro (1983), p. 132.
18. Kahn, A.J., and S.B. Kamerman (1987). *Child care: Facing the hard choices.* Dover, Mass.: Auburn House Publishing Company, p. 121.
19. Shapiro (1983), pp. 133–134.
20. Blow (1900), p. 42.
21. Kahn and Kamerman (1987), p. 121.
22. Spodek (1982), p. 176.
23. Fein and Clarke-Stewart (1973), p. 17.
24. Ibid., p. 18.
25. Kahn and Kamerman (1987), p. 127.
26. Kerr, p. 88, citing the 1929 *Year Book of the National Society for the Study of Education*, p. 160.
27. Fein and Clark-Stewart (1973), p. 19.
28. Lazerson (1971a). The historical antecedents of early childhood education. *National Social Studies Education Year Book*, Part 2: 33–53.
29. Lazerson (1971a), p. 51.
30. During the Civil War, a federally supported day nursery operated in Philadelphia for the children of women who worked in the wartime factories and hospitals. Kerr (1973), p. 158.
31. Fein and Clark-Stewart (1973), p. 22.
32. Kerr (1973); Steinfels (1973), pp. 67, 163.
33. Kerr (1973), p. 167.
34. Spodek (1982), p. 180.
35. Kahn and Kamerman (1987), pp. 126, 129.
36. Quoted in Fein and Clarke-Stewart (1973), p. 34.
37. *H.R. 2966, Background Materials*, p. 11.
38. Ibid.
39. Excerpts from a constituent's letter to Representative John Brademas cited in *H.R. 2966 Background Materials*, p. 83.
40. Rauth, M. (1976). *A long road to an unresolved problem: Comprehensive child care in the U.S.* Washington, D.C.: American Federation of Teachers, p. 2.
41. AFT Task Force on Educational Issues (1976). *Putting early childhood and day care services into the public schools: The position of the American Federation of Teachers and an action plan for promoting it.* Washington, D.C.: American Federation of Teachers.
42. Grubb, W.N. (1987). *Young children face the states: Issues and options for early childhood programs.* Rutgers, N.J.: Center for Policy Research in Education, p. 10.
43. In 1925 the most common entrance ages for kindergarten were four and five years. In 1961 the median admission age was four years, eight months. By 1984 nearly two-thirds of all school districts required a minimum age of five years by October 15th. (Education Research Service, 1986)
44. Grubb (1987), p. 8.

45. Blank, H., Savage, J., and A. Wilkins, *State Child Care Fact Book 1988*. Washington, D.C.: Children's Defense Fund, p. 159.
46. Kerr (1973).
47. Lazerson (1970), pp. 95, 97.
48. Spodek (1982), p. 175.
49. Lazerson (1971a), p. 93.
50. Grubb (1987), p. 6.
51. Lazerson, M. (1971b). *Origins of the Public Schools: Public Education in Massachusetts, 1870–1915*. Cambridge, Mass.: Harvard University Press.
52. Lazerson (1970), p. 85.

Chapter 2

FACTS AND FINDINGS FROM THE STATE AND DISTRICT SURVEYS

The purpose of this chapter is to provide the reader with basic information about state-funded prekindergarten programs and about the variety of local public school-operated early childhood programs (which include, but are not limited to, state-funded prekindergarten programs). The terms *early childhood* and *pre-kindergarten* refer to children younger than kindergarten entry age, that is, from birth through about the age of five years. *Public school-operated* denotes a program that is directly administered and operated by a local education agency, or a public school district. The information presented in this chapter is drawn from the state and district surveys conducted as part of the Public School Early Childhood Study.

First, the methods we used to gather the information will be explained. The discussion then moves through a summary of what was found about state prekindergarten programs across the country. Finally, profiles of three kinds of local school district-operated programs are offered as illustrations of the variety of programs school districts are actually providing. Knowing what the states have legislated and what local school districts do will help to set the stage for discussions of critical issues in later chapters.

The Public School Early Childhood Study

The Public School Early Childhood Study had three parts: *the State Survey*, a telephone and mail survey in 1986–1987 of state

20

agency personnel, Head Start Association directors, and child advocates in all 50 states and the District of Columbia; *the District Survey*, a mail survey of 1,225 public school districts in the spring of 1986; and *Case Studies* of prekindergarten programs operated by 13 public school districts in 12 states conducted during the winter of 1986–1987. The entire study focused on both practical operations and policy implications at the state, district, and school levels.

The State Survey

The purpose of the State Survey was to develop an overview of the status of child care and early childhood education for children kindergarten age and younger in the 50 states and the District of Columbia. Fiscal, programmatic, regulatory, and policy-related information was gathered from state departments of education, human services, day care licensing, and Head Start through structured telephone interviews and written surveys. In addition, reports, regulations, and other published materials were gathered from each state. The goal was to construct as complete a picture as possible of early childhood efforts in each state.

Seven telephone interview guides and seven survey instruments were developed for respondents from state agencies responsible for child care licensing, Title XX/SSBG, WIN, AFDC, Chapter I, Special Education, and state kindergarten and prekindergarten programs. Two additional telephone guides were developed for the chairpersons of state Head Start directors associations and state child advocates. Because neither had access to quantitative data, survey instruments were not developed for these respondents.

The survey instruments collected data on numbers of children served, by age and length of day; present and projected funding levels; regulations; staffing requirements; programmatic requirements; and coordination efforts for each program area. The telephone interview guides sought to confirm data collected via the survey and from review of published materials, and to collect information on the major early childhood issues and concerns in the state for each program and on any barriers to addressing these issues. In each state, interviews were conducted with state agency personnel in charge of child care regulation, the federal- and state-subsidized child care program (the federal Social Service Block Grant [SSBG] or Title XX), and other subsidized child care programs, such as those under Aid to Families with Dependent Children and the Work Incentive Program. Early childhood specialists in the state education department, special education staff, state (ECIA—Education Consolidation and Improvement Act) Chapter I coordinators, and Head Start officials and child advocates were also interviewed.

State program administrators were identified through lists provided by national organizations and federal agencies. Child advocates were selected in consultation with the Children's Defense Fund and represented persons knowledgeable and active in early childhood programs and policy in each state who could provide a bridge between child care and public school early childhood programs. Interviewers were trained in both the program areas and in interviewing techniques.

Cover letters, one-page program descriptions, and copies of the telephone interview guide and the survey instrument were mailed to program administrators. Telephone contact was established to ascertain the correct names, titles, and responsibilities of potential respondents. A second telephone contact immediately followed the mailing to monitor receipt of the materials and to set up convenient times for the telephone interviews. Both the cover letter and survey instruments contained a return date for the written materials as well as an addressed return envelop. Despite the fact that the telephone interviews were arranged in advance, many had to be rebooked several times over a period of weeks due to the busy schedules of respondents. The interview response rate was 97 percent; the overall response rate for both interviews and survey instruments was 89 percent.

The District Survey

The District Survey was designed to gather extensive data on the details of program operation for all types of programs for prekindergarten children operated by public school districts. The purpose of the survey was to describe the current state of public school-operated prekindergarten programs in the United States by answering two basic questions: What kinds of prekindergarten programs do school districts run? What are the operational characteristics of these programs in regard to children, staff, and parents? The District Survey was conducted in the spring of 1986; the data gathered were for the 1985–1986 school year. The targeted sample for the survey sought to include all U.S. public school districts operating any program for children younger than kindergarten entry age during the 1985–1986 school year.

Because no reliable federal sources exist for identifying all U.S. school districts operating prekindergarten programs, data from the federal Administration for Children, Youth, and Families were used to identify all public school districts participating in Head Start and were carefully merged with data from two reliable education data firms. The final sample included (1) all school districts which identify at least one school as having a prekindergarten classroom, (2) all districts with any central office personnel identified as an *early childhood supervisor*, and (3) all districts which either administer a Head Start grant or operate at least one Head Start classroom. There are approximately 14,000 operating public school districts in the United States; the sample consisted of 2,773 districts. This sample is not representative of all U.S. school districts in general and, because of the sample construction method, probably overrepresents Head Start programs. Therefore, the results of this survey are not generalizable beyond the sample.

Two survey instruments were constructed and field tested. The district overview, directed to the superintendent, was designed to collect basic data on the types of programs and their respective administrators, the total number of prekindergarten children served, by age, and the superintendent's opinions on prekindergarten programs and their future in the district. The program questionnaire was directed to each program's administrator and was designed to collect data specific to one program in regard to number and ages of children served; hours of operation, and day and year length; support services; ratios and class sizes; funding sources; cost per child; eligibility criteria; staffing, hiring requirements, and salaries; accommodations to working parents; and the administrators' opinions as to what were the most and least favorable aspects of their programs. Each district superintendent received a package of four questionnaires (one overview and three programs).

The total number of district overview questionnaires completed by school districts was 1,225, representing a 44 percent response rate for the district overview. From these district overviews, 1,717 programs were identified. The total number of program questionnaires received was 1,681, yielding a 98 percent response rate for the program questionnaire.

The responding districts and the nonrespondent group were compared on a number of dimensions: geographical distribution, urbanicity, per-pupil spending, relative poverty, ethnicity, and enrollment size of district. These comparisons show that the nonrespondents do not differ from the respondents, and thus the respondents do accurately reflect the targeted sample.

The Case Studies

The final part of the study was a group of in-depth case studies designed to provide, through face-to-face interviews and on-site observations, an understanding of public school early childhood programs in practice. Potential case study sites were located through a broad-based nomination process designed to reach all public school prekindergarten programs. The objective of the site selection process was to gather a large pool of generally good programs—ones representative of the range of programs operated by public schools for children younger than kindergarten entry age, and of the variation on school district demographic factors (for example, district size, geographic location, urbanicity, and ethnicity)—from which to select a dozen sites.

From the pool of over 200 nominations, the study selected 13 public school prekindergarten programs in 12 states, representing a wide range of program types. Programs varied in several dimensions: length of day (part-day, school day, or full working day); funding source (state-funded prekindergarten, Chapter I, local tax support, parent tuition); size and degree of urbanicity of district; and regional location. The 13 selected sites represent all major program types, all regions of the country, and all sizes of districts.

Data were collected through review of written materials, classroom observations, and individual and group interviews. Observations and interviews were conducted during site visits. Written materials collected during the nomination process were reviewed prior to the site visit. They included district demographic data, program reports and evaluations, parent handbooks and newsletters, curriculum guides/objectives, and personnel handbooks (or union contracts).

During a five-day site visit, a two-member team observed prekindergarten and kindergarten classrooms and interviewed the district superintendent, other district-level administrators, program administrators, teachers, parents, and representatives of the early childhood community. Districts with multisite programs were asked to choose one site (whichever they regarded as the best example of their program) as the focus for the visit. In these districts, the site visit team also attempted to observe briefly in a few other program sites. In districts with a small number of sites (fewer than 10), the team attempted to observe briefly in all program sites while keeping the primary focus on the one site selected by the district. Observations were made of all prekindergarten classrooms in this designated site. Teachers and parents from this site were also interviewed. A group teacher interview, to which all teachers in the designated site were invited, was scheduled at the time most convenient for the majority of teachers. All parents whose children attended the early childhood program at the designated site were invited to attend the parent group interview. Interviews were scheduled with the district superintendent, other appropriate district-level administrators, and the program administrator(s). To assess continuity of curriculum approach between prekindergarten and kindergarten, observations were done in at least one kindergarten class.

The site visit team also observed children and interviewed the directors in two local, nonpublic school programs chosen to be the closest alternatives for families to the designated public school site. Additional interviews were conducted with the child care resource and referral agency (in sites where one existed), as well as with presidents of local early childhood educators associations and the heads of local child care directors associations.

Two basic instruments were used for data collection on site visits: a three-part classroom observation form and six interview protocols. Classroom observations were guided by two previously developed and validated instruments: the *Early Childhood Environment Rating Scale* (ECERS) and the *Stanford Research Institute (SRI) Classroom Observation System*. The ECERS, developed by Thelma Harms and Richard Clifford at the Frank Porter Graham Child Development Center at the University of North Carolina at Chapel Hill, provides an overall picture of the quality of an early childhood setting as determined by the scores on seven dimensions: Personal Care Routines, Furnishings and Display for Children, Language-Reasoning Experiences, Fine and Gross Motor Activities, Creative Activities, Social Development, and Adult Needs. The scale was slightly adapted for use in this study, but essentially it was used as designed. A second instrument modified for use in this study was taken from the SRI observation system, developed by Jane Stallings for use in the national *Follow Through* evaluation. A classroom environment form was used to record summary information and data on the physical environment, including the organization of space and the presence of supplies and equipment. A third part of the observational record was designed by study staff. It was used to record staffing patterns; the ethnicity, gender, and number of staff and children; and a brief description of the activities observed during each classroom visit. The interview protocols included six categories of informants: superintendents, program administrators, teachers, parents, directors of child care resource and referral agencies, and directors of community early childhood programs.

Both district superintendents and early childhood program administrators were asked about the origins and history of the program, financing, and child eligibility. The protocol for program administrators was more programmatic in focus, concentrating on operational questions such as staffing, training, recruiting of children, curriculum goals, administrative structure, parent involvement, and relationship to other district early childhood programs and to other community programs.

Teachers answered a set of questions concerning their background, career path, current working conditions, supervisory support and staff development, evaluation, relationship to early childhood professional organizations, the relationship between the program and parents, and their opinion of the advantages and disadvantages of having early childhood programs in public schools.

The parent interview focused on four areas: how parents selected the program, what influenced their decision, and what the enrollment procedures were; their view of parent involvement, and the program's attitude toward parents and responsiveness to parents; whether they worked and/or attended school and had child care needs; and their overall opinion of the program.

The interview for resource and referral agency personnel covered local demographics (numbers of children by age, socioeconomic status of families generally, numbers of working parents); supply and demand for child care; the nature of the local early childhood community; an overall view of staff recruitment, retention, and training issues; and their opinion of the public school early childhood program and their relationship to it, specifically including perceived problems of competition for staff or children.

These community observations and interviews helped to paint a picture of each local early childhood community, providing a background context for viewing the public school prekindergarten program. Three technical reports, describing in greater detail the methodology and specific findings of each of the three parts of the study, are available.[1]

Patterns of Public Involvement in Early Childhood Programs

Public schools are involved in early childhood education in many ways, although the state-funded prekindergarten program for four-year-olds is the most widely known, having been the subject of much media coverage and public debate. While this is a prevalent

form of public school involvement, there are many other forms—
some old (like the Lanham Act child care centers discussed in the
previous chapter) and some new (like New York City's Project
Giant Step or Vermont's new Early Education initiative). One way
to view the prevailing patterns of public involvement in early
childhood education is to look at involvement at the three levels of
government: federal, state, and local. In the context of this discussion, involvement means either funding or directly operating a
particular program for young children.

The federal government does not directly operate any early
childhood programs. There are five ways that the federal government funds early childhood programs: *indirectly* via the Dependent Care Tax Credit of the Internal Revenue Code and *directly*
through the Social Service Block Grant (Title XX), Head Start,
Chapter I of the Education Consolidation and Improvement Act,
and the Education of the Handicapped Act (special education).

Similarly, states do not directly operate early childhood programs. There are six ways that states fund early childhood programs: *indirectly* through state dependent care tax credits and
directly through state/federal child care subsidy programs (all 50
states and the District of Columbia), through state-funded prekindergarten programs (22 states), through so-called permissive prekindergarten programs (reimbursed via state school aid formulas
in 4 states and the District of Columbia), through state-funded
parent education programs offered by public school districts (2
states), and through contributions to Head Start (8 states and the
District of Columbia).

At the local level, the picture becomes more complex because
local communities both fund and operate early childhood programs. Some cities and counties appropriate local monies for child
care and other forms of early childhood education, and others
operate child care programs directly. A municipality can simultaneously receive federal and state funds, appropriate other local
funds, and operate early childhood programs. In most communities, a multitude of local public and private agencies are the
ultimate recipients of the federal, state, and/or local funds from
the various sources, and these agencies are the direct operators of
early childhood programs. As one of several local agencies in a
given municipality, school districts may both operate and fund
early childhood programs.

The remainder of the chapter is dedicated to describing two
pieces in the pattern of involvement outlined above: state-funded
prekindergarten programs (those offering direct services to children younger than kindergarten entry age and those aimed at

parents of prekindergarten-aged children) and local public school-operated early childhood programs. Ten tables are included to summarize the information presented.

State-Funded Prekindergarten Programs

In the majority of states the state education agency has had some experience—mainly through federal legislation and funds—in providing prekindergarten programs for handicapped children, through the federal Education of the Handicapped Act, or programs for low-income or low-achieving prekindergarten-aged children, using federal Chapter I funds. However, prior to 1980 seven states had passed legislation and/or provided state revenues for state-created prekindergarten programs: New Jersey, Pennsylvania, New York, California, the District of Columbia (for counting purposes in this discussion, the District of Columbia is regarded as a state), West Virginia, and Maryland. The earliest of these is New Jersey's program, which began in 1903. Between 1965, when Head Start was created, and 1977 four states began to contribute state funds to Head Start programs operating in their states: Hawaii, Washington, Connecticut, and Alaska.

These state efforts to create early education programs (or in the case of Head Start contributions, to support existing ones) represent a distinct category of early childhood programs: Many of the programs in this category were conceived in the mid-1980s as part of a statewide education reform agenda, not as child care programs, and the majority are operated by public schools. Often these programs are an effort to extend early education to needy, unserved youngsters, usually between the ages of three and five. Programs that aim to serve a specific category of children—those who are poor, who cannot speak English, who are deemed to be educationally at-risk—are referred to as *targeted* programs.

The largely targeted state prekindergarten efforts resulting from this renewed interest in early childhood education recognize that nonhandicapped, low-income children are less than half as likely as higher-income children to enter school (at kindergarten) having had prekindergarten experience—despite the federal Head Start program, the use of Chapter I funds for prekindergarten in some states, and funding for child care through the Social Services Block Grant (Title XX). According to 1985 statistics from the federal Department of Education, two-thirds of four-year-olds whose families have incomes of $35,000 or more per year participated in prekindergarten programs. In contrast, fewer than one-third of four-year-olds whose families earn less than $10,000 per year were enrolled in prekindergarten programs.

This new category of programs directly serves children below the age of kindergarten entry. A close relation to this category is the state-funded parent education program provided through public schools. These programs are aimed at the parents of prekindergarten-aged children. Minnesota and Missouri have funded this kind of program, the former initiating it as a state-funded pilot in 1974.

Between 1980 and 1983, three states initiated direct service prekindergarten programs (Oklahoma, Florida, and Alaska—which already contributed to Head Start), and Missouri began its pilot parent education program, making a total of 15 states—10 with state-funded prekindergarten programs, 4 contributing to Head Start, and 2 providing parent education for the families of prekindergarten-aged children.

Fueled by the education reform movement, the tempo of state involvement increased beginning in 1984, when three states began prekindergarten programs: one each in South Carolina and Texas and two distinct programs—one permissive and one innovative grants—in Maine. Both Minnesota and Missouri expanded their parent education programs statewide. The pace accelerated rapidly in 1985, when six states appropriated funds for prekindergarten programs (Illinois, Louisiana, Massachusetts, Ohio, Washington, and Wisconsin). During 1986 and 1987 five more states joined the ranks (Delaware, Kentucky—with two distinct programs—Michigan, Oregon, and Vermont), and three states with existing prekindergarten programs passed legislation for additional programs (Florida, New Jersey, and Michigan). Furthermore, since 1984 four more states initiated contributions to Head Start programs (Rhode Island, Maine, Massachusetts, and Minnesota). In 1988, New Jersey began its third state-funded prekindergarten program, Rhode Island, Colorado, and Iowa created their first (all targeted at children at risk), and Illinois, New Hampshire, and Ohio began to contribute state funds to Head Start.

As 1989 begins, a total of 32 states are involved—27 fund 33 prekindergarten programs, 12 contribute to Head Start, and 3 fund parent education programs delivered through public schools. Table 2–1 summarizes these state efforts. Table 2–2 presents the ages and numbers of children served and annual funding levels for state prekindergarten initiatives, parent education programs, and Head Start contributions through FY 1988.

Other features of these state initiatives are summarized in Tables 2–3 and 2–4. Table 2–3 offers a typology for differentiating among

Table 2-1 State-Funded Prekindergarten Programs, Contributions To Head Start, and Parent Education Programs Updated Through 1989

States	Prekindergarten Programs	Contributions to Head Start	Parent Education via Public Schools
Alaska	✓	✓	
California	✓		
Colorado	✓		
Connecticut		✓	
Delaware	✓		
District of Columbia	✓	✓	
Florida	• ✓ ✓		
Hawaii		✓	
Illinois	✓	✓	
Iowa	✓		
Kentucky	✓ ✓		
Louisiana	✓		
Maine	✓ ✓	✓	
Maryland	✓		
Massachusetts	✓	✓	
Michigan	✓ ✓		
Minnesota		✓	✓
Missouri			✓
New Hampshire		✓	
New Jersey	✓ ✓ ✓		
New York	✓		
Ohio	✓	✓	
Oklahoma	✓		
Oregon	✓		✓
Pennsylvania	✓		
Rhode Island	✓	✓	
South Carolina	✓		
Texas	✓		
Vermont	✓		
Washington	✓	✓	
West Virginia	✓		
Wisconsin	✓		
Total 32	33	12	3

Table 2-2 Funding Levels And Children Served Via State Prekindergarten Programs, State Contributions To Head Start, And Parent Education Programs Through FY 1988

ates	Ages Served	Funding (FY 1988 unless noted)	No. Of Children Served (FY 1988 unless noted)	Funding Inc/Dec Over Prior Year
ıska	3-4	$197,000	45 (FY87)	decrease
ıska Head Start	3-5	2.7 million	1,625 (FY87)	increase
ılifornia	3-5	35.5 million	19,221	level
ınnecticut Head Start	3-5	400,000	–	increase
ılaware	4	189,000	99	increase
strict of Columbia	4	12.2 million	3,444	increase
C. Head Start	3-5	1.1 million	725	level
ırida	3-4	1.6 million	–	increase
ırida (migrant)	3-4	2.9 million	2,540 (FY87)	ncrease
ıwaii Head Start	3-5	291,790	–	increase
ıois	3-5	12.7 million	7,400	level
ıntucky	3-4	900,000 PACE	270 PACE	increase
		232,123 EIG	280 EIG	–
uisiana	4	1.8 million	1,272	decrease
aine (grants)	4	27,730	–	–
aine (permissive)	4	–	167	–
aine Head Start	3-5	1.9 million	724	level
aryland	4	3.3 million	2,820	increase
assachusetts	3-5	10.3 million	–	level
assachusetts Head Start	3-4	4.5 million	–	increase
chigan (grants)	4	300,000	800 (FY87)	decrease
chigan (formula)	4	1 million (FY87)	–	–
nnesota Head Start	3-5	2 million	3,500 over 2 yrs	–
nnesota Parent Ed.	0-5	22 million	72,000	increase
ssouri Parent Ed.	0-3	12 million	–	increase
ıw Jersey (permissive)	4	6.9 million (FY87)	5,794 (FY87)	–
ıw Jersey (grants)	3-5	1 million	–	–
ıw York	3-4	27 million	12,000	increase
ıio	3-5	18,000	–	decrease
ːlahoma	4	832,275	1,400	increase
ˈegon	3-4	1.1 million (FY88-89)	300	–
ınnsylvania	4	1.7 million (FY87)	3,260 (FY87)	–
ıode Island Head Start	3-5	365,000	–	increase
ıuth Carolina	4	10.9 million	10,715	small increase
ıxas	4	46.2 million	54,493	increase
ˈrmont	3-4	500,000	250	–
ashington	4	4.7 million (direct service)	2,000	increase
ashington Head Start	3-5	660,000 (FY89)	–	increase
est Virginia	3-4	258,574 (FY86)	215 (FY86)	decrease
isconsin	4	4.3 million	5,850	small increase

state-funded direct service prekindergarten programs by the target population of children served, the state agency administering the program, the local agencies permitted to operate the program, and the method of funding. Table 2–4 offers a typology based on the same information for those states making contributions to Head Start.

Characteristics

Each of the programs in the states that now fund direct-service prekindergarten programs represents a unique product of that

Table 2-3   A Typology of State Prekindergarten Legislation Through FY 1988

Older (pre-1980)	Newer (1980-1987)	Children Served	State Agency	Recipient of Funds	Method of Funding
N.J.*, PA., D.C.	Wis., Maine*	Any child; no target population	Department of education	Public schools	Permissive; K-type attendance formula reimbursement; enrollment reimbursement
	Ohio, Okla., Del.	Any child; no target population	Department of education	Public schools	Grants/contracts
	Tex., Mich., Ky, *La., Maine*	Targeted; at-risk	Department of education	Public schools allocations	Grants/contracts;
	S.C., Ill., Mass, Fla., Ky.*	Targeted; at-risk	Department of education	Public schools with subcontracts to other agencies permitted	Contracts; allocations
Calif., W.Va.	Vt, Oreg.	Targeted; at-risk	Department of education	Public schools with subcontracts to other agencies permitted; direct contracts to other agencies	Grants/contracts
	Wash., Alaska, N.J.*	Targeted; at-risk	Departments of community development; community and regional affairs; human services	Direct contracts to public schools and other agencies	Grants/contracts

* Both Kentucky and Maine have two distinct programs; New Jersey has three distinct programs.

Table 2-4 A Typology of State Contributions to Head Start Programs Through FY 1988

Older (pre-1980)	Newer (1980-1987)	Children Served	State Agency	Recipient of Funds	Method of Funding
Alaska, Wash., Hawaii	Maine	Targeted; at-risk	Departments of community development, community/regional affairs, community services	Direct allocation to grantees	Formula allocation
Conn.*	R.I., Minn.	Targeted; at-risk	Departments of human services; human resources; jobs and training	Direct allocation to grantees	Formula allocation
D.C.+	Mass.	Targeted; at-risk	Department of education; board of education	Direct allocation to grantees	Formula allocation

State Funding Levels and Numbers Served

State	Current Funding Level	Numbers of Children Served
Alaska	2.7 million	1,625
Conn.	.4 million	–
D.C.	1.1 million	725
Hawaii	.3 million	–
Maine	1.9 million	724
Mass.	4.5 million	–
Minn.	2.0 million	3,500
R.I.	.4 million	–
Wash.	.5 million	–

* Connecticut has contributed up to half of the 20 percent match since 1968. Funds were made available to Head Start programs through CAP agencies. In FY 1988, the state provided funds directly to Head Start programs to offset federal cuts.

+ D.C. contributes to Public School Head Start grantees only.

state's strengths and concerns combined with the particular array of actors and forces that converged to create the program. Although these programs each have a distinct history and course of development and each certainly has unique features, as a whole they are a category of early childhood program—state-funded direct-service programs for children younger than kindergarten entry age—and do share certain basic characteristics across states. For example, four-year-olds are the most common age group served in these programs; education departments are the usual state administrative agency; the vast majority of the programs are operated by local public school districts; and most are half-day, school-year programs.

What Ages of Children Are Served and What Criteria Are Used to Determine Which Children Are Eligible? The 30 state-funded prekindergarten programs operational at the time of the study are almost equally divided between those serving only four-year-olds and those extending program services to children between ages three and five. Two-thirds (20) of these state programs are targeted for children defined as being at risk due to their family's low-income status or to other conditions, such as limited English proficiency or a predicted lack of school readiness. (See Table 2–3 for states with targeted programs.) The majority of states with targeted programs offer some guidelines for defining risk status and require that school districts and/or grantees ensure that children served meet these guidelines; some state programs also require the screening of individual children to determine at-risk status. South Carolina, Illinois, and Louisiana are the states that admit children to the state-funded prekindergarten program on the basis of individual assessments of developmental status. Obviously, all state contributions to Head Start can be classified as targeted efforts since Head Start is by definition aimed primarily at poor children (with a small proportion of slots reserved for handicapped prekindergartners).

Among the eight states which do not target their early childhood programs to specific categories of children, five provide prekindergarten services under the school code (New Jersey, Pennsylvania, Wisconsin, the District of Columbia, and one of Maine's two programs). *Permissive* means that public school districts are permitted under the state school code to serve prekindergarten-aged children. These permissive programs theoretically allow any of the state's local school districts to serve four-year-olds or three- and four-year-olds, and the districts receive reimbursement under the state school attendance reimbursement formula. Although nontargeted programs imply that any child (of the appropriate age) is eligible, in fact this does not mean that all such children have access to the prekindergarten program in any of these states. In practice, the number of children served statewide varies from about 6,000 in either New Jersey's or Wisconsin's permissive programs to fewer than 200 children in Maine's. Three states (Ohio, Oklahoma, and Delaware) distribute their nontargeted prekindergarten program funds via competitive grants. The number of children served statewide ranges from about 100 in Delaware to about 1,400 in Oklahoma.

Which State Agency Administers the Prekindergarten Program and Which Local Agencies Are Permitted to Operate It? With only three exceptions (Washington, Alaska, and the two newer programs in New Jersey), state departments of education or public instruction have primary responsibility for the prekindergarten programs. One of New Jersey's newest prekindergarten programs is the nation's first to be jointly administered by two state agencies—education and human services. In contrast, state contributions to Head Start tend to be administered under the auspices of noneducational state agencies such as community development or human services. Fifteen of the twenty-eight state prekindergarten programs limit program operation to the public schools; five state programs permit the public schools to subcontract with other agencies for services; four states permit public schools to subcontract and also permit private agencies to contract directly with the state. Three states contract directly either with public schools or other agencies but permit no subcontracting. Table 2–3 lists the state prekindergarten programs by state agency auspice and types of contracting permitted. (Table 2–4 offers similar information for state contributions to Head Start.)

What Teacher Qualifications and Staffing Ratios Are Required? State prekindergarten programs are evenly divided between those requiring classroom teachers to have training and/or certification in early childhood education and those without any such requirements. Only six state prekindergarten programs permit staff–child ratios in excess of 1:10 for four-year-olds (Texas and the nontargeted programs in Maine, New Jersey, Ohio, Pennsylvania, and Wisconsin). Nine state programs require ratios of 1:8 or below (California, Delaware, Kentucky, Maine's targeted program, Massachusetts, both of Michigan's programs, New York, and Washington). Class size is limited to 20 or fewer children in 10 state programs (District of Columbia, Delaware, Florida [migrant], Maryland, Michigan, South Carolina, Washington, Kentucky's PACE, Massachusetts, and New York). Of these state programs, three limit class size to 15 or fewer children (Kentucky's PACE, Massachusetts, and New York).

With a few exceptions, the staff–child ratios and class sizes specified for state-funded prekindergarten programs are the same as or better than the states' child care standards regarding ratios and class sizes. Florida's two prekindergarten programs are notable in that both require twice as many staff per child (1:10) as the state child care standards, which allow a ratio of 1:20 for four-year-olds. Five states specify less favorable staff–child ratios in their prekindergarten programs than are required under their state's child care regulations. Four of these are permissive programs (Maine, New Jersey, Wisconsin, and Pennsylvania). The fifth is the targeted prekindergarten program in Texas, which requires a ratio of 1:22, while child care regulations specify 1:18–20. On the positive side, the Texas prekindergarten program does limit class size (to 22 children) in contrast to state child care regulations, which allow class sizes of up to 35 children.

What Services Are Required to Be Provided in State-Funded Prekindergarten Programs? Half of the state early childhood efforts specify, either in legislative language or through program regulations, that comprehensive services be provided. Comprehensive services typically include nutrition, health, social services, and parental participation requirements. Two-thirds (12) of the 20 targeted state prekindergarten programs require a full complement of comprehensive services. Permissive programs (with the exception of the District of Columbia's) do not specify that comprehensive services be offered. Table 2–5 notes which services are required in the state-funded prekindergarten programs.

Are Curriculum Elements Specified for These Prekindergarten Programs? The 8 states with permissive prekindergarten legislation have no curricular or comprehensive service requirements for these programs. In 18 state prekindergarten programs, some elements of a developmental approach are specified either legislatively or in program regulations; in 11 these elements are required (California, Florida, Kentucky's PACE, Massachusetts, Maryland, New Jersey's two newer programs, New York, Oklahoma, Oregon, South Carolina, and Washington). The remaining 12 state programs focus primarily on academic (or school readiness) curricula.

What Is the Daily and Annual Schedule of These Programs? Despite the fact that state policymakers generally claim that state prekindergarten initiatives are partially based on the need to assist the growing numbers of mothers in the labor force as well as to enhance the development of young children, the majority of state prekindergarten programs (16 states) are half-day

Table 2-5 Comprehensive Services Specified in State-Funded Prekindergarten Programs

es With kindergarten grams	Parent Education	Parent Participation	Screening/Health Assesment	Nutrition	Social Services	Staff Development
ska	✓	✓	✓	✓	✓	✓
fornia	✓	✓	✓	✓	✓	✓
aware		✓				
rict of Columbia	✓	✓	✓	✓		✓
rida (migrant)		✓		✓		
rida	✓	✓	✓	✓	✓	✓
ois	✓	✓	✓	✓	✓	
ntucky (PACE)	✓	✓	✓			
tucky (EIG)						
isiana	✓	✓	(screening only)			✓
ne (permissive and grants)						
yland	✓	✓	(screening only)			✓
ssachusetts	✓	✓	✓	✓	✓	✓
higan (both programs)	✓	✓	✓	✓	✓	✓
w Jersey (permissive)						
w Jersey (grants)	✓	✓	✓	✓	✓	✓
w York	✓	✓	✓	✓	✓	✓
o	✓	✓	(screening only			✓
ahoma	✓	✓	✓	✓		✓
gon	✓	✓	✓	✓	✓	
nsylvania						
uth Carolina	✓	✓	✓	✓	✓	✓
as	✓		(screening only)			
mont	✓	✓	✓	✓	✓	
shington	✓	✓	✓	✓	✓	✓
st Virginia						
consin						✓

These six elements are mentioned specifically in either the enabling legislation creating these programs and/or in the state agency's regulations further defining these programs.

programs; an additional 8 states specify that local programs may be provided for either half- or full-school days. Five states clearly permit children to be served for the full working day either by directly funding full-working-day programs or by encouraging the use of other funds to supplement state prekindergarten funds. Even with permission (or at least not prohibition) and some encouragement in these states (Vermont, Massachusetts, Illinois, New Jersey's newer programs, and both of Florida's programs), relatively few full-working-day programs have been funded to date. In Illinois none have been funded; in Massachusetts 16 full-working-day programs have been funded out of a total of more than 120 funded. One-third of Vermont's first-year grants were awarded to agencies that already offered full-working-day programs. The number of children who actually received full-working-day services funded under Vermont's early education program is not known.

The school year is the typical annual schedule. Although a few states permit special summer extensions of their prekindergarten programs (Texas, Illinois), no state funds year-round prekindergarten programs.

How Much Are States Spending on Their Prekindergarten Programs?   In terms of total state expenditures for prekindergarten programs, including direct service prekindergarten programs, state contributions to Head Start, and state-funded prekindergarten parent education programs, eight states spent in excess of $10 million in FY 1988 (California, Illinois, Massachusetts, Minnesota, Missouri, New York, South Carolina, and Texas), ranging from $10.9 million in South Carolina to $46.2 million in Texas. Twelve states spent less than $2 million annually. Some of these are the understandably smaller efforts of smaller states such as Delaware, Hawaii, and West Virginia; all are funded at less than $300,000 annually. Vermont is a small state spending a relatively large amount (first-year funding of $500,000 doubling to $1 million in the second year) for its prekindergarten program.

Texas serves the largest number of children and spends the largest total amount of state revenue on its prekindergarten program, followed by California and New York. It is important to note that if California's full-working-day child development programs and voucher child care programs (which, along with the state prekindergarten program, are administered by its Department of Education) are factored in, California spends well over $300 million on all early childhood programs, far exceeding other states. New York spends $27 million for its prekindergarten program and about $165 million on all its child care programs.

Like the total funding level, the state expenditure per child served varies tremendously across the states as well. The variation in program costs among state prekindergarten programs may be seen by comparing the number of children served in a state's prekindergarten program to the program funding level. Texas, for example, spent $37.5 million in state funds to serve 48,800 four-year-olds in FY 1987 or about $800 per child served. California anticipates spending $35.5 million to serve 19,221 four-year-olds in the state-funded prekindergarten program in FY 1988, or about $1,850 per child served. The enormous difference in the state expenditure per child served in these states' half-day targeted programs, funded at approximately the same levels, can be accounted for by three factors: differing staff–child ratios (California requires 1:8 while Texas requires 1:22), the comprehensive Head Start service model[2] used by the California programs (Texas does not require such services), and differences in the relative proportions of state/local funding. The California prekindergarten program is 100 percent state-funded; in Texas state funds support only a portion of prekindergarten program expenses, which varies according to the local district's relative wealth and ranges up to 65 percent.

The influence of staff–child ratios on cost may also be seen in smaller state prekindergarten programs such as those in Maryland and Wisconsin, which both provide half-day programs for four-year-olds. Wisconsin estimates it will spend $4.3 million in FY 1988 to serve 5,850 children; a staff–child ratio of 1:20 is recommended. Maryland will spend approximately $3.3 million in FY 1988 to serve 2,820 children; a staff–child ratio of 1:10 is required.

Are State-Funded Prekindergarten Programs Coordinated with Other State Efforts to Serve Prekindergarten Children? While in almost all states, a state-level coordinating body exists representing state agencies and in some cases parents, child care providers, and Head Start, no state has moved to truly coordinate funding for prekindergarten programs and child care across state agencies. Fewer than one-third of those states with prekindergarten programs have legislative or regulatory requirements regarding local-level coordination of these efforts with child care, Head Start programs, or other services for prekindergarten children. In some states the absence of local-level coordination has resulted in increased competition for children, staff, and space between Head Start programs, particularly those using space in public schools, and the state prekindergarten program. Table 2–6 presents a condensed description of each state's prekindergarten program, including each of the characteristics discussed above.

Table 2-6　A Summary of State-Funded Prekindergarten Initiatives Through FY88

State	Population Served	Hours of Operation	No. of Children Served	Resources	Ratios	ECE Training	Method of Funding
Alaska enacted 1983	3- and 4-year-olds Head Start eligibility	Half day; 5 villages	45 (FY87)	$197,000 (FY88) $250,000 (FY87)	Unknown	Unknown	Targeted grants for Head Start-like programs
California enacted 1966	3- to 5-years-olds (low-income)	Half day; 185 contracts; 500+ sites	19,221 (FY88)	$35.5 million (FY88 estimate)	1:8	Unknown	Reimbursement on average daily attendance; contracts with school district which may subcontract; grants may also go directly to private nonprofits
Delaware enacted 1986	4-year-olds	Half day; 3 pilot programs (FY88)	99 (FY88)	$189,000 (FY88)	1:8	Unknown	Competitive grants, school districts only
Florida state funds used to supplement migrant program since 1981	3- and 4-year-old migrant children	Full school day; 18 programs	2,579 (FY86) 2,540 (FY87)	$2.9 million (FY88)	1:10	No	Districts may subcontract to nonprofits; 60% state funds, 40% federal funds
Florida enacted 1986 begun 1986-1987	3- and 4-year-olds targeted at risk only	Half or full day incl'g full working day; 19 districts (FY88)	1,000 (FY88)	$1.6 million (FY88)	Local option, 1:10 recommended	Yes	Project grants to school districts; may subcontract
Illinois enacted 1985 begun 1/86	3- to 5-year-olds at risk of academic failure	Half or full day incl'g full working day; 97 programs (FY88)	7,400 (FY87)	$12.7 million (FY88)	1:8 preferred, may not exceed 1:10	Yes	Project grants; no local match; may subcontract to nonprofits
Kentucky parent and child education enacted 1986	3- and 4-year-olds at risk	Half and full day; 12 districts, 18 classrooms	270 (FY87-88)	$900,000 (FY88)	1:7.5	No	Competitive grants to school districts; eligibility based on district with 60% or more adults without high school diploma
Kentucky innovation grants enacted 1986	3- and 4-year-olds at risk	3 programs (FY87-88)	280 (FY87-88)	$232,123 (FY87-88)	Unknown	Unknown	Competitive grants to school districts; may be subcontracted
Louisiana enacted 1985 begun fall 1985	4-year-olds at risk	Most full day; 50 of 66 districts, 71 classes (FY88)	1,272 (FY88)	$1.8 million (FY88)	1:10 with aide 1:15 without	No	Project grants; up to 4 per district; no local match

Table 2-6 *Continued*

State	Population Served	Hours of Operation	No. of Children Served	Resources	Ratios	ECE Training	Method of Funding
Maine innovative grants enacted 1984	4-year-olds at risk	Half day		$27,730 (FY88)	1:15 recommended	No	Competitive 1-year grants to teachers or districts
Maine enacted 1984	4-year-olds	Most half day; one full day; 5 districts (FY88)	167		1:15 recommended	No	School districts only reimbursed under school aid formula after second year of program
Maryland enacted 1979	4-year-olds at risk	Half day; 15 districts, 72 classes (FY88)	2,820 (FY88)	$3.3 million (FY88)	1:10	Yes	Project grants; selection based on low 3rd grade test scores
Massachusetts enacted 1985 begun fall 1986	3- to 5-year-olds, low-income	Half or full day, incl'g full working day; 121 programs (FY87); 56 pre-K and day care		$10.3 million (FY88)	1:7.5	Yes	Competitive grants to districts; may subcontract; 75% of funds to low-income districts
Michigan pilot project began Jan. 1986	4-year-olds at risk	Most half day; 29 programs (FY87)	800 (FY87)	$1 million (FY87) $300,000 (FY88)	1:8	Yes	Competitive grants to school districts; 30% local match; may subcontract with school operated Head Start only
Michigan enacted 1987	4-year-olds living in districts meeting funding formula requirements	Half day		$2 million (FY88)	1:8	Yes	Only school districts which meet state funding formula requirements
Minnesota parent ed. enacted 1974	0-5 years old	Less than half day, once per week; 280 districts	72,000 (FY88 est.)	$22 million (FY 88)	1:10	Yes	Public school districts (subcontracting allowed)
Missouri parent ed. enacted 1981	0-3 years old	4 home visits per year; 543 districts	51,000 (FY88 est.)	$12 million (FY 88)	Home visit program	Yes	Public school districts (subcontracting allowed)

Table 2-6 *Continued*

State	Population Served	Hours of Operation	No. of Children Served	Resources	Ratios	ECE Training	Method of Funding
New Jersey since 1903	4-year-olds	Half day 72 school districts (FY87)	5,794 (FY87)	$6.9 million (estimated FY87)	1:25	No, but most teachers have nursery school endorsement	School districts regular school aid formula based on enrollment
New Jersey enacted 1987 begun Nov. 1987	3- to 5-year-olds at risk; Head Start requirement	Full working day, full year		$1 million (FY88)	1:10	Yes	Allocation by county & competitive grants to programs; priority to Head Start but school districts and nonprofits may apply; matching requirement determined by county; range 10-25%
New York enacted 1966	3- and 4-year-olds; 90% low-income	Most half day; 90 districts (FY88)	12,000 (FY88)	$27 million (FY88)	1:7.5	No	Project grants via a proposal process; 11% local match; new programs limited to half day only
Ohio enacted 1985-1986	3- to 5-year-olds	Half or full day pilot models; 8 districts (FY87); 3 programs (FY88)		$18,000 (FY88)	1:12 (3 years); 1:14 (4- to 5-year-olds)	No	Project grants via RFP to school districts; new programs half day only
Oklahoma enacted 1980	4-year-olds	Half or full day; 37 programs (FY88)	1,400 (FY88)	$832,275 (FY88)	1:10	Yes	Project grants via RFP to school districts; maximum grant per district $27,000 (FY88); private schools may also apply
Oregon passed 1987 implemented 1988-1989	3- and 4-years-old; 80% must meet Head Start eligibility	Half day	300 (FY88)	$1.1 million (FY88-89)	Unknown	Unknown	Competitive grants to school districts which may subcontract; direct contracts permitted
Pennsylvania since 1965	4-year-olds	Half day; 9 districts (FY87)	3,260 (FY87)	$1.7 million (FY87 estimate)	Local option	Unknown	State aid formula for kindergarten used
South Carolina enacted 1984; Chapter I funding since 1971	4-year-olds with deficient "readiness" based on individual assessment	Half day; 86 districts (FY88)	10,715 (FY88)	$10.9 million (FY88)	1:10 recommended	Yes	Allocation to districts based on students "not ready"; districts may subcontract

Table 2-6 Continued

State	Population Served	Hours of Operation	No. of Children Served	Resources	Ratios	ECE Training	Method of Funding
Texas enacted 1984 began fall 1985	4-year-olds; low-income or limited English proficiency	Half day; 405 districts (FY86)	48,000 (87) 54,493 (88)	$37.6 million (FY87); $46.2 million (FY88)	1:22	Yes, with exemptions	Formula allocation; matching grant based on local property value
Vermont enacted 1987	3- and 4-year-olds at risk; low-income, limited English proficiency; other handicap'g conditions	Half or full day, including full work day	250 (FY88 est.)	$500,000 (FY88) maximum $30,000 per grant	1:10	No	Competitive grants based on RFP; preference to communities without other early childhood programs; grants to school districts which may subcontract; direct contracts permitted
Washington enacted 1985	4-year-olds; Head Start eligibility	Half day	2,000 (FY88)	$4.7 million (FY88); $6.2 million (FY89)	1:6	Yes	Competitive grants to school districts; Head Start and private nonprofits
District of Columbia enacted 1968	4-year-olds	117 full day + 27 half day (FY87), 170 full day (FY88)	3,444 (FY88)	$12.2 million (FY88)	1:10 half day 1:15 full day with aide	Yes	Local district regular school aid formula; used Chapter I funds prior to 1982
West Virginia programs operated since 1972 *	3- and 4-year-olds at risk and low-income	Half day and full day 6 programs *	215 (FY86)	$258,574 (FY86)	1:15	Yes	4 programs are run by the DOE as fiscal agent; 2 are run by counties under contract with DOE
Wisconsin enacted 1985	4-year-olds	Half day 25 districts (FY87)	5,850 (FY88 estimate)	$4.3 million (FY88)	1:20 recommended	No, local option	State aid formula to local districts; average local contribution is 52%

* School code revised in 1983 to permit local county school boards to establish prekindergarten programs for children under age 5. The programs listed are those not primarily for handicapped children.

Summary

State-funded prekindergarten programs usually reach a targeted population of four-year-olds and provide a part-day, school-year program. Many of these programs began in the 1980s as part of education reform legislation; nearly all are located administratively in state departments of education. Funding levels and expenditure per child vary considerably among states, as do staff–child ratios and requirements for comprehensive services. Coordination is common at the state level but usually not required at the local level. Although there is clearly a good deal of variation among these state-funded programs, those that specify and fund a reasonably good quality program (favorable staff–child ratios, well-trained teachers, comprehensive services, an appropriate curriculum for children, local coordination mechanisms) do represent a promising resource for extending the benefits of early childhood education to more needy young children. About one-third of the state-funded prekindergarten programs appear to offer this promise, notably the long-standing programs in New York and in California and the newer programs in Washington, New Jersey, Massachusetts, South Carolina, and Illinois. Permissive programs, as they are presently structured, do not appear to be as promising because they are not aimed at the most needy children and because they generally lack specific staffing, curricular, and service requirements. But whatever the state legislates or funds, local school districts will ultimately determine the nature and quality of the program that children actually receive. In the final section of this chapter, we turn to the practices of local school districts.

Prekindergarten Programs Operated by Local Public School Districts

As noted earlier, the local picture of involvement in early childhood education is a complicated one. The following discussion will focus only on those local programs for children younger than kindergarten entry age that are directly operated by public schools, that is, public school-operated prekindergarten programs. Even taking this relatively narrow focus, there are about 15 different kinds of prekindergarten programs. One way to categorize them is by funding source: federal, state, or local. The federally and state-funded categories are the ones already mentioned (Head Start, Chapter I, special education, state-funded and federally funded child care, state-funded prekindergarten, and parent education). Local funds can mean local property taxes (school tax), local government appropriations, and fees paid directly by parents. Also included are programs that have mixed funding sources (some federal, some state and/or some local monies) but that are locally determined, such as magnet prekindergartens used for desegregation purposes. This category of programs is broad and includes bilingual prekindergartens, magnet prekindergartens, parent cooperative nursery schools, child care supported by parent tuitions, child care for the children of teen/student parents, and nursery schools operated by high school students.

Our survey of school districts included 1,225 districts nationwide reporting on 1,681 programs serving approximately 200,000 children under age five. These programs fell into more than 20 distinct categories, which we have called program types. The basic distinguishing feature of a program type is its *funding source*: federal, state, and/or local public funds or parents' fees. The second distinguishing characteristic of a program type is its *purpose*. Although all the many categories of early childhood programs are educational, some are intentionally compensatory (like Chapter I) or comprehensive (like Head Start) or are designed to meet the child care needs of families (subsidized child care). Chapter I and Head Start are both federally funded programs but have differing purposes. The third distinguishing characteristic is *clientele*. Although both are federally and state-funded and designed to meet child care needs, a program for teen parents (and their infants) differs from a subsidized child care program for other low-income families. For example, the typical teen parent child care program probably operates during school hours and expects daily participation of the teen parent, whereas the typical subsidized child care program operates for nine or ten hours daily, year-round, and involves parents in a variety of ways. This combination of funding source, purpose, and clientele defines *program type*.

There are so many different types of programs that local school districts operate that it is impossible to discuss a "typical" public school prekindergarten program. The next section offers, with the help of Tables 2–7, 2–8, and 2–9, a brief description of the basic elements of all the program types included in the District Survey. These basic elements include expenditures per child, ratios and class sizes, and support services offered, such as meals and transportation.

To give a fuller picture of these local program types and to illustrate the differences among them, the discussion of basic elements is followed by a section that profiles three types of public school-operated early childhood programs. These profiles are composites compiled from the survey responses given by all programs of a particular type and do not represent one actual program. It is important to remember that the survey collected information *only* from public school-operated prekindergarten programs. The three examples profiled represent different funding sources: federal (Head Start), state (state-funded prekindergarten), and local (parent tuition-funded child care). The first two are public sources; the third is private. The first two program types serve somewhat similar clientele, as Head Start primarily serves children living in poverty and most state prekindergarten programs are targeted to "at-risk" children, whereas the third program type is organized for a different purpose and clearly serves a different clientele—families who can afford to pay the fees.

The Basic Elements of Local Prekindergarten Program Types

What Are the Sources of Funds and the Per-Child Expenditures in Local School District-Operated Prekindergarten Programs?   In general, the majority of public school programs operate part-day for the school year only and serve only four-year-olds. Public funds (state, federal, and local) are the major source of support for nearly all (90 percent) programs. The total expenditure per child is obviously influenced by the program's schedule, that is, number of hours of operation daily and number of weeks of operation per year. Table 2–7 presents data on the factors that affect program expenditures (daily, weekly, and annual schedules) for all the major program types included in the District Survey.

Unlike the considerable differences in per-child expenditure among states based on differences in staff–child ratios and required comprehensive services discussed earlier, the local expenditure per child in a given program type is not greatly influenced by staff–child ratio or by group size. This is mainly because the average staff–child ratio and group size do not vary greatly, within a program type or among the various program types. The greatest influence on per-child expenditure at the local level appears to be the salaries paid to teachers, which is strongly related to the source of program funds. All other factors being equal, expenditures are lower in program types supported by parent fees (because teacher salaries are much lower than for other district-employed teachers) than in those supported by public funds. The variance can be seen in the differences between the two child care program types, both of which are operated for the full working day, throughout the calendar year. The average annual expenditure per child in subsi-

Table 2-7   Elements of Program Expenditures

	Factors Affecting the Level of per Child Expenditures			
	---	---	---	---
	Daily Hours *	Days/week +	Annual Schedule	Expenditure/ Child + +
	(N = 1,537)	(N = 1,537)	(N = 1,629)	(N = 1,018)
Program Types				
Head Start	4.3	4.4	School year	$2,241
Chapter I prekindergarten	3.3	4.2	School year	$1,592
Special education	3.6	4.5	School year	$3,896
State-funded prekindergarten	3.4	4.6	School year	$1,841
Locally funded prekindergarten	3.1	4.0	School year	$2,162
Subsidized child care	8.7	5.0	Calendar year	$3,678
Parent tuition child care	7.0	4.2	Calendar year	$1,929
Parent education	2.3	1.5	School year	$1,855

Note   All data are from the District Survey (N = 1,681) and pertain to the 1985-1986 school year.

* Daily hours is the mean length of a daily session for 4-year-olds.

+ Days per week is the mean number of sessions per week for 4-year-olds.

+ + Expenditure per child is the mean annual expenditure per child reported.

dized child care is about $3,700, while the average in parent-tuition supported child care is just under $2,000.

What Are the Structural Elements of the Program: Staff–Child Ratio, Class Size, Staff Qualifications, and Staff Development? Reported staff–child ratios and class sizes are generally reasonable across all program types. The reported levels of early childhood certification and previous experience possessed by currently employed teachers are both higher than the minimum requirements. Most teachers are minimally required to have both a B.A. degree and some form of teacher certification, usually in early childhood education. Teachers are rarely required to have previous experience working with young children. Most districts reported that teaching staff are offered some form of inservice training and allowed to make observation visits to other local early childhood programs. Table 2–8 summarizes the average staff–child

Table 2-8   Structural Elements of Quality

Elements of Quality for 4 Year Old Children

Program Types	Mean Staff:Child Ratio (N = 1,508)	Mean Class Size (N = 1,508)	Level of Training * (N = 1,567)	Staff Development + (N = 1,658)
Head Start	1 : 7.5	17.7	39.1%	Preservice, inservice, program visits, pay for conferences
Chapter I prekindergarten	1 : 8.3	16.1	48.4%	Program visits
Special education	1 : 4.2	7.3	52.0%	Professional days, program vi
State-funded prekindergarten	1 : 9.1	16.8	58.2%	
Locally funded prekindergarten	1 : 10.1	16.3	54.4%	
Subsidized child care	1 : 8.2	18.1	83.8%	Inservice, program visits
Parent tuition child care	1 : 9.2	17.7	59.3%	Pay for conferences
Parent education	1 : 6.2	12.1	50.9%	

Note   All data are from the District Survey (N = 1,681) and pertain to the 1985-1986 school year.

*Level of training is the mean percentage of teachers currently employed who when they were hired had both early childhood education certification and at least one year of experience teaching children younger than five.

+ At least 75% of programs of each type offered this form of staff development. Forms are preservice training, inservice training 3 or more times per year, professional days, visits to other programs, reimbursement for attending conferences.

ratios, class sizes, teacher training and experience levels, and common forms of staff development reported by program type.

What Other Services Are Offered in Local School District-Operated Prekindergarten Programs?   Support services provided by professionals other than classroom teachers are available in many programs; the most common professionals used are nurses and speech therapists. Head Start and early childhood special education are the program types offering the highest level of services. Snacks, but not other meals, are usually provided in all program types; the exceptions are Head Start and subsidized child care, which are the only program types offering both meals and snacks to children. Transportation is not a common service, and transportation to other child care settings is rare. Head Start, special education, and state-funded prekindergarten are the program types most likely to offer transportation. Table 2–9 summarizes these service components by program type.

Profile: Head Start

Head Start is a federally funded and regulated program under the auspices of the federal Department of Health and Human Services (HHS). Funds flow directly from the federal source to local agencies (called "grantees"). The local grantee may choose to operate all the Head Start programs for which it receives funds, or it may

Table 2-9 Other Service Components

Service Components

Program Types	Other Professionals* (N = 1,329)	Transportation+ (N = 1,643)	Meals++ (N = 1,647)
Head Start	Nurse, social worker, speech therapist	School - home	Breakfast, snack lunch
Chapter I prekindergarten		None	Snack
Special education	Speech, language, physical, occupational therapists	School - home	Snack
State-funded prekindergarten		School - home	Snack, lunch
Locally funded prekindergarten		None	Snack
Subsidized child care	Nurse	None	Breakfast, snack, lunch
Parent tuition child care		None	Snack, lunch
Parent education		None	

Note   All data are from the District Survey (N = 1,681) and pertain to the 1985-1986 school year.

*Other professionals are those professionals, other than direct teaching staff, reported as used frequently (more than once a month) by at least 50% of programs of each type.

+At least 50% of programs of each type reported providing this form of transportation.

++At least 50% of programs of each type reported serving these meals.

choose to delegate the operation of some or all to other local agencies (called "delegate agencies"). Program standards, called Head Start Performance Standards, are specified at the federal level and each local Head Start program is monitored for compliance with them through the ten federal regional offices of HHS. Grantees are responsible for fiscal and programmatic oversight of the operations of each of their delegate agencies. About one-fifth of all local Head Start programs nationwide are operated by public schools. In some cases the public school district is the grantee and operates the Head Start programs itself; in others the public school is a delegate agency operating Head Start under the supervision of a grantee. In our survey, 11 percent (189) of the 1,681 public school-operated prekindergarten programs were Head Start programs.

While Head Start programs in our survey were located in all regions of the country, rural public school districts and school districts in the southeastern region were more likely to be operating Head Start programs than other types of prekindergarten programs. Head Start programs comprised 11 percent of all the programs but were serving 20 percent of the children—over 39,000 out of 200,000—represented in our survey. About half of these public school-operated Head Start programs were started between 1965 and 1969, during the birth and earliest years of Head Start.

Location, Schedule, and Cost   Head Start programs are more likely than other types of programs to be located in a site other than a public school building and to operate for more than three hours a day. Some operate for four hours per day and a few for the full school day. Head Start is federally funded (with a required local match of 20 percent); the average total cost per child is $2,000 per year. Some Head Start programs are licensed by the state and/ or local regulatory agencies responsible for licensing child care programs.

Class Size and Staff–Child Ratios   Class size for public school-operated Head Start programs is about 18 children. Staff–child ratios are somewhat more favorable than those of other program types, averaging 1:7.5 for four-year-olds. This favorable ratio is probably partially due to the use of parents as classroom volunteers.

Staff Qualifications, Salaries, and Development   Unlike other public school prekindergarten teachers, Head Start teachers are not always required to have teacher certification or a B.A. degree. About half these Head Start programs require a B.A.; about one-third require teacher certification. Head Start is the only program type in our survey that reported requiring a Child Development

Associate (CDA) credential; about one-third of the programs reported the CDA as one form of teacher qualification.

These public school Head Start teachers—whether they have bachelor's degrees and teacher certification—earn on average $13,000 for the school year, significantly less than teachers in all other program types (except for those employed in parent-tuition supported child care, who earn even less). Of the Head Start programs in our survey, 55 percent (103) reported that their teachers were on a different (lower) salary scale than other teachers employed by the same school district. Further, 15 percent (28) reported that the Head Start teachers were not district employees.

Head Start programs are more likely than other program types to offer both preservice and inservice training and to pay for staff to attend professional conferences; more than 75 percent reported offering these forms of staff development. Nearly three-quarters of programs of all types reported that their staff attended local early childhood conferences and read local early childhood organizations' publications. Head Start respondents reported their staff to be somewhat more involved in the local early childhood community than staff in other program types. For example, more than half the Head Start programs reported their staff to be members of local organizations and presenters at local conferences, in addition to attending local conferences and reading newsletters.

Eligibility and Services   The child's age and any special needs, as well as the family's income, are the typical eligibility criteria reportedly used by Head Start programs in selecting children. This is consistent with Head Start's mandate to serve a combination of poor (90 percent of children served must be from families living below the poverty level) and handicapped (10 percent of those served must be children with identified handicaps) children.

Federal Head Start performance standards require that comprehensive services be provided in Head Start programs. These public school-operated Head Start programs appeared to be well in compliance. Based on data reported in the District Survey, the frequent use of other professionals is common. The Head Start programs reported using nurses (70 percent), speech therapists (80 percent), and social workers (60 percent). Dentists (41 percent), psychologists (34 percent), and language therapists (42 percent) were also reported. All these Head Start programs reported serving breakfast and lunch, and nearly all (77 percent) serve children breakfast, a snack, *and* lunch. Head Start programs are more likely than other program types to offer transportation between home and school (84 percent of Head Start in comparison to 60 percent among all other program types). Head Start is the only program type beside special education that offers transportation to other child care settings (27 percent of Head Start and 47 percent of special education programs provide transportation to child care in comparison to 6 percent of all other program types).

Parents Parent involvement is a hallmark of Head Start, and the public school-operated programs in this survey support that concept. Most Head Start programs (over 75 percent) reported having parent advisory boards, using parent volunteers in classrooms, distributing a parent newsletter, conducting parent education workshops, and encouraging communication among parents. In addition, more than half also employed parents in the classroom, involved parents in fund-raising efforts, and encouraged parents to advocate for the program with governmental officials. Among all other program types, the only form of parent involvement reported as common (by more than 75 percent of programs of each type) was holding parent-teacher conferences. No other program type approaches the levels of parent involvement that appear typical in Head Start.

Profile: State-Funded Prekindergarten Programs

As is clear from the first part of this chapter, the 24 states with state-funded prekindergarten programs are found in all regions of the country. Prekindergarten programs in 19 states in all regions of the country responded to our survey. Programs in those states that started their prekindergarten programs after 1986 (Delaware, Kentucky, Michigan, Oregon, and Vermont) are not included in our survey because they were not in operation when the data were collected. In sheer numbers of children served, the Southwest appears to predominate largely because Texas is the only state that requires every local district with 15 eligible children to operate the state prekindergarten program. (Eligible children are defined in Texas as district residents who are four years old and are either poor or unable to speak and comprehend English.)

Overall, state-funded prekindergarten programs comprised 16 percent of all programs in our survey (272 out of 1,681), serving 15 percent of the children (30,000 out of 200,000). School districts with larger enrollments, those with higher proportions of families below the poverty level, and those with higher proportions of minority students are more likely to operate state-funded prekindergarten programs than are other types and sizes of school districts. State-funded prekindergarten programs are relatively new; the majority have been started since 1980.

Location, Schedule, and Cost Most districts operate these

programs in multiple locations throughout the district, nearly always in public school buildings. Nearly all (80 percent) of these programs are not licensed (they are not required to be); those that *are* licensed are primarily in California. The overwhelming majority operate for three or fewer hours per day (86 percent) and for the school year only (94 percent). The average cost per child was $1,800 for the 1985–1986 school year.

　　Class Size and Staff–Child Ratio　Based on reported data from the District Survey, class sizes and staff–child ratios among state-funded prekindergarten programs nationwide average 17 four-year-olds and 2 adults, with the notable exception of Texas, where the recommended format is a class of 22 children with one teacher. In contrast, New York State limits the class size to 15 children and requires both a teacher and an aide.

　　Staffing　Teachers in state prekindergarten programs are required to have both a B.A. degree and state teacher certification, with about half requiring certification in early childhood education. Experience is not required as a condition of hire, but about half the teachers did have at least one year of experience teaching young children. All state prekindergarten teachers are paid on the same salary scale as all other district teachers, with beginning teachers earning an average of $16,000 for the school year. Teachers in state prekindergartens are less likely to be offered as much preservice or inservice training as teachers in other program types. They also appear to be somewhat less involved in the local early childhood community than their counterparts in other program types.

　　Eligibility and Services　The child's age and family income are the usual eligibility criteria, although not speaking or understanding English is an additional criterion reportedly used in about half of these programs. As noted earlier in the chapter, comprehensive services are required in about half the state prekindergarten programs. The practices reported by local districts operating state prekindergarten programs confirm this. (Support services provided by professionals other than teachers are used less often than in other types of programs.) Nurses, speech therapists, and librarians were reported to be used frequently in about half these programs. Only about half these programs reported serving snacks and lunch to children. When transportation is provided, it is limited to trips between home and school.

　　Parents　Beyond parent-teacher conferences, other forms of parent involvement appeared to be less common in state prekindergarten programs than in other types of programs, especially Head Start. In about half the state prekindergarten programs, parents are welcomed as classroom volunteers, are given a news-letter, and are offered workshops. Only about one-quarter of these programs reported scheduling parent-teacher conferences after parents' work hours.

Profile: Parent Tuition-Supported Child Care Programs

Like all the programs in our survey, these child care programs are operated by local public school districts. Tuition paid by parents is their major source of direct financial support. These programs represented 3 percent (43) of all programs in the survey and served less than 3 percent of the children (4,500 out of 200,000). Whereas Head Start and state-funded prekindergartens enroll mainly four-year-olds (who make up, respectively, 84 percent and 88 percent of their reported enrollments), these programs include children of all ages from infancy through age five. Eleven percent of the reported enrollment in parent fee-supported child care programs is children under age three; an additional 33 percent of their enrollment is three-year-olds.

Nearly two-thirds of these programs are located in the central region of the country—the Midwest, broadly defined. Notwith-standing the "human factors" needed to get any program started, many of these programs are the direct result of a combination of two other necessary factors: the availability of school buildings (due to declining enrollment) and the presence of district residents who can afford to pay for a program. Declining enrollment in middle-class school districts is most common in the Midwest. Middle-sized, suburban districts with a low proportion of poverty-level families are most likely to operate these programs. They are also newer programs; most (60 percent) of those in our survey started since 1980.

Location and Cost   Usually, these programs are located in one site, nearly always a public school building. Tuition paid by parents is the source of funds; the average cost per child was $1,900 in 1985–1986. These programs are usually (85 percent) licensed by the state and/or local regulatory agencies responsible for licensing other child care programs, even though these public school-oper-ated programs may be technically exempt from licensure. It is common for state child care regulations to exempt certain pro-grams from the licensing procedures: church-operated programs, public school-operated programs, programs operating for fewer than three hours daily, or, in many cases, any program that is part of an elementary school, whether the school is public, private, or parochial.

Schedule, Class Size, and Staff–Child Ratio   Typically, these programs operate for at least seven hours per day. About two-thirds are open for the calendar year; one-third are open during the school year only. Most offer both full-day and part-day options. Classes usually consist of about 18 children, staffed by two adults.

Teacher Qualification, Salaries, and Staff Development   Teachers in about half (55 percent) of these programs are required to have B.A. degrees, about half (54 percent) are required to have teacher certification in early childhood education, and 40 percent require at least one year of experience teaching young children. Nearly two-thirds (65 percent) of teachers in parent tuition-supported child care programs are not on the same pay scale as other district teachers; 10 percent of these programs reported that their teachers are not district employees. Beginning teachers in these parent-tuition supported programs earn, on average, $12,000 for the school year or $12,500 for the calendar year—significantly less than teachers in all other program types.

Teaching staff in these programs have somewhat fewer opportunities for preservice and inservice training than teachers in other program types but are more likely to be reimbursed for attending professional conferences. These teachers are much more likely to be involved in the early childhood community. More than three-quarters of these programs reported their staff were members of local early childhood organizations, attended local early childhood conferences, and read local organizations' publications. More than one-quarter (about the same proportion as Head Start programs reported) were involved with local child care councils and served on boards of other community early childhood programs.

Eligibility and Services   Generally, all children *whose parents can afford the tuition* are eligible to apply. The only stated eligibility criterion is the child's age. Support services provided by professionals other than teachers are generally not available, with the exception of speech therapy. Nearly all these programs provide snacks to children, and many offer lunch as well. Transportation is not usually provided.

Parents   Parent involvement is greater than in state prekindergarten programs. About half of parent tuition-supported child care programs have a parent advisory board, encourage parent classroom volunteering, offer parent workshops, and engage parents in fund-raising efforts. More than three-quarters report regularly distributing a newsletter to parents and encouraging communication among parents. As in all types of programs in the survey, 95 percent reported that parent-teacher conferences are regularly scheduled.

Summary

Local education agencies—that is, school districts—operate a wide variety of programs funded solely or by a combination of federal, state, and local sources, including parent tuition. Expenditures per child vary mainly by length of day and year. Teachers are generally required to have prior training and education and usually state teacher certification. Regardless of their degrees and certification, teachers earn lower salaries in Head Start and child care programs; the lowest salaries are in programs funded by parents. Class sizes and staff–child ratios are reasonable as measured against accepted standards of the early childhood profession (a ratio of not less than one adult for every 10 four-year-olds in groups of 20 or fewer). The majority of programs are half-day, school-year only and enroll only four-year-olds. The level of additional services and parent involvement varies by program type, with Head Start programs providing the highest levels of services and parent involvement.

One way to sum up would be to ignore local variations and say that public schools are providing mainly part-day programs for a limited population of children. However, although state-funded or locally funded prekindergarten programs are the most common program types found in public school districts, an amazing variety of programs are currently being operated by public schools. Even though, from a state-level perspective, it might appear that only a few prekindergarten program types are operating in local schools (Chapter I, special education, and state-funded prekindergartens), the local variety cannot be ignored. In a sense, this local variety itself is another aspect of the promise of public school involvement in early childhood programs. From the descriptions of programs operated by school districts, there are clearly many different types of programs with different purposes, funding sources, clients, and other features—which offers some hope that public schools are more flexible program operators than they are often given credit for being. The parent-tuition-supported child care programs offer some evidence that at least some public school districts have the capacity to be community institutions that respond to community needs. The fact that the average class sizes and staff–child ratios for all program types in our survey were within the boundaries of good practice set by the early childhood profession is certainly good news.

But all this promise must be translated into practice, and practice cannot be discerned from written responses on a questionnaire. Practice must be observed in action. The dynamic aspects of the quality of these programs, such as the child's experience in the program, parents' opinions about it, and the views of other members of the local early childhood community, come from the case studies of 13 school districts in 12 states. The 13 districts were selected as examples of good practice, as nearly as could be judged from written materials, telephone interviews, and local references. They were also selected as illustrative examples of program type. We purposely selected districts that operated more than one type of program. The 13 sites we visited included 20 different prekindergarten program types: five state prekindergarten programs, four subsidized child care programs, four child care programs supported primarily by parent-tuition, two parent education programs, three Chapter I programs, and two locally funded prekindergarten programs (one was a magnet program and one a parent cooperative nursery school). Table 2–10 summarizes the basic facts of operation and the criteria used to select these local programs.

In these visits to districts around the country, we were able to observe children in classrooms and collect the views of parents whose children were enrolled in programs and the views of representatives of the early childhood community in each site. Much of the rich detail that illustrates the issues discussed throughout the rest of this book comes from these site visits.

Endnotes

1. The complete results of the Public School Early Childhood Study are available in three technical reports: *The State Survey, The District Survey,* and *The Case Studies.* All three reports are published by and may be ordered from Bank Street College of Education in New York City.
2. The Head Start model specifies four program components that must be provided in addition to educational services: health, social, and nutrition services and parent participation. These services may be provided directly by each local program or by referral to other community services. Parental participation includes both working in the classroom and having decision-making power in regard to the overall program.

Table 2-10   Selected Facts About Districts Chosen as Case Study Sites

	Pomona Unified School District, Pomona, Calif.	School Board of Palm Beach County, West Palm Beach, Fla.	Chicago Public Schools, Chicago, Ill.
Prekindergarten program type	State subsidized part-day and full-working-day programs	Chapter I migrant program	Chapter I Child Parent Centers (CPC) & state-funded prekindergarten (pre-K)
Date of origin	1969	1968	CPC 1967, pre-K 1986
Group size for 4-year-olds and staff–child ratio	16 (1:8)	20 (3:20)	17 (2:17)
Teacher qualifications	Children's Center permit	State certified in elementary (pre-K–3)	State certified in elementary (K–3)
Comprehensive services	By referral to school district personnel and community agencies	On-site community resource coordinators and by referral to school district personnel	Nurse and school/community representative, also by referral to other district personnel
Curriculum	High/Scope Cognitively Oriented	Florida Migratory Child Compensatory Program and High/Scope	
Parent involvement	Active parent association	Monthly meetings and frequent conferences	CPC parents required to be on site 2 days/month; (pre-K) monthly parent workshops; volunteering in classrooms 2 hrs/month parent participation req'd
Schedule	11 hour day year-round	10-hour day, 5 days/wk, from Sept–June with transportation	3 hour sessions, 5 days/weeks, September–June
Staff participation in local early childhood community	Some program administrators active in local AEYC affiliates; very active in Calif. Child Development Directors' Association	District administrators are active in AEYC affiliate and early childhood committees	A few personnel are members of local AEYC affiliate
Region	West	Southeast	East central
Urbanicity	Urban/suburban	Urban/suburban/rural	Urban
School district ethnicity	45% Hispanic, 25% white, 24% black, 6% Asian and others	63% white, 27% black, 8% Hispanic, 2% Asian and others	60% black, 23% Hispanic, 14% white, 3% Asian and others
Size (K–12 enrollment)	23,107	89,450	431,000

Table 2-10 *Continued*

	Northville Public Schools, Northville, Mich.	*Duluth Public Schools, Duluth, Minn.*	*School Districts of Affton and Lindbergh, St. Louis, Mo.*
Prekindergarten program type	Parent tuition supported, part-day and full-working-day programs	Parent education	Parent education; part-day and full-working-day programs supported by parent tuition
Date of origin	1985	1975	1971
Group size for 4-year-olds and staff–child ratio	20 (3:20)	16 (1:8)	20 (1:10)
Teacher qualifications	ECE experience & training; some are certified teachers	State certified	ECE experience and training; some teachers are state certified
Comprehensive services	Speech therapy by referral to school district personnel	Lending library, social workers, referral to district & community agencies	Developmental screening on site; others by referral
Curriculum	Locally designed; play-based with emphasis on art	Local design based on state defined curriculum elements	High/Scope Cognitively Oriented
Parent involvement	Volunteer in classrooms; visit informally	Program is primarily for parents	Weekly parent breakfasts; volunteer in classroom/field trips; active parents' association
Schedule	10.5-hour day year-round	1.5-hour sessions weekly	11.5-hour day year-round; parent ed: 5 home visits per year
Staff participation in local early childhood community	Some staff are members of local AEYC affiliates; director attends local directors' coalition	No staff active in local AEYC affiliate	Program director is president of local AEYC affiliate, and many teachers are members
Region	Central	North central	West central
Urbanicity	Suburban	Urban	Suburban
School district ethnicity	White	89% white, 9% Native American, 1% black, 1% Asian	White
Size (K-12 enrollment) (Pre-K enrollment)	3,368 112	13,700 2,500	7,100 800

Table 2-10 *Continued*

	Westside Community Schools, Omaha, Nebr.	Buffalo Public School District, Buffalo, N.Y.	School District of Philadelphia, Philadelphia, Pa.
Prekindergarten program type	Part day & full working day programs supported by parent tuition	Locally funded magnet prekindergarten	Locally funded parent co-op nursery (PCN) and child care (CC)
Date of origin	1968	1980	PCN 1954, CC 1944
Group size for 4-year-olds and staff–child ratio	16 (1:8)	20 (1:10)	20 (1:10)
Teacher qualifications	ECE experience and training; state certification for head teachers	State certified in elementary	School-district-administered examination
Comprehensive services	By referral to school district personnel and community agencies	On-site community resource coordinators and by referral to school district personnel	Nurse and school/community representative; also by referral to other district personnel
Curriculum	Locally designed (Learning Through Play)	Locally adapted (Early Intervention Program and Talents Unlimited)	Locally designed
Parent involvement	Volunteer in classroom, active parent association	Monthly calendar of home activities; some volunteering in classrooms	Parents must volunteer 1 day/week in classroom (PCN); parent councils in each site (CC)
Schedule	11-hour day year-round	Full school day from September–June, with transportation	PCN: half day, 5 days/week, school year CC: 11-hour day, 5 days/wk, year-round
Staff participation in local early childhood community	Head teachers attend local AEYC affiliate	Some teachers are members of local AEYC affiliate	District administrator is member of local AEYC affiliate
Region	West central	Northeast	Northeast
Urbanicity	Suburban	Urban	Urban
School district ethnicity	White	47% black, 45% white, 8% Asian and Hispanic	64% Black, 24% White, 9% Hispanic, 3% Asian and others
Size (K–12 enrollment) (Pre-K enrollment)	4,900 228	46,000 2,446	195,552 5,943

	School District of Greenville County, Greenville, S.C.	Dallas Independent School District, Dallas, Tex.	Fort Worth Independent School District, Fort Worth, Tex.
Prekindergarten program type	Federal, state, and district subsidized full-working-day program; state-funded prekindergarten	State-funded prekindergarten	Chapter I/state-funded prekindergarten
Date of origin	1972	1985	1968
Group size for 4-year-olds and staff–child ratio	20 (3:20)	22 (1:11)	22 (1:11)
Teacher qualifications	State certified in ECE	State certified in ECE, elementary w/K endorsement or TYC certificate	Elementary certification or TYC (Teacher of Young Children)
Comprehensive services	Social worker on site; also by referral to school district personnel	Developmental screening, by referral to district personnel	By referral to school district personnel
Curriculum	Local design based on High/Scope and adaptation of state kindergarten objectives	Local design based on state-defined elements	Locally designed; standardized throughout district
Parent involvement	Monthly parent meetings, active School Improvement Council	Volunteer in classroom/field trips	Focused on home activities to reinforce school activities; some volunteering in classrooms/field trips
Schedule	10-hour day year-round Pre-K: 3 hrs, 5 days/wk, school year	3 hours, 5 days/wk, school year	Full school day, 5 days/wk, school year
Staff participation in local early childhood community	Program director is active in local early childhood committees	District administrator is member of early child care task force; a few teachers are members of local AEYC affiliate	Some teachers are members of AEYC local affiliate
Region	Southeast	Southwest	Southwest
Urbanicity	Urban/rural	Urban	Urban
School district ethnicity	76% white, 24% black, 1% Hispanic, Asian, and others	80% black, Hispanic, and others; 20% white	36% black, 36% white, 25% Hispanic, 3% Asian and others
Size (K–12 enrollment) (Pre-K enrollment)	54,000 600	132,388 2,500	65,100 2,290

Table 2-10 *Continued*

	South Central School District, Seattle, Wash.
Prekindergarten program type	Part-day and full-working-day programs supported by parent tuition
Date of origin	1984
Group size for 4-year-olds and staff–child ratio	20–25 (3:25)
Teacher qualifications	ECE experience and training
Comprehensive services	By referral
Curriculum	High/Scope in part-day program; no prescribed curriculum in full-day program
Parent involvement	Volunteer in classroom and field trips
Schedule	11.5- hour day
Staff participation in local early childhood community	A few teachers are members of local AEYC affiliate
Region	West
Urbanicity	Suburban
School district ethnicity	82% white, 7% black, 2% Asian, 5% Hispanic and others
Size (K–12 enrollment)	1,600
(Pre-K enrollment)	94

Chapter 3

ADMINISTRATION OF
EARLY CHILDHOOD PROGRAMS

Administration refers both to the choice of state agency and to the internal structure for managing the program that is adopted (or adapted) by that agency, as well as to the internal management structures of local school districts. Decisions about the administration of early childhood programs—which agency is responsible for the state-funded prekindergarten program at the state level and how the variety of prekindergarten programs are integrated into school district hierarchies at the local level—profoundly affect the success of these programs. The content of the program, how it is regulated, the nature of services offered, and many other aspects are affected by these administrative choices. This chapter discusses a variety of administrative forms—and their effects—from both state and local perspectives.

The administrative location of early childhood programs (at the state or community level) has implications not only for the basic nature of the program itself but also for the funding mechanisms utilized; the technical assistance, monitoring, and evaluation available; and the coordination of the program with other programs serving similar populations. In turn, these issues will affect the outcomes for the children and families served by the program. Given the limited state dollars available for social and educational programs, which agency administers a program may in large measure determine which priorities are addressed. For example, a national consensus has emerged on the need for affordable, available, quality child care; however, while one rationale for state-funded prekindergarten programs is often the pressing need for child care, few of these programs actually provide funds for full-working-day programs or support the creation of integrated packages to serve the care and education needs of the children and families using the state prekindergarten service. Instead, various child care and education programs are created separately and exist in parallel fashion, each with its own funding stream, distinct mission, specific goals, and sets of federal and/or state regulations. Administrative differences among agencies, even those providing similar services or concerned with similar clientele, create diverse implementation strategies. These disparities can develop into a competitive, rather than a cooperative or collaborative, relationship among the various agencies responsible for these early childhood programs, which in turn leads to the need for interagency groups at both the state and local level to develop coordinated policy and engage in long-term planning activities.

Grubb points out that choosing which state agency should administer early childhood programs entails subtle choices with varying consequences.[1] The dominant purpose of an agency and the backgrounds of its personnel may partially determine the content of its program, the regulations governing it, and other smaller decisions that shape programs. Most federally and state-funded child care is administered through welfare or social or human service agencies, while prekindergarten programs are usually placed in state departments of education to emphasize their educational orientation. Grubb feels that neither alternative is completely satisfactory. Welfare agencies carry an unavoidable stigma and are not viewed as focusing on "normal" children or on educational goals. Education agencies do focus on educational goals, although for older children (K–12); they are unfamiliar with early childhood programs and are often unsympathetic to child care concerns. The alternative Grubb suggests is administering early childhood programs in an independent state agency, such as an office for children or, like the state of Washington, through the Department of Community Affairs, which already administered state Head Start funds before the prekindergarten program was enacted. Another approach is the interagency coordination model adopted by South Carolina which, while permitting the Department of Education to administer the state-funded prekindergarten program, retains the Interagency Coordinating Council—representing all state agencies which serve children—as the body with authority to approve overall plans for the program.

These more neutral choices (offices for children, or interagency councils, or departments other than education or social services) have some programmatic advantages. Their focus is neither strictly on education nor on welfare. Instead, they may be focused on the client (offices for *children*, departments of *community* development) or on a cross-system holistic approach to providing services (as would an *interagency* council). But there are also pragmatic disadvantages. These agencies can be effective only if they are strong enough to carry the early childhood programs (powerful enough to be able to garner sufficient state funding and sustain popular, legislative, and gubernatorial support for the programs). Education departments are usually more powerful and have greater clout with legislators and the governor than social service or welfare agencies. Education, due to its size and tenure, is certain to be a more powerful agency than a newly created agency and does not suffer from the turf battles among agencies inherent in an interagency council. Given the political and economic power wielded by departments of education—especially in the education reform era—DOE was, in the last analysis, more likely than Human Services to be the single agency chosen to administer prekindergarten programs.

Administrative Locus of State-Funded Prekindergarten Programs

With only three exceptions (Washington, Alaska, and the new program in New Jersey), state departments of education or public instruction and state boards of education are the agencies with primary responsibility for administering state-funded prekindergarten programs. Within the state departments of education, the most common placement of these prekindergarten programs is in the unit dealing with instructional services or curriculum and instruction. Only three states (California, New York, and Massachusetts) have created departmental units to deal specifically with child development or early childhood education.

While it is customary for education-related federal programs such as Chapter I and special education to be administered by state departments of education, it is interesting to note that state contributions to Head Start, which provides early childhood education that includes a wide range of supportive services, are predominantly under the auspices of non-educational agencies, ranging from departments of human services or community development to employment and training. The only exception among the states which contribute funds to Head Start is Massachusetts, which provides both salary support and expansion funds to Head Start programs through the state Department of Education. Clearly, Head Start, like the publicly subsidized child care programs, is not customarily viewed by the states as belonging under the auspices of education.

Given that education reform spawned many of the newer state-funded prekindergarten programs, it is no surprise that many are administered by state departments of education. The administrative locus of a state-funded prekindergarten program is essentially a political decision. Gubernatorial, legislative, and public support for education programs and education appropriations is much stronger currently than that for social programs. Even though early childhood programs are a hybrid, combining elements from both education and social services, they are most often viewed as one or the other. When a proposed early childhood program is seen as more social service related, or is closely modeled on Head Start as a few of the newer state-funded prekindergarten programs were, then the natural choice is a noneducation state agency. When early childhood programs are perceived as education, as the state-funded prekindergarten programs that were part of education reform packages certainly were, then the state department of education is the obvious recipient of the new program. The education agency is usually not the state agency with the most experience in managing programs serving young children; it is the agency that has experience with education (for older children).

The perceived principal need which a program is designed to meet affects decisions about administrative locus. New Jersey offers an example of these administrative choices in its three prekindergarten programs. New Jersey's long-standing permissive prekindergarten program was very clearly educational. It was begun in 1903, long before there was any delivery system for publicly funded early childhood education other than public schools. It is an education program administered by the Department of Education. By contrast, the state's newer prekindergarten program, which is modeled on Head Start and designed to encourage full-working-day services, is administered by the Department of Human Services. It's newest (third) program (also following Head Start guidelines) is jointly administered by both departments.

Although political perception of a program's purpose is a strong factor, and adequately explains the choice of noneducation agencies for locating Head Start contributions and some Head Start-like prekindergarten programs, the choice of which noneducation state agency to administer a program is further influenced by factors unique to each state. For example, because the program is targeted to a small number of native villages, Alaska located its small state-funded prekindergarten program in the Department of Community and Regional Affairs. The choice of the Department of Community Development for Washington's state-funded pre-kindergarten program reflects the influence of at least three factors. First, creation of the prekindergarten program was strongly supported by the Business Roundtable, which viewed it as part of an economic development strategy (for example, early education can better prepare tomorrow's work force). Second, while the state constitution guarantees state funding of basic education for all citizens, the state's economic health was not strong enough to support funding of a universal program for all the state's prekindergarten children. Therefore, the education department would not have been a fiscally pragmatic choice. Finally, the new program is modeled closely on Head Start, and the state's preexisting (and ongoing) contribution of state funds to Head Start programs already resided in the Department of Community Development.

There are programmatic consequences of these choices about locus. Education departments, while clearly in the business of education, have little or no experience with providing the supportive services that are a necessary part of early childhood programs. They also appear to be less likely to foster collaborative efforts with other state agencies and to encourage collaborative efforts at the local level among community agencies (which is one means of delivering comprehensive support services). State education departments are likely to leave curricular matters to local option or to focus on more academic curricula and programmatic approaches rather than on the full range of child development domains commonly addressed in good early childhood education curricula. Indeed, all permissive, state-funded prekindergarten programs not targeted to specific populations of children (the programs in New Jersey, Pennsylvania, Wisconsin, and Maine) are administered by departments or boards of education and are located in public schools. These programs do not require comprehensive services or specify elements of a child development-based curriculum. Most are half-day programs and are guided by standards similar to those for public school kindergarten. These programs offer little evidence of coordination with other state programs serving similar populations. Some of the newer targeted programs, such as in Maryland and Washington, do specify some elements of comprehensive service, sometimes directly referencing Head Start's array of service components.

While a decision about administrative locus is, theoretically at least, not irrevocable, there is practically no chance that the administrative agency will change. Once a program is an established part of one state agency it is extremely unlikely to move into another state agency. The forces of turf protection and program ownership are very strong. Whatever drawbacks the state administrative agency presents must be reckoned with through internal and external advocacy for incremental change within that agency, unless a comprehensive state policy is developed guiding reorganization of the administration of children's services into a more rational structure.

Some states have recognized (usually through the influence of organized advocacy from the child care and/or Head Start community) that the majority of existing early childhood education is provided in the community beyond the public school system. The basic principle of efficiency in public policy—maximize use of existing resources—also suggests the need to draw on these extant providers (child care and Head Start centers, for example) at least to some degree. While the state education department may still be selected as the administrative locus for all the reasons previously discussed, the range of possible providers of a state-funded prekindergarten program can be extended to the wider early childhood education community beyond (and including) the public schools. This is accomplished by permitting subcontracts between local school districts and other local agencies and/or direct contracts between the state agency and local agencies other than public schools. Subcontracts keep local administrative control in the public school system, while allowing all or part of the prekindergarten program services to be provided at the local level by community agencies.

This practice has the potential—unfortunately only partially realized in practice—to promote some local collaboration among schools and other community agencies.[2] The targeted programs for at-risk preschoolers in South Carolina, Illinois, Massachusetts, and Florida provide examples of state-funded prekindergarten programs which permit subcontracting and (except for Illinois) have explicit provisions for interagency collaboration at both the state and local level. Local collaboration is required in Massachusetts, in Florida, and in certain circumstances in South Carolina; it is encouraged in Illinois. The subcontracting provision has been used somewhat in Massachusetts and in Florida, very little in Illinois, and not at all in South Carolina. While not all of these states' prekindergarten programs provide comprehensive services that include child care, their programs are more likely than the permissive state programs to include other services supportive to families.

The use of direct contracts allows any local agency—including the public schools—to apply for funds. This practice encourages healthy competition and offers opportunities for local coordination. The prekindergarten programs in California, Vermont, and Oregon fall into this category; in each, the state department of education is still the overall administrative agency. In Washington, Alaska, and the two newer programs in New Jersey, maximum flexibility has been achieved at the state level with program administration residing in, respectively, the departments of community development, community and regional affairs, and human services jointly with education. These states' programs are modeled, more or less explicitly, on Head Start and therefore promise a comprehensive range of services supportive of families. Programs in Washington, New Jersey, and Oregon require specific local-level coordination.

Before turning to examples of state administrative practice, it is important to point out that even *within* state departments of education, few states have created administrative structures which bring together on an ongoing formal basis the various categorical programs serving prekindergarten children (special education, Chapter I, bilingual, and migrant programs). Failure to create coordinating mechanisms within the education department itself both impedes the orderly planning necessary to enhance service provision and makes fruitless competition—both within the department and in the schools—more likely.

Examples of State Administrative Practices

Single State Agency for Child Care and Early Childhood Programs California is unique among the states insofar as it houses all early childhood and child care programs in the state Department of Education in the Child Development Division. All early childhood programs under the Department of Education are subject to licensure by the Department of Social Services and must also comply with the additional curriculum and staffing requirements of the Department of Education's "Funding Terms and Conditions," which apply to all programs receiving state Department of Education funds. Programs providing the part-day prekindergarten and/or full-day child development services receive technical assistance, fiscal and program monitoring, and inservice training from the Child Development Division. Programs also engage in an annual self-review process, using instruments developed by the Child Development Division.

Because of the single state agency model used in California, coordination of child care with other programs for prekindergarten children is greatly enhanced. For example, funds from the federal preschool special education incentive grant are used to train personnel in state-subsidized child care programs in serving special needs children. Coordination of Chapter I funds and state funds to provide both child care and child development programs for migrant children is another example of the benefits provided by administering multiple programs through a single state agency. The enactment of GAIN (Greater Avenues to Independence), the state's welfare reform legislation, has led to increased coordination between the Child Development Division and the Department of Social Services (which administers the workfare program). Although the process has not gone particularly smoothly, according to some respondents, it is seen as evolving and improving.

At the local level in California, countywide community child care councils are important vehicles for coordination among various agencies. The statewide network of child care resource and referral agencies also contributes to local-level coordination. All child care and child development programs funded by the Child Development Division may be operated directly by school districts *or* subcontracted to nonprofit or for-profit community agencies. Nonprofit agencies may also contract directly with the Department of Education. These practices encourage a wide diversity of program types and expand choices for families among services.

The District of Columbia, which has provided funds for at least one classroom of its full-school-day program for four-year-olds in each of the District's public schools, has established the Office of Early Childhood Development as a single administrative unit to coordinate children's services throughout the District. The creation of this office was part of a five-year plan of the mayor's Commission on Early Childhood Education to improve funding, resources and standards for child care, and early childhood programs in the schools and the private sector.

Department of Education Administered Program Provided by Public Schools Only Delaware provides an example of a state-funded prekindergarten program administered by the Department of Education and delivered by public schools. It is a small, nontargeted grants program. The governor's Early Childhood Education Study Committee evaluates and monitors the prekindergarten program. This 36-member committee is broadly representative of Head Start, early childhood educators, public schools, and the legislature. In addition, Delaware, as is true of some other states, has a Human Resources Cabinet which coordinates all human services programs and advises the governor on various issues, including child care and early education.

Public School Administered Programs with Subcontracts to Other Agencies and the Involvement of State Councils Florida has mandated coordination between the Department of Public Instruction and child care programs since 1974. As a result, many interagency agreements and coordination groups are operative in the state. Chapter 228, which established the Prekindergarten Early Intervention Program, also created a State Advisory Council to assist and advise the superintendent of Public Instruction on the implementation of the prekindergarten program. (Many of the tasks carried out by the council are more commonly lodged within the purview of state departments of education.) The council is charged with reviewing and recommending rules for the program; providing technical assistance to school districts in developing prekindergarten proposals and programs; assisting the department in monitoring and evaluating district programs; and conducting studies on the effectiveness of the state prekindergarten program and other early childhood programs. The council members are broadly representative of the state agencies, the child care provider community, the public schools, health services, and the state legislature. To further ensure coordination, school districts applying for funds are directed to develop, implement, and evaluate the prekindergarten program in cooperation with a district interagency coordinating council on prekindergarten education, which mirrors the state council.

Florida is one of only five states permitting full-working-day child care programs to be funded under its prekindergarten program. This fact, and the administrative structure which has been adopted for the program, increases the likelihood that the educational, social, medical, and child care needs of families served will be addressed at both the state and local level.

Massachusetts has developed a structure similar to Florida's both in establishing funding priorities under its state-funded prekindergarten programs and in using state and local advisory groups. In addition to these features, the state has created an Office of Early Childhood Education within the Department of Education, which provides technical assistance to local district and subcontracted programs through the Department of Education's regional offices. The state has also created a child care policy group within the governor's Executive Office of Human Services, which includes Department of Education representation and which has attempted to make teacher requirements across child care and early childhood programs more uniform through revision of child care licensing standards.

Florida and Massachusetts offer examples of what can be achieved by the use of interagency groups to guide and monitor both the planning and implementation process. States like Washington have chosen the department of community development as the state administrative agency, rather than the department of education. Within the department, the Division of Community Services, which oversees the state's contribution to Head Start, has assumed a monitoring and evaluation role very similar to the role of state departments of education in other states. The Early Childhood Education and Assistance Program Advisory Committee has played a very similar role to that of other state advisory committees in developing program guidelines and overseeing program activities. New Jersey's new program, which is administered by the Department of Human Services, Division of Youth and Family Services, operates through extant county human service advisory councils to oversee the coordination and consolidation of all state-funded human service programs operating in their localities.

While California's single administrative agency for child care and child development provides one quite successful model, state efforts to use interagency groups and offices for child development within the Department of Education may prove to be equally effective administrative structures in the development of high-quality early childhood programs. However, they are not as yet free of both potential and actual problems. Despite their having achieved some degree of connection between early childhood programs under the auspices of the public schools and those provided by other state agencies, much remains to be done in both planning and implementation to minimize the likelihood that state prekindergarten programs may supplant existing Head Start and subsidized child care programs. Competition for children, space, and staff can be alleviated via collaborative efforts that begin in the planning stage and continue beyond. Further, programs provided under the auspices of state departments of education, using categorical funds such as federal special education and Chapter I, do not appear to be well integrated into the administrative structure of the state-funded prekindergarten effort. The result is duplication of administrative structures and the adoption of dissimilar requirements for funding, staffing, and monitoring these programs—even though they exist within the same state agency.

Two facts—that nearly all of the state-funded prekindergarten programs are administered by state education departments and that some local school districts are now engaged in providing a variety of prekindergarten programs—will profoundly influence the public debate over whether child care programs belong in schools. This debate raged fiercely around the Comprehensive Child Development Act of 1971 when the public schools were proposed as the logical sole proprietor of publicly funded child care. One of the major arguments against this position was that public schools have no experience with young children or with the realities of providing full-working-day, year-round programs. Public schools, it was argued, could not provide the necessary comprehensive services, would offer inappropriate education for young children, and would hire improperly trained staff (unemployed elementary school, or even high school, teachers). While it may have been true that public schools lacked experience then, the situation has changed. In 1971 very few state education departments (or local school districts) were involved with children younger than five. Those states that were involved provided either very small programs (West Virginia), permissive programs that were not widely used (New Jersey and Pennsylvania), or newly begun replicas of Head Start (California and New York).

In contrast to their position in 1971, today most state education departments (and many local school districts) can claim knowledge and experience with younger children based on their administration of state-funded prekindergarten, prekindergarten special education, and other programs for younger children that are now under their jurisdiction. Although their experience with younger children has certainly grown, it is nevertheless true that the vast majority of public schools do not have experience with the realities of providing full-working-day programs that include longer hours and year-round schedules.

Administration of Early Childhood Programs in Local School Districts

The form and structure of program administration at the school district level appear to have major influences on the nature and quality of the services delivered to children and families. In those districts we visited, the quality of the program itself appeared to be strongly affected by the administrative structure itself and by the personnel who staff it.

Among all districts with prekindergarten programs about two-thirds (67 percent) reported that a single person coordinated all the districts' prekindergarten programs (in addition to each program's own administrator). Smaller districts and those with fewer than 50 prekindergartens enrolled district-wide were more likely (75 percent) to report having a single district prekindergarten coordinator. In contrast, larger districts and those with more than 1,000 enrolled prekindergartners were less likely (52 percent) to have one district prekindergarten coordinator. Rather, these districts have one coordinator for each prekindergarten program.

Forms of Administration

The administrative structure of early childhood programs in public school districts usually takes one of three basic forms. Which form a district follows depends more on the number and extent of the district's programs than on the size of the district per se. Larger districts can be found using all three of the forms discussed below, while smaller districts tend toward one of the two single-administrator forms. The building principal's direct role differs among the various forms, but the principal's support for and understanding of the realities of programs for young children is always a crucial element in the success of early childhood programs.

Single Site or Single Program/Single Administrator Some districts operate a single type of program (such as state-funded prekindergarten only) or operate a variety of program types which are all located in a single site (for example, one building which houses child care, prekindergarten, prekindergarten special education, and parent education). Typically, one administrator is responsible for the district's total early childhood program and reports directly to the district superintendent (or, in a very large district, one bureaucratic level below the superintendent, for example, to a deputy superintendent). In a smaller district this central administrator is responsible for hiring, firing, and training program personnel and functions as the building (single site) principal. In a larger district operating one program type in multiple sites, the building principals generally have some authority (more than in a smaller district) in personnel matters in the classrooms in their building, while staff training and curriculum development remain centralized under the district administrator.

Affton-Lindbergh Early Childhood Education, a joint program of the Affton and Lindbergh school districts in St. Louis County, Missouri, is a good example of the single-site administrative form. There is one director of Early Childhood Education, who is on the principal level and is the direct supervisor of all program staff. All programs operate in one site in a former middle school building in the Lindbergh district. Programs include early childhood education (part-day, part-week); early childhood extended day (full-working-day hours, year-round); extended day kindergarten (surrounding the part-day kindergarten hours, year-round); early childhood special education (integrated into any of the other programs); and the state-funded parent education program (Parents as First Teachers).

The director shares personnel hiring, firing, supervision, and evaluation responsibilities with the assistant director. All staff are employees of the Affton district. Policy decisions for the Early Childhood Education program are the responsibility of a coordinating council. The council includes five representatives: two from each district's central office and the director of Early Childhood Education. The high degree of commitment both districts feel to the program is evident in the level of their choices for the council: Affton appointed the superintendent and the business manager; Lindbergh appointed the associate superintendent and the assistant superintendent.

Curriculum and training are, in a sense, neither centralized nor decentralized when all programs are in one site. Curriculum and training are consistent across programs. The director at Affton-Lindbergh, who functions both as district early childhood administrator and as building principal, selected (in collaboration with teaching staff) a curriculum for use in all the programs. The selected curriculum (High/Scope) is somewhat modified by each classroom teaching team. Training in the High/Scope curriculum, required of all staff, is provided along with other training opportunities in the form of support for attendance at local and state early childhood education conferences.

Multiple Program Types (and Sites) with Separate (Multiple) Administrators Some districts operate many different program types in multiple sites throughout the district, with each type having a separate district-level administrator. Since programs are usually differentiated by their funding sources (and their associated program and fiscal regulations), the federally funded Chapter I program is directed by one administrator, while the state-funded prekindergarten program is directed by another. This differentiation is related not only to funding source but also to evolution. A new program usually requires a new administrator (unless the new program is relatively small and has purposes similar to an extant program and can be added to that administrator's responsibilities).

Individual school buildings may house one or more of the various program types. Typically, the building principals (rather than district administrators) have more direct personnel and supervisory responsibility (usually including complete authority over hiring/firing of classroom personnel) in this form, particularly if their building houses more than one program type. Training of personnel and program monitoring usually remain the responsibility of the central program administrator—especially if a standard curriculum is used throughout the district. Particularly in large districts, the various program administrators rarely reported directly to the superintendent. It is more common to report either to an associate superintendent for curriculum and instruction (or elementary education) or to an associate superintendent specifically charged with early childhood education. This associate superintendent can exert more or less influence on the philosophy and content of each of the separate programs, drawing them into a unified whole or allowing for a great deal of variation in philosophy and curriculum approach.

The Chicago Public Schools offer an example of this second administrative form. The Bureau of Early Childhood Programs is within the Office of Instruction. (*Office* is the highest bureaucratic level in the district; the order proceeds from *office, department, bureau,* to *division.*) The director of the Bureau of Early Childhood Programs is responsible for Head Start, state-funded prekindergartens, and the Chapter I Child/Parent Centers (CPCs). There are two administrators in the bureau: one for Head Start and state prekindergarten, and one for CPCs. Their offices are located within the central district office. All bilingual/multilingual prekindergarten programs are in a different bureau (Bureau of Multilingual Programs), as are prekindergarten special education programs (Bureau of Special Education).

Chicago's state prekindergarten classrooms are within school buildings (usually one classroom per school); the building principal is directly responsible for their operation. Child/Parent Centers are in separate buildings near schools or on school grounds. CPCs have head teachers who supervise a parent coordinator and other classroom personnel. Although CPC head teachers report to the building principal, CPCs are essentially separate operations.

The CPC curriculum is loosely structured by the Bureau of Early Childhood Programs, but is largely the product of the head teacher and her or his staff. The curricula for Head Start and the state prekindergarten are centralized and supervised more closely.

Multiple Program Types (and Sites) with a Single Adminstrator
In other school districts that operate many types of early childhood programs, also usually differentiated by funding sources, one early childhood administrator is responsible for all the various program types. Again, individual school buildings may house one or more program types. The building principal's role is limited and often does not include directly hiring classroom personnel (although the principal may be heavily involved in a consultative role). Training for all program types is centralized and more often conducted jointly across all program types in this form of administration. This

form usually results in a more unified philosophical approach across all program types. The administrator usually reports directly to the district superintendent.

The Pomona Unified School District in California is a good example of this third form of administrative structure. Pomona has one Child Development administrator for all of its programs, which include Head Start, state prekindergarten, Children's Centers, the child care resource and referral service, the school age parent and infant development program, school age child care, respite care, and the alternative payment system. The various programs are located at numerous sites throughout the district. Most Head Start and state prekindergartens are in separate buildings on school grounds; some Children's Centers are in separate wings of school buildings, some are in portable structures on school grounds, and others are in rented space in churches. Sites in school buildings vary in the degree to which the building principal is involved.

The Child Development offices are in one location, away from the district offices. The Child Development administrator is the link with the district office. Otherwise, contact between the staff of the district and Child Development offices is infrequent except for the processing of personnel applications. The district office screens and processes personnel applications. All early childhood teachers and paraprofessionals are unionized, along with other district personnel, and are represented by two district-wide bargaining units. Head teachers are not considered administrators (they are members of the teachers' bargaining unit). The administrator of Child Development hires, fires, and evaluates all teachers and other staff, including the head teachers.

There is an assistant administrator for Head Start and prekindergarten, and one for Children's Centers and other programs. Each program site has a head teacher who is responsible for day-to-day supervision and educational direction. One of the assistant administrators is a High/Scope trainer who offers sessions for all teachers in all programs. Whereas training is centralized, the curriculum is neither centralized nor standardized. The program for children varies somewhat by site within a basic High/Scope framework, depending on the head teacher and the staff of each site.

The Effects of Form

The form of administration affects how early childhood services are delivered in a school district. If the district is very large and operates extensive early childhood programs, more centralized structures, like the first and third forms already described, can be more efficient in using scarce resources, such as training and staff development funds. As a result, they may cost less in total admin-istrative expense. Less centralization, as in the second form described above in which various program administrators and the building principals have more responsibility, can increase local control (*local* in the sense of building personnel, as opposed to central office personnel). But it may also increase the variation in program quality, in that service delivery is supervised directly by building principals who may have widely varying preparation for supervising early childhood programs.

Categorical funding is a powerful reality that affects administration, and therefore direct services, in programs for young children. There are now, and will probably continue to be, many separate funding sources for early childhood services. Each dictates a set of funding and programmatic regulations. Certain programs—such as special education, Chapter I, bilingual, and a few state-funded prekindergarten programs—require individual testing of children to identify those eligible. Many programs require eligibility tests of family income (including some state prekindergartens), and/or determination of employment status, or frequent redetermination of eligibility (as do subsidized child care programs). The central office administrators for these programs are responsible for implementation *and* for meeting these requirements, monitoring compliance, maintaining records, and they are ultimately accountable for the entire district's behavior in regard to the program they administer. This kind of accountability is more likely to be tested (through audits and other means), and therefore can come to be valued more highly, than the quality of service delivered to children or the efficacy of staff development efforts. The highly centralized administrative structures of large districts often concentrate heavily on meeting this array of varying, often conflicting requirements—sometimes to the detriment of the actual service delivered to children.

Clearly, the program content, or, more broadly, the quality of services delivered, is affected by the administrative structure. A more coherent philosophical, or unified programmatic, approach to early childhood education appears to be more likely in a centralized administrative form with a certain type of administrator. However, the most significant variable in determining the quality of a program is the people who inhabit the administrative structure.

The Critical Element: Leadership No matter what the size of the district (and to a certain extent no matter what the administrative form), the best early childhood programs (those that deliver higher-quality service to children, satisfy parents, and earn the respect of their early childhood community peers) are characterized by strong leadership. As in all effective education, the leader is a critical ingredient. (The vast literature on effective schools consistently cites the principal as a major influence.) The effective early childhood leader has three essential characteristics: She or he is well prepared in early childhood education/child development, is "close to the customers," and is close to the source(s) of power. The administrator who is well prepared has been well trained as an early childhood educator. Usually, this entails being formally trained (educated or credentialed) in early childhood or child development, but it also means having direct experience with children as a teacher or administrator of early childhood programs outside the school system before becoming the district's administrator. This experience can be, for example, teaching in a Head Start program or in a child care center. "Close to the customer" means both close to the classrooms (that is, known to and influential with the teachers, involved in training, and knowledgeable about the children) and close to the parents (aware of and responsive to parents' concerns and needs). "Close to the power" means respected and influential in the district office and particularly with the superintendent, so that the early childhood programs are a high priority to the district. The effective early childhood leader clearly communicates the mission and philosophy of the early childhood programs to personnel, parents, and the power structure.

This crucial leader/administrator appeared more often in either the single-site/single-program administrative form or the multiple-program/single-administrator form than in the multiple-administrator form. The multiple-administrator form may be able to support leaders who each have some of these characteristics, but it very rarely allows one leader to emerge with all three of the essential elements. In smaller districts this crucial leadership role is played by one person. In larger districts with developed bureaucratic structures, this role can be played either by a partnership or by one person surrounded by a strong team.

This kind of leader is necessary to ensure good early childhood programs in public schools. Knowing that they are necessary is only the first step. Superintendents must seek out these leaders and support them with appropriate administrative structures. Since these effective leaders are probably in short supply, we recommend trying to create more of them. From the leadership examples we encountered in our site visits, it appears that this kind of leader develops somewhat organically from a particular combination of experiences, opportunities, and personal qualities. We recognize that it is easier to specify the salient characteristics of these effective leaders than it is to specify how to create more of them. But it is certainly worth trying, given how critical these leaders are to a quality early childhood program. One route would be to identify and nurture promising candidates from within a district—for example, among principals with early childhood backgrounds. Another would be to look in the community for influential directors of child care centers or Head Start programs, and support their further administrative training. A promising candidate would be someone who has direct experience in early childhood, accompanied by a high degree of political savvy. Another route would be to increase the amount of leadership training included in preservice preparation programs for early childhood educators, with a concentration on developing critical public relations and advocacy skills and an understanding of the practical realities of effective leadership.

Recommendations

- The primary purpose of an administrative structure should be to support and improve the quality of service delivered to children and families in each and every early childhood program. For early childhood programs operated by a school district, select the administrative structure appropriate for the district's size that will be most effective in accomplishing that purpose.
- In selecting an administrative structure at the state level, a range of options—for example, a single state agency, joint management by two agencies, or the creation of a new agency focused on children's services—should be considered. Amidst the political and economic considerations, the selection should be based on the capability of the state agency (or agencies) to fulfill the purpose and intent of the early childhood program and to improve the delivery of services to children and families.
- For administrators at all levels, increase the knowledge base in early childhood education, child development, and program quality factors.
- At the state and local levels, hire early childhood administrators who have both direct experience working in programs for young children and who can develop and communicate a

strong, clearly articulated philosophy of early childhood education.
- School districts should target staff development resources to principals with prekindergarten programs in their buildings.
- Include program administrators in early childhood training offered to teachers. A school district should include both central office personnel and building principals in such training sessions.
- Seek out experienced early childhood personnel—throughout the early childhood ecosystem—who have potential to become effective administrators and support their further development.

Endnotes

1. Grubb, W.N. (May 1987). *Young children face the states: Issues and options for early childhood programs.* Rutgers, N.J.: Center for Policy Research in Education (p. 63).
2. For a thorough discussion of the issues and consequences of various coordination mechanisms, see Chapter 7.

Chapter 4

FINANCING EARLY
CHILDHOOD PROGRAMS

Educational programs for children are supported by two distinctly different systems of financing, depending on whether the children are over or under age five. Educational programs for children over age five are easily separated into categories by auspice: public or private. The public school system is supported by public funds—federal, state, and local—in relative proportions that vary from state to state. In contrast, the private school system is supported by private funds—from parents and from other private sources, such as religious institutions. Very small amounts of public funds do find their way into the private education system to support specific items or services, such as textbook aid or transportation. However, for the most part, it is fair to state that the public education system is supported with public funds and the private education system is supported with private funds.

In contrast to the easily delineated public/private funding system for programs for children five and over, services for children *under* age five are delivered through a diverse array of public and private organizations which are financed by a mixture of public and private funds. Many private organizations receive public funds, and many public organizations utilize private funds. For example, a private organization offering a variety of child care services may have diverse funding sources. Services to children whose families are eligible for full subsidy are supported, mainly or entirely, by funds from public sources (state and federal). Services to children whose families are required to pay a portion of the total fee are financed by a combination of public and private funds. Child care services may also be offered to families who can afford to pay the full fee; these services are entirely privately financed (by the parents). Families who are ineligible for subsidy but are unable to pay the full fee may be supported partially by private funds in addition to their own funds (for example, scholarships funded by organizations such as United Way).

Even the essentially private portions of the early childhood system are supported indirectly by public funds. For example, nursery schools are private organizations which are typically either nonprofit corporations, cooperatives, or for-profit enterprises and are funded primarily by parents' fees. However, when used as a child care arrangement, nursery schools are partially supported by public (tax) funds through the Dependent Care Tax Credit or an employer-provided Dependent Care Assistance Plan.

A public organization, such as a municipality or a school district, may offer the same variety of subsidized and nonsubsidized child care services as a private organization and would use a similar mix of funding sources. Some public school districts offer both full-working-day child care and part-day nursery school programs funded almost entirely from private sources (parents' fees). Part-day programs for children under five, such as certain states' funded prekindergarten programs, may be offered by both public schools and other public and private organizations. While public (state) funds may be the major source of support, they are supplemented in some instances by local public tax dollars and in some cases by private funds from parents or foundations.

In many ways, the system of services for children under age five is strikingly similar to the higher education (postsecondary) system. A variety of public and private colleges and universities throughout the nation are supported by direct public funding (state tax dollars), indirect public sources (guaranteed student loans, property tax exemptions), and private funds (tuition). The similarities with higher education, rather than with K–12 education, may be more useful in considering the appropriate role of public funding in the early childhood system. The major differences between the financing systems in place to support programs for children over five and programs for children under five inevitably lead to conflicts as public support increases for programs for children under age five.

Allocation of Resources

"The Love of Money Is the Root of All Evil"[1]

Money itself is at the heart of the conflicts about public schools and early childhood programs. Competition—real or perceived—

for resources is the root of the conflict. The long-standing arguments about the proper role of schools in the early childhood system have heated up precisely because there is more interest (the potential for more resources) in early childhood education. In the absence of resources for expansion, philosophical debates about the proper role of the schools can continue for decades without resolution. But when the potential exists for resources to become more plentiful (as they did when the Child Development Act of 1971 was passed and then vetoed), the pressure for resolution increases. Currently, there is ample public interest in child care and early education, which means potential for resources and the competition for them—and pressure to resolve the debate and "choose a system."

The multibillion dollar price tags on many of the 200-odd bills with child care provisions introduced in the 1988 session of Congress represent potentially large increases in resources and serve to fuel the debates about which providers and which mechanisms (supply or demand subsidy, tax code or vouchers) are most appropriate. Nearly all of these bills, including the Act for Better Child Care and Smart Start, were not passed, but both the Family Support Act of 1988 (so-called welfare reform) and the reauthorization of Chapter I (which officially extended services to three- and four-year-olds and created Even Start, a joint parent-child education program) were approved. Chapter I, being essentially a "public schools only" program, will increase the public schools' role in the early childhood system, while the Family Support Act is more likely to affect the subsidized child care market in which public schools play a minor role (except in California).

The rapid creation of state-funded prekindergarten programs over the past five years and the increases in state funds for child care (in some states) are evidence of greater interest at the state level in the early years of childhood. The increased interest (and resources) in these states have further fueled the debate about the proper role of schools. New and expanded initiatives in the field come at a time when demand for services is at an all time high and gives no evidence of declining. More parents are working; more parents recognize the value of early education. The demand side of the equation (parents) wants more choices that combine education and care, lower costs, higher quality. The supply side of the equation (the providers of service—public schools and all others) is ready to expand but not to give up any ground; each provider is zealously protecting currently held financial turf. In the climate of increased pressure from all sides, policymakers will certainly have to recognize the reality of turf, but they must look well beyond it to make wise choices for the allocation of public resources that will both satisfy demand *and* improve and expand supply.

Mechanisms for Financing Early Childhood Programs

A financing mechanism is not a substitute for program definition. Rather, it is a means of achieving the goals and objectives of a well-defined program. Ideally, the goals and objectives of the program to be funded (or the services to be purchased) are clearly and specifically defined. Given that, the most efficient financing model is one that is broad in defining eligible providers of service in order to utilize the best elements of the early childhood system; recognizes the relationship between funding level and program quality, thereby allowing for reasonable per child funding; specifies the accountability measures for meeting the program objectives; recognizes the shared responsibility for funding and requires a degree of local participation in funding that takes account of the differing ability of communities. In practice, each of the mechanisms used by states to finance their prekindergarten programs has its own pros and cons in terms of fiscal and programmatic accountability, support for quality, and flexibility or adaptability to local conditions in different communities across the state.

A financing mechanism that limits service provision to public schools is sometimes perceived by policymakers as a way to ensure that programs are "educational" without specifying a whole set of program regulations. Public school is perceived as synonymous with education; the public education system is where public funds for educational programs go. This is generally true for kindergarten through grade 12; however, it is not the case for children younger than kindergarten entry age. In the arena of early childhood—that is, children under age five—many publicly supported educational systems (Head Start, child care programs, and the like) are outside the public school system and merit the attention of policymakers as vehicles for prekindergarten education.

The Prekindergarten Pie

Generally, the public and private school systems for children over age five are not in direct competition (except in some sense for students); they peacefully coexist. Each has its own basic financing system, culture, clientele, and buildings. Because the two systems have separate funding sources, they do not compete directly for resources.[2] The ratio of public to private enrollment nationally for grades K–12 is a stable pattern that has held steady for decades at roughly 10 percent private to 90 percent public enrollment (obviously with some local variation).[3]

The prekindergarten pattern is dramatically different. The ratio of public to private prekindergarten enrollment is practically the opposite of K–12 enrollment—about 1 percent of children under age five attend public schools.[4] However, the pattern is changing. The recent increase in public school-operated prekindergarten programs over the past five years has caused the public schools to play a more significant role in the (mainly nonpublic) early childhood system.

The concern expressed in the early childhood community over the growing presence of public schools as providers is fundamentally financial. It is a widely held belief that there is a limited enthusiasm for public investment in early childhood and therefore a finite "pie" of resources. More interest may not mean more resources—just a reallocation of present resources. The fear is that the public school system—being an extensive, well-respected, generally trustworthy, public institution with longevity and great clout—will get "more than its fair share" of the finite resources, leaving the rest of the early childhood system with less. The portion of the finite pie left for the nonpublic school sector will be sliced in ever smaller pieces.

Child Care and Prekindergarten Funding in the States   Is the pie bigger? Are the pieces smaller? These questions are, in part, a matter of perspective. Is the early childhood community justified in its concern? The record on public funding levels is favorable. Of the states with direct service prekindergarten programs operating during both the 1986–1987 and the 1987–1988 school years, about half increased funding for prekindergarten programs and half decreased or level-funded (no change in funding from one year to the next) those programs. Three-quarters of those states that contribute state funds to Head Start programs increased their contribution in this same period; Head Start contributions remained the same in the District of Columbia and in Maine.

Attention to the need of low- and middle-income parents for full-working-day programs for the care and education of their preschool children remains largely under the auspices of the Social Services Block Grant (Title XX) and/or the state-subsidized child care programs. Among the 21 states with funded prekindergarten programs in operation during FY 1987, only two states, Louisiana and West Virginia, decreased funding for both their state-subsidized child care program and prekindergarten program over the prior year. Maine and California level-funded both program areas; thus there was no increase in funding for either their child care or prekindergarten programs from one fiscal year to the next. Ten states managed to increase funding in both programs, five of them increasing their child care funding between 20 and 30 percent (despite serious fiscal problems in states like Kentucky and Michigan). Alaska and Oklahoma, both experiencing significant declines in state revenues, maintained their commitment to the prekindergarten program while decreasing child care funding, although in Alaska child care funding was restored in the FY 1988 budget. Only one state, Ohio, showed an actual decrease in its prekindergarten funding while increasing child care funding by 7 percent. In New York and in Texas, prekindergarten funding expanded significantly, while child care funding rose only 3 to 4 percent in FY 1987, allowing for very little expansion. Illinois and Massachusetts level-funded their state prekindergarten programs while increasing child care funding (although additional funding was provided to Head Start programs in Massachusetts).

Taken as a whole, these states present a pattern of gradual increases in funding for both prekindergarten and child care programs. The increased presence of public schools in the early childhood arena does not appear to have limited the size of the whole resources pie or to have decreased the size of those pieces allocated to the nonpublic school sector.

Competition The various nonpublic school parts of the early childhood (prekindergarten) system have always competed for public funds (for example, for Head Start grants or contracts to provide child care services). This competition is perceived to be more or less equal (and fair) because all the competitors are generally similar in size, clout, and ability to provide the service. As public schools continue to play a part in providing programs for children under five, competition for public funds will increase and the element of unfairness will be introduced. The public schools are clearly *not* similar—in size, clout, or perceived ability—to the other competitors in the early childhood system.

Competition for public funds is a thorny issue, but another form of competition—for private funds—poses even more difficult problems. There are two quite different perspectives on the danger of the public school as entrepreneur: that of the private sector, which feels direct competition, and that of the public education system as a whole, which feels its base of public support may be threatened. From the perspective of the private sector of the early childhood system, public schools that offer child care services for a fee are perceived as unfair competitors because the schools are using publicly financed resources (such as buildings) to offer child care at bargain rates in the private sector, thus undercutting the competition. From the perspective of the public education system, private fees charged to parents in a public system are an attack on the foundation of the whole system of free public education. Charging fees to individual parents for their own children contradicts the shared public responsibility to provide education for every child in a community. If fees for prekindergarten services in public schools become common practice, the question can be raised: Why not for older children?

For this reason, the Council of Chief State School Officers recently voiced its opposition to any fees for prekindergarten programs provided by public schools:[5]

> *[An approach] might be to make eligibility for child development programs universal but to establish a fee schedule for parents able to afford it. Such an approach could set an undesirable precedent for chipping away at the basic precept of a "free public education." A variation on this approach would be to make poverty the prime determinant of eligibility but to make a limited number of seats available to children who are not income-eligible and whose parents are willing to pay a fee. (Under Head Start, 10 percent of the slots are available to such children.) Such an approach might be justified as an interim measure leading to universal participation.*

Fees charged to parents are seen as a destructive wedge (like vouchers) that could reach beyond prekindergarten and undermine public support for all education. Rather than risk having the public question its total support for public education, some policymakers have become advocates for free prekindergarten education.

This position ignores the fact that local public schools in some states are already permitted to, and do, charge parents fees for some locally developed and funded programs, such as nursery schools; that public schools participate in the subsidized child care system, particularly in California but also in many states throughout the South; and that some midwestern school districts operate child care programs entirely on a fee-for-service basis. These public schools routinely collect fees from parents for their share of the cost of prekindergarten, their share of subsidized child care based on sliding fee scales, or the total cost of child care. This practice has not undermined public support for education to any noticeable degree in these communities. However, the extent of public school involvement in these fee-collecting forms of prekindergarten is still relatively small compared to the currently expanding role of public schools in providing other publicly funded forms of prekindergarten programs.

Competition from the public sector may result in some improvements. One of the most promising aspects of greater public school involvement in the early childhood system is that the higher wages and status enjoyed by public school teachers may extend to early childhood teachers, who are often viewed as glorified babysitters rather than as educators. As more public school prekindergarten teachers are needed, not only may some qualified teachers in the nonpublic school sector gain access to higher-paying jobs but the presence of those higher-paying positions may exert an upward force on all wages in the early childhood system as a whole. From the perspective of the early childhood system, this kind of healthy competition is tolerable because it will benefit the system in the long run, even though the flow of qualified teachers into the public schools will increase staff recruitment/retention difficulties for the nonpublic school sector in the short run.

Categorical Funding Streams

Clearly, a varying mixture of both private and public funds support early childhood programs. Generally, there are no overt restrictions on the use of private funds beyond the obvious ethical condition that they be put to the use for which they were intended. Public funds, however, carry many restrictions. Most of the existing public funding streams (except for the tax code provisions) that support early childhood programs, whether operated under public or private auspices, are categorical; that is, the funds are authorized for a specific category of service or type of recipient. Examples of categorical funding streams are Head Start, Chapter I, special education, subsidized child care, and many state-funded prekindergarten programs. Each has its own funding (as well as programmatic) requirements in terms of eligibility of recipients and service providers, accountability for the use of funds, restrictions on the type and nature of service provided, the form and complexity of recordkeeping, and the like.

The categorical nature of public funding creates difficulties for service providers who operate in more than one categorical stream. For example, meeting differing audit requirements of two or more categorical funding sources requires a more complex record-keeping system; differing eligibility requirements may require maintaining a number of different recruitment and enrollment procedures and policies. Notwithstanding the problems of categorical funding, the diverse mixture of public and private services and funding is one of the strengths of the early childhood system. Diversity of funding sources can be viewed as providing stability rather than complexity. From the program operator's viewpoint, financial stability may be more likely when all the funding eggs are not in one basket.

Policymakers, too, must fit new efforts into the existing categorical maze. From the policymaker's viewpoint, securing funding increases for an array of many small early childhood programs may be easier than for one large program, in that each increase appears relatively small in comparison to the entire state (or federal) budget and each *is* smaller than the sum of all the increases for various early childhood programs taken together (a sum usually not computed for fear of the political consequences).

One reason that so many categorical programs (with their associated funding streams) exist is precisely because it is often easier to mobilize support for funding a new effort than it is to appropriate the same amount of funds to expand an existing program. This is particularly true if the new effort is seen as "solving a pressing problem" or is associated with a powerful policymaker. Funding increases (and policy change generally) occur incrementally, not in giant leaps.

Dealing with the Categorical Confusion   As new categorical streams are created that are similar to old ones, conflicts erupt. For example, the Head Start advocates see Smart Start as a threat to their existence rather than as a new source of funds for Head Start programs. Even though a state-funded prekindergarten program allows community agencies to apply for funds, child care providers may oppose it.

Abolishing all the categorical streams and then creating one single funding scheme with an equivalent allocation of resources is too risky, politically and practically. No one—legislator, program advocate, or beneficiary—will watch his or her program die and then naively trust that it will be faithfully resurrected in any new financing scheme. Although a single funding stream is a temptingly simple solution, we can't start over. Categorical funding streams are a reality that will likely persist (as will the turf protectors for each category). Rather than starting over, the policy task is to rationalize the system by dealing at the margin—that is, any new funding streams, any increases in appropriations for existing programs. To rationalize is to maximize use of the early childhood system and support a uniform level of service quality throughout the system.

From a state policymaker's perspective, it is not simple to get a handle on the array of funding sources for early childhood programs because some have a state presence and others only a local one (for example, Head Start and Chapter I are both direct federal-local funding streams). However, the effort is likely to be fruitful in terms of coordinating programs and developing an integrated funding package. In New York the legislature has commissioned a study of the financing and rate-setting methods in use for all early childhood programs. This kind of information can enable policy-makers to make more efficient use of existing (as well as new) funds.

In the process of rationalizing the early childhood financing system, the fears of turf protectors can be satisfied by assurances that no tampering will occur with their existing base of funding. Regulations governing existing categorical funds can be reconciled so that any new streams, or increased appropriations within old ones, will mesh. Thus all new funds will be more widely available (accessible to more types of service providers), will support a uniform level of quality, and can be easily merged at the provider level so that funds from a variety of sources can be used in a continuous and coherent manner to serve children eligible for more than one funded service.

Quality Versus Quantity Given limited resources, debates about serving more children or improving the quality of services (to a smaller number of children) will continue. The political temptation is to try to serve the largest number of children for the lowest total cost. Moreover, it is easier to judge accountability for numbers than for quality. It is certainly easier to count children served or dollars spent than it is to precisely measure improve-ments in quality. However, a basic level of quality is necessary to ensure that public dollars are not being wasted. Given how critical the quality of the program is to the eventual outcomes for children and for society, and how many aspects of quality are related to per-child funding levels, quality should always take precedence over quantity in debates about funding.

The Consequences of Financial Decision Making If diversity is an accurate descriptor of both the service delivery and financing systems for early childhood programs, it also applies to the process of financial decision making. Policymakers faced with decisions about the wise use of public funds for early childhood programs—whether for continuing current efforts, creating new programs, or increasing budgets for existing programs—are necessarily operat-ing within the diversity of the public/private early childhood system that has evolved. Financial decisions have consequences, intended or not, for the whole early childhood system. For exam-ple, a new early childhood funding stream such as a state-funded prekindergarten program, even if it is intentionally limited to public schools or to Head Start operators, will affect the whole early childhood system. The policy objective that led to creation of the new program may be to expand the opportunities for quality early education for poor children. If the new funds appropriated to meet this objective are restricted to one type of service provider, they will make use only of that limited portion of the system, automatically increasing that provider's share of the early childhood market, and will bypass other parts of the system which might be equally capable of meeting the objective (and may even undermine these other service providers). These unintentional consequences may or may not coincide with the desired policy objective of expanding educational opportunities for young children. Policy objectives must not be confused with service providers. Clearly specifying the objective and then capitalizing on (and extending) the strengths of the whole system may be a more effective strategy than assuming that one part of the system is better able than others are to meet the objective.

In the best case, diversity offers choices—both for the parent who is looking for what best suits her child and for policymakers looking for options to satisfy different policy objectives. The diverse system that has been allowed to evolve is the product of the differences among communities (and states) and has proven to be adaptable to changing conditions in those communities. A single system, although easier to understand, offers one choice with no alternatives and is less adaptable.

Current Funding Levels for the Early Childhood System

The conflicting views of the proper role of schools (whether schools should charge parents fees, quality versus quantity, among others) can coexist relatively peacefully as long as the stated end goal is not a universal prekindergarten system available *only* in public schools. Universal access to prekindergarten may be a reasonable policy goal when pursued in the context of the entire early childhood system and the public's enthusiasm for funding such services. But unless the public is willing to expand its commitment to public education by shouldering the multibillion dollar cost[6] for universal prekindergarten, a more effective route toward universal prekindergarten may be a commitment to gradual expansion of public funding for programs for children under age five, offered in a variety of settings, with an assumption of shared financial responsibility among parents, the public, and the private sector (for example, employers).

The best estimate for the nation as a whole is that between $250 and $300 million state funds are spent annually on prekindergarten programs (including state-funded prekindergarten programs, state contributions to Head Start, and state-funded parent education programs) for roughly 200,000 children between the ages of three and five, with the majority being four-year-olds. By contrast, total federal funding for Head Start is over $1 billion and serves roughly 450,000 children, mainly four-year-olds, nationwide. Head Start funds must be matched at the rate of 80 percent federal to 20 percent local; funds from local matches increase the Head Start total by about $300 million. It is close to impossible to estimate SSBG/Title XX expenditures and service levels, but considering both federal and state funds together, subsidized child care is probably roughly equivalent to the size of Head Start in dollars and numbers of children served—close to $1 billion is spent on services to over 400,000 children under age five. The total tax expenditure for the federal Dependent Care Tax Credit exceeded $3.9 billion in FY 1988 for services provided under various auspices to an unknown number of children. Some estimates for the total national expenditure on child care from all public and private sources (including the Dependent Care Tax Credit and payments by parents) range from $10 to $20 billion.

Sources of Funds for Prekindergarten Programs Operated by Local Public School Districts

In the variety of prekindergarten programs they operate, local school districts are not creating financing mechanisms; they are responding to funding opportunities much like any other member of the early childhood system. They apply for funds from public sources that are also available to many other agencies (such as Head Start, subsidized child care, some state-funded prekindergarten programs) as well as from sources that are open only to them (such as federal Chapter I funds or most state-funded prekindergarten programs). Like other members of the early childhood system, public schools use combinations of funds from various sources. They operate programs on a fee-for-service basis like any private entrepreneur might do in response to demand. In terms of their prekindergarten programs, public schools behave more like their early childhood system peers than like the K–12 education system.

Funding sources for prekindergarten programs operated by public school districts can be categorized into four groups: public funds from federal, state, or local sources, and private funds supplied by parents in the form of tuition. Across all program types, the District Survey found that 90 percent of all programs reported public funds as their primary source of support. The remaining 10 percent relied on parent-paid tuition. Among those relying on public funds, 40 percent reported state funds, 20 percent local public funds, and 30 percent federal funds as their major source of support. (It should be noted that the federal contribution may be somewhat overstated because Head Start, which is federally funded, was overrepresented in our sample.) Combining funds from a variety of public sources is common; 58 percent of programs that reported public funds as their primary source of support relied on funds from two or more sources. Those programs that rely on parent-paid tuition tend not to use other sources in combination; 72 percent of them reported only one source of funds—tuition.

Two program types rely almost exclusively on federal funds: Chapter I prekindergarten programs and Head Start programs. Nearly all the programs placing themselves in these categories reported federal funds as their major source of support. State-funded prekindergarten and state-subsidized child care programs are the two program types that rely mainly, as their names indicate, on state dollars. Special education programs receive funds from both state and federal sources, as do programs for teen/student parents.

Locally funded prekindergartens are an interesting program type; about half reported local public funds as their major source of support, and about one-third reported parent tuition as their major source. About half the parent education programs in the District Survey reported state funds as the major source, but about one-third are supported with local public funds. Those programs supported primarily with local public funds are similar to those public school-operated child care programs supported by parent fees. The decision to use local public funds (and to charge parents fees) to offer a nonmandatory service, such as parent education or nursery school or child care, is another example of the public school district acting contrary to what one might expect of the K–12 education system. In this case, the school district is a pro-active funder responding to community needs rather than a respondent to mandates or to offers of state or federal funds.

Cost Per Child and Contributing Factors

The major contributing factor to the overall cost of a prekindergarten program is staffing: staff salaries, staff–child ratios, and group sizes. Equipment, supplies, and facility expenses certainly contribute to the overall true cost of an early childhood program, but they are not the major contributors to cost. Class size is a cost factor often discussed in relation to cost per child in programs for older children because the typical classroom has only one teacher. Because young children require more staff (at least one for every eight to ten children) than third graders do, the ratio in prekindergarten classrooms is more important than group size in terms of contribution to cost.[7] Obviously, the cost per child is also affected by the length of the school day and the school year. Oddly, the cost per child also appears to be related to the source of funds (because of wide variation in teachers' salaries among program types), with programs supported by parent tuition reporting the lowest cost per child.

Ratios and Group Sizes   The annual cost per child reported by programs in the District Survey ranged widely among programs within types and across program types. Special education programs are more expensive than programs of all other types, primarily because the staff–child ratio is quite low (1:7) and special education teachers are paid higher salaries, on average, than other district (K–12) teachers. Group sizes are slightly larger in child care programs, but somewhat lower staff–child ratios were reported. Overall, group sizes and staff–child ratios do not differ significantly among program types. However, length of day and year differ both among and within types.

Length of Day and Year   Prekindergarten programs can be divided into part-day, full-school-day, and full-working-day categories. Not surprisingly, part-day programs cost least per child, averaging about $1,900.[8] Full-school-day programs cost, on average, $2,400 per child. Full-working-day programs averaged $3,250 per child. The relationship between hours per day and cost is not linear; a school-day program is about twice as long as a part-day one, but the cost is not twice as great because some expenses, such as administration or facilities, are not related to the length of day. The length of the year also contributes to cost. School-year programs (of all program types and lengths of day) cost about $1,950; calendar-year programs cost about $3,600 per child. Length of day and year are not necessarily independent variables: Most public school-operated prekindergarten programs are both school-year and part-day, while those that are calendar year programs tend also to be full-working-day.

The Apparent Effect of Funding Source on Cost Per Child After allowing for the effects on cost of length of day and year, significant differences appear among programs' reported costs per child that are directly related to their funding source. In part-day, school-year programs (of any type), cost per child ranges from $3,000 in programs supported by local public funds to $1,700 in programs supported by parent-paid tuition. In full-working-day, calendar-year programs (again, of any type), the highest average cost per child, between $4,000 and $5,000, is in programs supported by state or local public funds. The lowest, $2,100, is in parent-tuition supported programs. Differences in teachers' salaries explain these large differences in cost per child.

As described in Chapter 2, certain program features vary among program types—for example, length of day, teacher qualifications, and eligibility criteria. Some of these variations are directly related to the program's source of funds. Teacher salaries are the feature that varies most dramatically among program types *and* is the major factor in explaining differences in cost per child.

Mean teacher salaries (starting ten-month salary for a teacher with a B.A. and no prior experience) reported in the District Survey ranged from $12,480 in parent-tuition child care programs to $16,594 in special education programs. The teacher salaries in parent-tuition child care and in Head Start programs were significantly lower than salaries in all other program types. At first glance, it appeared that differences in teacher qualifications (teachers in these program types are not always required to be certified) explained this salary difference. However, further analysis revealed that teachers in Head Start or child care programs are paid significantly less *regardless of certification status*. Teachers with the same level of certification will be paid less if they are employed in a public school-operated Head Start or child care program than in any other type of public school-operated prekindergarten program.

There is a clear indication that teacher salary differentials are related to the program's funding source. Teacher salaries are dramatically lower (and the difference is statistically significant) in those programs supported by parent-paid tuition than in programs supported by any source of public funds. The mean teacher salaries for all program types supported by federal, state, or local public funds are close—approximately $16,000—a sharp contrast to the mean salary of less than $13,000 in parent-tuition child care. Public school districts commonly put teachers employed in their child care programs on a different (lower) salary scale than their K–12 teachers, even when the same certification is required. Such disparity implies that prekindergarten teaching deserves less reward than K–12 teaching. Maintaining disparate pay scales is an attempt, perhaps, to justify keeping salaries, and thus program costs, low. This finding is particularly disturbing considering that one of the more hopeful aspects of the emergence of public schools in the early childhood system is the promise of higher salaries for appropriately prepared early childhood professionals and of higher status generally afforded public school teachers.

How States Fund Their Prekindergarten Programs

Decisions about administrative auspices and financing mechanisms are not independent of one another. Finance mechanisms for state-funded prekindergarten programs usually follow directly from the choices of administrative auspice, whether the prekindergarten program is limited to public schools and whether the program is targeted (designed to serve a particular group of children at risk). For example, the earliest state-funded prekindergarten programs (as in New Jersey and Pennsylvania), which were not designed as interventions to affect the later school success for disadvantaged children, were essentially extensions of the principle of local control over education—districts may choose to enroll children who are younger than kindergarten entry age at their discretion—with modest financial support from the state; state funds do not cover the full cost of the prekindergarten program. The programs are limited to public schools only and the financing mechanisms used are familiar public school methods. Funding is based on enrollment (or attendance), modified by the state's equalization formula, and is often related to the formula used for kindergarten reimbursement.

Many of the more recent state-funded prekindergarten programs were clearly part of an education reform agenda and, quite naturally therefore, were placed under state education department auspices. However, many of these programs are targeted to disadvantaged (at-risk) children and therefore tend to have programmatic regulations (as opposed to the earlier permissive programs). These states' prekindergarten programs are more likely to use a grant or contract method of financing to ensure that local operators follow the programmatic regulations. Some use competitive processes for distributing funds; others do not.

Some of the later targeted prekindergarten efforts of states, such as Washington, do not rely solely on the public education system. A variety of providers throughout the early childhood system, including public schools, are eligible for funding. Competitive grant/contract funding mechanisms are used in these prekindergarten programs both to ensure programmatic compliance of all grantees/contractors and to appropriately include nonpublic school operators. The eight states and the District of Columbia which channel state funds to Head Start programs to improve the quality of the programs and/or expand the number of children served distribute funds using an allocation formula based on the number of children served. In addition, several states have more than one state-funded prekindergarten program and use different funding mechanisms in each program. In addition to methods of funding, other elements which vary within and among states include allowable expenses (salaries, equipment, facilities, transportation), requirements for cash or in-kind matches, and permission to levy fees to parents for the program.

Funds to Public Schools Only: Nontargeted Programs

Eight of the thirty state-funded prekindergarten programs are not targeted to specific children and are available only to public school districts.

Kindergarten-Type Formula Reimbursement   Five states (New Jersey, Pennsylvania, Wisconsin, Maine, and the District of Columbia) fund prekindergarten programs operated by local public school districts through a kindergarten-type reimbursement formula. These programs are provided under the school code and are permissive (the program may be offered at the discretion of the local district). The programs are not targeted to any category of children; once the district has decided to provide the program, children eligible by age and residence are entitled to attend and are usually admitted on a first-come, first-served basis. However, the district often has to make a substantial financial commitment to the program before becoming eligible for state funding. In Pennsylvania, for example, state funds (which totaled $1.7 million in FY 1987) are unavailable for prekindergarten programs until after the first year of operation.

Under Maine's permissive legislation school districts are reimbursed after the first two years of operation. Once the programs become eligible for funding, children served are included in the district's total student count for state aid; the kindergarten formula is used to determine reimbursement. Only 167 children were served through this program in FY 1988. Funds secured through this process cover a portion of teaching and ancillary program cost, with poorer districts usually receiving a larger proportion of cost reimbursement under the state's equalization formula.

The District of Columbia is unusual in that it makes prekindergarten programs an integral part of the school system. Since 1982, the prekindergarten program has been completely absorbed in the general education budget as a line item totaling $2.2 million for FY 1988. Each of the District's schools provides at least one classroom for four-year-olds. Each school's share of prekindergarten funds is based on enrollment and the availability of space. If enrollments in one school are too small to fill a class, children are sent to another school which offers the program.

Competitive Grants Another method of funding local district programs is a competitive grants process among districts. Delaware, Ohio, and Oklahoma use this process to fund nontargeted prekindergarten programs. On the basis of a proposal submission process, Delaware awarded $189,000 in grants to three pilot programs (one per county). Grant funds may cover the costs of teacher and aide salaries plus transportation; the district is responsible for all other costs. Ohio initially funded nine model demonstration programs in FY 1986, three of which were for prekindergarten education. The following year, limited funds ($6,000 per project) were made available to other local districts to replicate the prekindergarten models created the previous year. Eight districts applied and were funded to replicate prekindergarten demonstrations. The following year (FY 1988) only three districts applied for and received funds. Grant monies for these demonstration and replication projects may be used for staff salaries, materials, inservice training, and general program expenses. Ohio does permit the district to charge fees to parents. Oklahoma appropriated just over $832,000 for competitive grants in its prekindergarten program and set a maximum amount of $27,000 per district for a full-school-day program. Districts are expected to contribute between 25 and 30 percent of total program costs through in-kind contributions, which include space and utilities.

Funds to Public Schools Only: Targeted Programs

Among the seven states which limit programs to public schools and target their programs to at-risk children, three methods are used: a noncompetitive allocation process (Maryland, Louisiana, and

Texas); formula funding (one of Michigan's programs); and a competitive grant process (New York, Kentucky, and Maine).

Noncompetitive Allocations In Maryland, eligibility to provide the program for four-year-olds is restricted to schools whose third grade reading comprehension scores are at least six months below the national norm. Schools with the lowest scores are given additional consideration. School systems must reapply annually for program grants and demonstrate that they continue to meet the requirements. The amount received depends on the salaries and fringe benefits for a teacher and aide for each classroom plus substitute fees, if necessary. State funds may not be used for materials, supplies, or equipment. In-kind contributions from the district are expected. In FY 1988, $3.3 million was appropriated for the program.

Louisiana uses a system based on the total student enrollment in the prior year to determine the number of projects to be awarded to each school system. Beginning with the 1985–1986 school year, the Department of Education was required to award funding for qualified Early Childhood Development Projects to each city or parish school system. The funds cover one program in districts with student enrollments under 20,000 and up to a maximum of four programs in districts with enrollments of 60,000 or more. No local cash or in-kind match is required. Funds may be used for supplies and equipment, as well as for salaries and fringe benefits. The FY 1988 appropriation was $1.8 million.

The Texas state-funded prekindergarten program is unique. While it is close to being mandatory and is certainly targeted, it nonetheless shares many characteristics with other states' nontargeted, permissive prekindergarten programs. Most targeted prekindergarten programs specify many aspects of the service that local districts must provide and tend to use a grant or contract system of financing. The Texas prekindergarten program offers less programmatic definition and direction to local districts than some other states' targeted programs. Funding is based on an allocation formula rather than on a grant or contract.

Under Texas House Bill 72 (the education reform bill that created the prekindergarten program), any school district *may* provide prekindergarten classes, but districts that identify 15 or more resident four-year-olds who are poor or have limited English proficiency *must* provide the prekindergarten program. While districts are required to provide a local cash match of one-third of the program costs, each district's allocation for the program is based on a funding formula which provides higher levels of support to poorer districts. Program funds may be used for salaries, supplies, parenting resources, and staff development. Transportation is not required, but if provided, it is funded under the general school transportation system. The state appropriated $46 million for the prekindergarten program in FY 1988.

Formula Funding Michigan uses a formula allocation process in one of its prekindergarten programs. This program is limited to school districts eligible under the state aid formula to establish or continue prekindergarten programs in conjunction with federal funds available under Chapter I or Head Start for programs for at-risk four-year-olds. Districts are ranked according to a calculation based on a percentage of the number of children eligible for the free and reduced lunch program times their average kindergarten enrollment. Districts with at least 13 percent (or 50) of four-year-olds meeting these criteria are eligible to receive an allocation. Approximately 15 of the states 500 districts are estimated to be eligible. Allocations per child are limited to $2,000.

Competitive Grants New York targets its program for at-risk children and uses a competitive grant process to distribute funds, as do one each of Michigan's, Kentucky's, and Maine's programs. The New York State Prekindergarten Program awards grants through a competitive proposal process, in which local districts make application to the state Department of Education. Community need for the program (the number of eligible families in the district) must be documented as part of the proposal. State funds support up to 89 percent of program costs; a minimum 11 percent local match is required. The state appropriation for FY 1988 was $27 million. Program funds cover staff salaries, staff development costs, materials, and social, health, and nutritional services. Transportation is a district option.

The second of Michigan's two prekindergarten programs provides funds for high-risk four-year-olds through competitive grants. Local school districts or intermediate (regional) school districts and Head Start or other preschool programs *operated* by public schools are eligible to apply for funds.[9] Applications for funds are reviewed by the Departments of Education and Social Services. Priority for funding is given to schools which comply with the Board of Education Standards of Quality, involve parents in the program, and employ teachers and support staff with suitable training in early childhood development. Applicants are required to collaborate with local early childhood development programs and to supplement grant funds with other federal, state, or local funds. While total grant levels are not specifically limited, state funds may not exceed $2,000 per child served. A total of $300,000 was appropriated for this program in FY 1988.

Funds to Public Schools with Subcontracting Permitted: Targeted Programs

South Carolina, Illinois, Massachusetts, Florida, and Kentucky target their prekindergarten programs for at-risk children and permit local public school districts to subcontract for services with other community agencies, such as Head Start, child care centers, or other local early childhood programs. However, permission to subcontract does not necessarily mean that local districts use this option for providing services. Both the competitive grants process and noncompetitive allocation formulas are used by states in this group. It is possible that the method of reimbursement (allocation versus competitive grants) may also act to inhibit or to encourage the subcontracting process. Districts funded under an allocation or formula reimbursement mechanism are possibly less likely to engage in either the effort or the documentation necessary to include nonpublic school agencies in the program via subcontracts. The use of competitive grants may make subcontracting more likely if the community agency is seen as offering an edge in securing the grant or if school/community collaboration is specifically rewarded in the grant-making process.

Noncompetitive Allocation Formulas   South Carolina's prekindergarten programs are formula-funded, with reimbursements based on costs per kindergarten child for a half-day program. Applications for prekindergarten program funds are accepted from school districts only, but subcontracting is allowed if all provisions of the program regulations are met. None of the currently funded programs are run by nonschool entities. Funding for the entire Education Improvement Act (EIA), of which the prekindergarten program is one part, was provided by a one-cent increase in the state sales tax; $10.9 million was appropriated for the prekindergarten program in FY 1988. All school districts are eligible to apply for funding for the program for four-year-olds. Each district's proportionate share is based on the number of students judged "not ready for first grade" as determined by the most recent first grade readiness test scores and the total amount of funding available for the program in the state's budget. No local match is required, although some districts do provide additional funds.

The program is free to participating families, and costs covered may include the full range of teaching and administrative costs, equipment and supplies, and supportive health, social, nutritional, and parent services. Transportation is not a required provision but may be offered on a space-available basis.

Competitive Grants   Massachusetts and Florida both make use

of the competitive grants process for their prekindergarten programs. In Massachusetts a total of $10.3 million was appropriated
for competitive discretionary grants, which are available to local
school districts in three service categories: prekindergarten programs for three- and four-year-olds, enhanced kindergarten and
transitional first grade, and programs seeking to develop creative
approaches to combining early childhood education and child care.
Seventy-five percent of the funds must go to low-income school
districts, as determined by the number of children aged 5 to 17
years old living in families receiving AFDC. First priority is given
to school districts where more than 10 percent of enrollment is
low-income. Second priority is given to individual schools which
qualify under Chapter I guidelines. The remaining 25 percent of
funds may go to schools or districts which do not meet the low-
income criteria but which offer innovative models. No screening
procedures for individual program participants are required, but
local programs may give priority to lower-income children at their
discretion. Half-day, full-school-day, and full-working-day programs may be funded.

Local school districts may subcontract with both public and
private agencies to provide services. Under Massachusetts law, no
local matching funds are required, but the Department of Education must give priority to proposals which describe linkages with
other human service agencies and which seek to combine a number of funding sources (including Title XX/SSBG-funded child care
and Head Start). Programs must be designed to supplement, not
supplant, services provided under other state and federal auspices.
To make optimal use of all resources, school districts are explicitly
encouraged to coordinate funds from special education, bilingual
education, and occupational education.

Florida provides two prekindergarten programs for at-risk four-
year-olds. The Early Childhood Migrant Program ($2.9 million for
FY 1988) is administered and monitored by the Department of
Public Instruction's Bureau of Compensatory Education Programs.
Funds are allocated on a formula basis to local school districts,
which may subcontract the program to private nonprofit agencies.
No local matching funds are required. All programs must meet
both federal regulations for Chapter I/migrant preschool education
and local school district regulations. In FY 1987 the program was
administered by 17 school districts and one private nonprofit
agency.

In establishing Florida's second prekindergarten program,
Chapter 228 the Prekindergarten Early Intervention Program, the
intent of the legislature was to encourage and assist school districts

in implementing developmental programs for three- and four-year-olds, which provide preventive interventions for children at risk of educational failure and enhance the educational readiness of all children. The competitive grants program is administered by the Department of Public Instruction and $1.6 million was appropriated for its first year (the 1986–1987 school year).

Florida's school districts may submit proposals for implementing new services, enhancing existing prekindergarten or child care programs, or subcontracting for the provision of these services. After the initial year, school districts which received funding are not required to resubmit full proposals but need only submit amendments to their original proposals (if there are any changes). As originally conceived, the program was designed so that at least 50 percent of the children served were economically or educationally disadvantaged. Children not meeting these criteria could be served on a sliding fee scale thus promoting socioeconomic integration. During the FY 1988 appropriation process, the legislature changed the original intent of the legislation by limiting new funding to programs that exclusively serve economically and educationally disadvantaged three- and four-year-olds.

Program costs allowed under the prekindergarten grants include teaching staff, home visits, parent education, administrative and supervisory costs, materials, health and developmental screening, social service referral, and program monitoring and evaluation. Program funds may not be used for the construction of new facilities. Transportation is a covered service and provided free of charge.

A wide range of community agencies received funding through subcontracts from school districts in both fiscal years, including several child care programs and Head Start programs. For FY 1989 the Florida legislature appropriated $22 million for the prekindergarten program and changed the competitive grant system to an allocation formula designed to fund programs in each of the state's 67 school districts.

Funding Permitting Subcontracting and Direct Contracting with Community Agencies: Targeted Programs

Seven states which target their programs for at-risk preschoolers currently allow Head Start and other community agencies to apply directly to the state administering agency for funds through a competitive grant process. Subcontracting to community agencies can proceed under other funding mechanisms (allocation formulas or noncompetitive grants), but direct contracting to community agencies other than public schools requires a competitive grant process. The programs in California, West Virginia, Vermont, and Oregon are administered by state departments of education, while programs in Washington, Alaska, and two of three programs in New Jersey are under the administrative auspices of other state agencies.

Administered by State Departments of Education   In California the state-funded preschool program, which provides a half-day program for three- to five-year-olds, was authorized in 1966 as part of the school code. The intent of the program is to serve low-income children in order to facilitate later school success. The program is administered by the state Department of Education, as are other child care and child development programs in the state. In FY 1988, $35.5 million was appropriated for the prekindergarten program.[10] State reimbursement is made on a per-child enrollment basis. School districts and school boards may also contract with other organizations (both private and nonprofit and for-profit agencies may be used) to provide services. Nonprofit organizations may also contract directly with the Department of Education. Programs are not required to provide a local match and the majority are 100 percent state funded, although a few programs use local funding as well. In FY 1987 approximately half of the 186 contracts for the prekindergarten program were with organizations other than public school districts.

In May 1987 Vermont enacted legislation for prekindergarten programs, beginning in September 1987, to serve disadvantaged three- and four-year-olds, with priority to those children with special needs. Twenty percent of the first year's funds ($100,000) is restricted to support programs using mainstreaming models for handicapped three- and four-year-olds; this restriction is designed to bring the state into compliance with PL 99-457. The remaining 80 percent of the funds is available to serve children who are economically disadvantaged (families with incomes up to 125 percent of the state median income), have limited English language skills, or have suffered from, or are at risk of, abuse and neglect. Grants are awarded competitively, with priority given to communities with the greatest needs. The goal of the program is to extend existing successful programs to serve additional children with unmet needs.

Allowable expenses include salaries; administrative costs; social, health, and nutritional services, and parent education. Transportation is an allowable expense and must be part of the program design. No local cash or in-kind match is required. School districts, family centers, Head Start, private preschools, and child care centers are eligible to apply directly for funds; grantees may also subcontract for services. Applicants for funds must show evidence of need and demonstrate that they will engage in a collaborative effort with other programs or agencies in the community. Eleven programs were funded in the first round of applications; several programs were for the full working day. Half of those funded were school district operated programs; one was a Head Start program. The legislature increased the appropriation to $500,000 for the second year of the program and to $1 million the third year.

Oregon legislation enacted in 1987 for the 1988–1989 school year calls for comprehensive, developmental half-day programs which include social, health, and nutritional services. The legislature appropriated $1.1 million for the first year of the program, which is administered by the Department of Education. Grants are awarded competitively to school districts, which may subcontract, and to Head Start grantees and other nonsectarian organizations, which may either apply directly to the state education department or may participate via subcontracts from school districts. In approving grant applications, the Department of Education is required to distribute funds regionally, insofar as is practical, based on percentages of unmet need. Funds must be used to establish or expand programs but must not be used to supplant existing programs supported by federal Head Start funds. There is no local match requirement, but local support is encouraged. To prevent duplication of service and maximize local resources, the legislation mandates coordination with existing Head Start programs and other organizations serving young children.

Administered by State Agencies Other Than Education   The Washington legislation authorized $2.9 million for FY 1987 to establish the Early Childhood Education and Assistance Program (ECEAP) to serve 1,000 four-year-olds from families at or below the federal poverty level. ECEAP is administered and regulated by the Department of Community Development's (DCD) Division of Community Services, which also administers the state's contribution to Head Start.

Eligibility for the program is based on age and family income only. Four-year-olds whose families meet the federal Head Start poverty level guidelines are eligible. Grants are competitively distributed through a Request for Proposal process. School districts, Head Start, nonsectarian child care and preschools, and newly established community-based projects may apply for funds. School districts may also subcontract to provide services. Applicants are expected to demonstrate the level of unmet need in their communities as well as linkages with schools and the private service sector. Priority is given to counties with a high percentage of families below 100 percent of the federal poverty level whose children are not being served in existing intervention programs. The ECEAP Advisory Committee determined that 60 percent of available funds are to be set aside for counties where 20 percent or fewer eligible children are served by Head Start. The remaining 40 percent of funds is available to counties serving more than 20 percent of eligible children. A recent policy change by the Advisory Committee sets aside 10 percent of the slots (or at least 200 slots) for migrant or Indian children. No local funding match is required, but in-kind contributions are strongly encouraged.

ECEAP grants cover costs for space (including renovation), teaching staff, administration, health, social and nutrition services, transportation, parent education, home visits, and program monitoring and evaluation. There is no charge to parents for program services. During the first program year, total program costs (for administration and operation) supported with ECEAP funds were not permitted to exceed $2,700 per child enrolled. This ceiling was removed in the FY 1988–1989 reauthorization. Administration costs are limited to no more than 15 percent of the total contract. Additional funding is available to ECEAP programs for the education and training of staff. Programs may receive up to $50 per year for each child enrolled to support staff development activities.

Programs may provide half-day, full-school-day, or full-working-day services. First- and second-year grantees are providing only half-day programs of three hours or less per day. Only one full-working-day program received ECEAP funding; the child care portion of the program is funded by the state Department of Social and Health Services.

New Jersey's prekindergarten grants program was funded at $1 million for FY 1988.[11] The comprehensive child development program, for at-risk three- to five-year-olds, is similar to Head Start. Ninety percent of the children served must meet Head Start income guidelines; 10 percent may be handicapped. The same eligibility priorities used for Title XX/SSBG child care apply to the new state initiative: protective service cases; handicapped children; children of teen mothers; children of single parents participating in education or training programs, particularly those participating in the new state employment and training program (REACH); children from low-income single-parent or two-parent families where the parent(s) works and no one is available to care for the children. The program is administered by the Department of Human Services, Division of Youth and Family Services. Application for program funding is via a Request for Proposal to county Human Service Advisory Councils. Priority is given to Head Start programs to expand their programs to full-year, full-working-day programs, but public schools, private nonprofits, and Title XX/SSBG-funded child care centers may also apply.

The total amount of funding available per county is based on the Department of Human Services' fair funding formula (based on poverty, among other indicators). County allocations under the grant program will range from about $6,000 to $200,000. The per-child reimbursement rate is based on the highest state-subsidized child care rate plus a separate additional rate for supplementary services and transportation. One-time expenses for startup are permitted. Programs are required to provide a 10–25 percent cash match depending on each county's DHS-determined matching requirement (only government agencies may provide in-kind matches).

Conclusion

The various models and funding mechanisms used by the states for their prekindergarten programs serve different needs and reflect different priorities for service provision. The most efficient financing mechanisms make maximum use of the entire early childhood system in a state (or community), offer reasonable funding levels and specify clear programmatic requirements that help to ensure quality, and encourage shared responsibility for funding by requiring local matches (tailored to community ability).

Local school districts, as operators of prekindergarten programs, are much like any other member of the early childhood system. They do not create financing mechanisms; they respond to them. Public school districts participate in the opportunities offered by public funding sources available to them and, in certain cases, can become entrepreneurial competitors in the private sector when responding to community demands for child care. Few local school districts create prekindergarten programs using their local public (tax-based) resources. Public school districts represent one part of the early childhood system that state (and federal) policymakers are acting within when they create and finance prekindergarten programs.

On the whole, the current use, in a few states, of state-aid formulas and per-pupil reimbursement, while providing school districts with a familiar funding mechanism, does little to encourage districts to provide prekindergarten programs. These formula funds usually cover only a fraction of the cost of high-quality programs. As a result, discrepancies between rich and poor districts (even with state equalization formulas) are likely to result in perpetuation of service differences among districts. Wealthier districts are more able than poorer districts to fund these programs. In those states with permissive, nontargeted prekindergarten programs (New Jersey, Pennsylvania, and Wisconsin) where prekindergarten standards for staffing ratios, staff qualifications, and/or program content are either not specified or are the same as for kindergarten, the program offered may not be developmentally appropriate for three- and four-year-olds. It is also very unlikely that ancillary support services, such as health and social services or parent participation and education, will be a part of these programs. Formula-funded programs which are targeted, such as Michigan's, do specify staffing, curricular, and service standards and are therefore more likely to be offering appropriate programs with comprehensive services.

The District of Columbia offers a vision of what a nontargeted, reimbursement-type program with explicit standards might look like. Unless program standards are clearly spelled out, programs funded by grants (whether provided either directly by local schools, under contracts with the schools, or by direct contract with local agencies) vary tremendously in the extent to which these programs are, or are not, comprehensive and do, or do not, coordinate with other community programs.

Clearly, it is possible to restrict programs to operation by public schools and still focus on coordination and comprehensiveness (as does New York); however, it is less likely that such programs will provide the extended hours necessary to serve the needs of working parents. The combination of grants or contracts and the ability to both contract directly and through the public schools would appear at present to provide the best solution to ensuring both competition and diversity among programs, as well as coordination between programs serving similar populations. Massachusetts, Florida, Illinois, California, Vermont, and Washington serve as examples of what can be achieved in terms of expanding the delivery sources of prekindergarten services to include community agencies while maintaining state control over the content of the program. However, while this may be an effective means of testing experimental programs or different models of service provision, it may also give unfair advantage to sophisticated community organizations and school districts with the capacity for writing successful proposals. What is needed, if these models are to expand to statewide implementation, is an allocation process which provides districts and community organizations in high-poverty areas with special inducements to participate, while holding all programs to explicit standards for developing programs appropriate for children and effecting coordination in communities.

Recommendations

- Financing mechanisms for state-funded prekindergarten programs should be designed to encourage all parts of the early childhood community, including public schools, to participate as providers.
- Both subcontracting and direct contracting mechanisms should be used so that wide participation is encouraged. Some local community agencies may be more successful in securing subcontracts from a local public school district, while others will be more successful in a direct relationship with a state agency.
- The conflicting requirements of various categorical funding sources must be reconciled so that eligible children can be served in a coherent and continuous manner. That is, funds from more than one source should be easily combined at the local level.
- Local matches should be required as evidence of local commitment to providing a program.
- Local matches should be reasonable and variable, allow for the variable financial ability of different providers in the early childhood community, and be weighted in favor of poor communities in a state.
- Allowable costs should include start-up expenses, capital expenses, training, and transportation.
- Funding should be tied to clearly specified programmatic regulations (staffing, curriculum, comprehensive services) that promote quality.
- Funding levels should be sufficient to meet the specified programmatic standards and to support reasonable staff salaries and benefits.
- Any funds appropriated to improve quality, expand supply, or raise salaries in early childhood programs should be available to the entire early childhood system.

Endnotes

1. King James version of the Bible, 1 Timothy 6:10.
2. Public funds do not, even indirectly, support private educational programs

once children reach compulsory school age. The federal tax code provision (Dependent Care Tax Credit) that supports child care expenses for children from birth to age 14 clearly prohibits claiming credits for those expenses attributable to education for children of compulsory school age.

3. Stern, J.D., and M.O. Chandler (Eds.) (1988). *The condition of education: Elementary and secondary education* (vol. 1, CS 88-623). Washington, D.C.: U.S. Government Printing Office, U.S. Department of Education, National Center for Education Statistics.

4. Roughly 200,000 children out of 18 million children under age five attend public schools. The precise number of children under age five in public schools is not known. However, data from the District Survey (197,000), the National Center for Education Statistics (185,000), and the State Survey (200,000) converge on a rough estimate.

   Stern, J.D., and M.O. Chandler (Eds.) (September 1988). *1988 education indicators* (CS88-624). Washington, D.C.: U.S. Government Printing Office. U.S. Department of Education, National Center for Education Statistics.

   Mitchell, A.W. (1988). *The Public School Early Childhood Study: The District Survey*. New York: Bank Street College.

   Marx, F., and M. Seligson (1988). *The Public School Early Childhood Study: The State Survey*. New York: Bank Street College.

5. Council of Chief State School Officers (1987). *Elements of a model state statute to provide educational entitlements for at-risk students* (p. 6). Washington, D.C.: Author.

6. If all three- and four-year-olds were to be guaranteed a free school-day, school-year program, the total annual cost would be likely to exceed $15 billion [7 million three- and four-year-olds × $2,500/child = $17.5 billion].

7. In terms of contribution to program *quality*, group size has been shown to be a stronger factor than staff/child ratio. Ruopp, R., W.L. Bache, C. O'Neil, and J. Singer (1979). *Children at the center: Final results of the National Day Care Study*. Cambridge, Mass.: Abt Associates.

8. Special education programs, because of their much higher cost per child, were excluded from these calculations.

9. In FY 1988 eligibility was broadened to include nonprofit community agencies.

10. If all the prekindergarten programs administered by the Department of Education (for example, Children's Centers and other full-working-day programs) were included, California's total expenditures on early childhood programs would far exceed those of any other state.

11. The third, and newest, of New Jersey's prekindergarten programs was created in 1988, with an FY 1989 appropriation of $10 million. Head Start agencies and public school districts are eligible to apply. Program standards and child eligibility guidelines for this program are the same as for Head Start. It is designed to be a comprehensive child development program providing full-working-day services to up to 50 percent of enrolled children if needed. This new program is jointly administered and funded by the Departments of Education *and* Human Services.

Chapter 5

REGULATING PROGRAMS FOR YOUNG CHILDREN

The basic purposes of regulation are to protect the health and safety of children and to establish minimum standards of good practice in programs for young children. Some regulations seek to ensure higher than minimum standards of practice and even to distinguish among levels of program quality. This chapter discusses the major regulatory systems that apply to the variety of early childhood programs operated by public schools.

Regulation of programs for children is primarily a state and local function. Because of basic disagreement over whether, and to what extent, the federal government should regulate children's programs, there are no federal regulations for children's programs generally, despite federally funded studies in the late 1970s (the National Day Care Study, for example) designed expressly to determine which regulatable aspects of children's programs most affected the quality of those programs. The Federal Interagency Day Care Requirements (FIDCR) were promulgated in 1968, written and re-written based on the outcome of these studies, never fully implemented or enforced, and finally rescinded in 1981. Nonetheless, some federal regulations do exist to govern specific programs that are federally funded, such as Head Start or Chapter I. In the antiregulatory climate of this decade, some of these federal regulations have been relaxed (for example, Chapter I) and others effectively eliminated through consolidation (federal requirements for day care funded under Title XX were eliminated when Title XX became part of the Social Service Block Grant in 1981).

Opposition to regulation centers mainly on the effects of regulation on cost. It is generally presumed that to comply with regula-

112

tory changes (such as the FIDCR) requiring smaller group sizes, more staff per child, and better trained staff would increase program operating costs. Increased costs would increase the price of child care for parents, raise the price of the state and federal share of costs in publicly supported programs, and reduce profits in the case of for-profit operators.

Regulatory reform, at whatever government level, considers the trade-off between quality and cost. The lack of federal regulations and federal guidance for state and local regulation leaves regulatory tasks entirely to the states and localities. The recent antiregulatory clouds seem to have been centered over Washington, in that, during the same period, states have enacted volumes of school reform or school improvement legislation; furthermore (according to Morgan), when states have changed their day care regulations it has generally been in the direction of higher quality.[1]

The Many Forms of Regulation

Regulatory systems that apply to services for young children come in many different forms. Every state has a set of regulations, generally referred to as the *day care code*, that governs day care services and the issuance of licenses or permits to operate day care services (either to all or to some specified subset of service types). Every state has a body of law and regulations, referred to as the *school code*, that governs public school facilities and operations. These kinds of regulatory systems are mandatory; school codes apply to all public schools and day care codes to all regulated forms of day care. These codes establish the minimum standards of practice acceptable in each state and vary significantly from state to state.

Another form of regulation is *program standards:* the set of regulations that define acceptable practices for a certain program, such as the federal Head Start Performance Standards, or a particular state's prekindergarten program regulations. Program standards seek to specify a higher level of acceptable practice than day care codes or school codes. In some states a different (usually stricter) set of regulations is applied to day care services that receive public funds; these are called purchase-of-service (POS) or funding standards. Program standards are mandatory only to those agencies providing the particular program or service.

A third form of regulation—or more accurately, standard-setting—is *accreditation* systems. These are completely voluntary and aim to distinguish higher-quality early childhood services from lower-quality ones. Some states, through their state departments of education, offer registration systems that permit any early childhood program which certifies that it meets the standards defined by the DOE to be registered as an educational program.

Some states have established procedures for accreditation of public school districts. There are also regional school accreditation systems. These broader accreditation systems may include a few standards specific to kindergarten and prekindergarten programs. The only nationally available accreditation system for center-based programs for young children is the NAEYC's National Academy of Early Childhood Programs.

There are obvious and subtle differences among these regulatory systems. Some are voluntary (accreditation); others are mandatory (day care and school codes). Some are specifically addressed to young children (day care funding standards, prekindergarten program standards, and NAEYC accreditation); others address a broad age range of children (school codes and school accreditation systems). Some are monitored and enforced by both state and local public employees (day care codes); some combine self-monitoring with outside enforcement (Head Start and some states' day care POS standards); others involve self-certification with little or no monitoring (voluntary registration). The content and specificity of each regulatory system, how compliance is monitored, the frequency of monitoring, whether technical assistance toward compliance is offered, and the degree and type of enforcement mechanisms used—all differ as well. As programs for prekindergarten children (and the funding streams that support them and the variety of community institutions that provide them) proliferate, so do the regulatory systems that govern them. The proliferation of often conflicting regulations creates confusion.

Day Care Codes

Every state has a day care code or day care regulatory system. The system includes building codes, fire safety regulations, health code requirements, and zoning requirements. Overall responsibility for enforcing day care regulations and for granting permission to operate usually resides with the state human service or health agency. Regulations, usually defined in state day care codes, include requirements related to general health and safety of children and staff, food service, fire safety, staff–child ratios, the qualifications of staff, and programmatic issues, such as the balance of indoor and outdoor activities, a stated educational philosophy, or the offering of age-appropriate activities. The content of these regulated areas varies widely among the states.

Probably the greatest variation among state day care codes is in staff qualifications. Acceptable qualifications for persons in charge of a group of children range from no requirements whatsoever to a college degree. Idaho and Mississippi specify no minimum age and require no prior education, training, or experience and no ongoing training for persons in charge of a group of children. In contrast, regulations in New York City require possession of an early child-hood teaching certificate including a bachelor's degree and supervised teaching with preschool-aged children for persons in charge of a group of children.

The regulations that comprise the day care code may be enforced at either the state or local (county or city) level or both, and may involve inspectors from different state and local public agencies for different aspects of compliance. Typically, for example, a day care center must be visited by a fire inspector, a building inspector, a sanitarian, and a child care licensor. Inspection for fire, building, and health code compliance is usually a local (city or county) function, while the licensor is more commonly a state employee. Typically, monitoring for compliance to regulations is ensured through annual visits, with immediate inspection in response to serious complaints of code violations.

In a given state most organized programs for young children, such as child care centers and nursery schools, are subject to these state and/or local regulations and are issued a license or permit to operate in a specific location. Each program site must be licensed; if the program moves to a new location, a new license or permit must be acquired. If the program expands in the same site, the existing license must be amended or a new license acquired to include the expansion. While staff qualifications are one aspect of compliance that must be demonstrated to acquire a permit to operate, individual staff members are not licensed in the sense that certified teachers are individually licensed by state education departments. Some states exempt from licensure certain types of services (such as those in operation for only a few hours per day or week or enrolling a very small number of children) or exempt certain categories of service providers (such as churches or Montessori schools). It is standard practice to exempt from licensing those programs for young children that are part of a public, private, or parochial elementary school. The rationale is that these programs are the responsibility of another state agency—the department of education.

School Codes

Every state has a school code consisting of the entire body of laws and regulations that have been built up over the decades (in some states, centuries) of the existence of public education, in combination with locally determined facility regulations such as fire codes, building codes, and zoning regulations. State school codes generally cover the preparation and licensing of teachers, the instructional program, instructional materials and equipment, and ancillary services (library, guidance). School codes change little by little over time, generally in response to major trends and forces such as the education reform movement (which prompted the school improvement/reform legislation of which many of the new state-funded prekindergartens were a feature). Because school codes govern public education from elementary through postsecondary levels, they are not particularly age-specific. There is some differentiation among requirements for elementary and middle and high schools, but not the age-specificity (among infants, toddlers, young preschoolers, older preschoolers) typical of day care regulations.

School facilities (buildings) are not regulated at the state level but through local building, fire, and zoning regulations. Codes vary widely in content, with the general rule being very few age-specific regulations. One community may require shorter drinking fountains in a school building housing kindergarten children, while another may make no differentiation. In some states uniform building codes include requirements for school buildings, and in others the state education agency offers facility planning guides to local districts.[2]

School codes are not monitored or enforced in the same sense that day care regulations are. A fairly high degree of state control is presumed in child care—the state is exercising its power to permit or deny certain activities (by granting licenses to operate) and to protect citizens from below-minimum services. By contrast, the principle of local control—rather than the exercise of state power—is a strong force in public education. Local control is manifested in the governance of public education by citizen committees in every state (local school boards and state school boards). The influence of the principle of local control can also be seen in the relationship between state departments of education and local school districts. State departments tend to exercise influence, exert leadership, and offer guidance rather than to enforce or compel local districts. The strength of local control in education varies from state to state. In general, the degree of state control is directly related to the proportion of state funding of education;

more state funds mean more state control. State control can be exercised through personnel, materials, and curriculum. Statewide textbook adoption is a means of exercising curriculum control. Closely specifying the certification requirements for teachers is a means of exercising control via personnel. There are also less direct ways to exert influence over local programs such as through state education department publications of guidelines or planning documents.

Public school district-operated prekindergarten programs of all types, because they are part of public schools, are technically subject to the state school code. Typically, there are no special provisions in the code for prekindergarten (or even for kindergarten) programs. Differentiation by age of children in school codes is in terms of differences among elementary and middle and high schools. The school code may specify that class size be smaller in elementary schools than in high school. However, the teacher–pupil ratio may be more favorable in high school because more special subject teachers are required. Items like bathroom location or size of toilets are not covered in these state regulations but in local building codes which do not differentiate between school buildings with and without kindergartners.

Purchase-of-Service or Funding Standards

Every state has a day care code, and nearly every state has publicly subsidized day care services. About half the states require that child care provider institutions receiving public funds meet a set of standards different than that for child care providers in general. Because public funds are generally not expended on unregulated child care, the remaining states require only that recipients of public day care funds be licensed under their basic state day care code in order to receive funds. Thus child care operators who might otherwise be exempt from regulation (public schools or churches) are allowed to participate.

Although the need for greater accountability is assumed for the expenditure of any public funds, the existence of day care purchase-of-service or funding standards is mainly due to federal direction. When Title XX was enacted in 1975, enforcement of federal funding standards for the purchase of day care with Title XX funds (the Federal Interagency Day Care Requirements, or FIDCR) that had been drafted originally to regulate child care purchased under Titles IV-A and -B appeared imminent. States, particularly those with less stringent day care standards, developed their own funding standards (in response to Title IV or to Title XX) in order to meet the apparent requirements of FIDCR which specified relatively high-quality day care in such areas as group size, ratios, and staff training.

Day care funding standards are both an accountability tool and a quality lever. Establishing higher quality standards than those in the basic day care code can raise the level of day care quality, at least for the funded portion of the state's day care services, and may by example influence the quality of other day care services. In fact, many states with day care funding standards (Alabama, Florida, Georgia, Louisiana, Mississippi, North Carolina, South Carolina, Texas, Virginia, and West Virginia) are in the South, a region with generally lower day care standards than other regions of the country.

Typically, state purchase-of-service standards are stricter than the state's day care code and cover areas not included in the code. Fire safety may be more strict (alarms connected directly to fire stations rather than those sounding only on the premises or more exits may be required); smaller class sizes may be specified (class sizes for preschoolers are not limited in the general day care codes in 32 states[3]) under purchase-of-service standards. Fiscal practices and accountability of child care providers are never included in day care codes but are common in purchase-of-service standards. These day care funding standards remain in force, even though Title XX (replaced by the Social Service Block Grant) no longer exists, because the standards continue to serve their dual purpose: meeting fiscal accountability demands and raising day care quality by example.

Another manifestation of funding standards is the regulations governing those state-funded prekindergarten programs that are not permissive. The content and specificity of these regulations vary. Local school districts may be implementing a closely defined program that requires the provision of specific services to certain children, or one that may be broadly defined as any program provided for a child of a given age, with very few other specifications. Certain program standards may be included in the state legislation creating a program, such as eligibility requirements or extent of services to be offered. Others, covering such areas as curriculum components and the qualifications of staff, may be defined by the state agency charged with oversight of the program or may be left to the local district. Some areas are jointly determined. For example, state legislation may require that a certain category of at-risk children be served, but the choice of a specific screening instrument to select children is left to the local district.

Regulation in States with Prekindergarten Programs

Turf, history, and purpose are forces that influence the type of regulatory system a state employs for its state-funded prekindergarten. For example, permissive programs are very clearly on education turf and in every instance are governed only by school codes. Prekindergarten programs born of education reform are very likely to be the responsibility of state education departments but may be governed by some additional regulations beyond the school code because school improvement legislation carried with it many new and amended regulations.

The regulation of state-funded prekindergarten programs draws on four regulatory systems: the general school code, specially designed new program standards within DOE, the state's day care licensing regulations, or Head Start program standards. These four systems are the basis for the states' regulatory systems. While a few states do offer a pure example of using only one of these basic systems, other states have created systems drawn from more than one.

The general school code is the only regulatory mechanism governing state-funded prekindergarten in four of the states with permissive prekindergarten programs (Maine, New Jersey, Pennsylvania, and Wisconsin). Only five states require that standards for their state-funded prekindergarten programs meet or exceed their state day care licensing standards (California, Massachusetts, Michigan, Ohio, and Vermont). Vermont is the only state which requires the prekindergarten program to meet only day care standards; it has not as yet developed additional Department of Education standards.

In several states, there is some similarity in staff–child ratios between DOE standards and state purchase-of-service standards for Title XX/SSBG (which can differ from day care licensing). Two states, Oregon and the new grants program in New Jersey, require programs to meet the federal Head Start standards. In Oregon state DOE standards apply as well. The remaining majority of states have created some form of program standards for their state-funded prekindergartens. Table 5–1 summarizes the regulatory systems applied to state-funded prekindergartens for those states with prekindergarten programs.

Combining the Day Care Code and Program Standards

California presents an example of a dual regulatory system using both the basic day care code and additional program standards for

Table 5-1 Regulation of State-Funded Prekindergarten Programs

State	State Department of Education Regulations	Day Care Licensing Standards	Head Start Standards
Alaska	✓ [1]		
California	✓	✓	
Delaware	✓		
District of Columbia	✓ [4]		
Florida (migrant and grants)	✓		
Illinois	✓		
Kentucky (both grants programs)	✓		
Louisiana	✓		
Maine (grants and permissive)	✓ [4]		
Maryland	✓		
Massachusetts	✓	✓ [2]	
Michigan	✓	✓ [2]	
New Jersey (permissive)	✓ [4]		
New Jersey (grants)			✓ [5]
New York	✓ [3]		
Ohio	✓	✓ [2]	
Oklahoma	✓		
Oregon	✓		✓
Pennsylvania	✓ [3, 4]		
South Carolina	✓		
Texas	✓		
Vermont		✓	

table continues

Table 5-1 *Continued*

States	State Department of Education Regulations	Day Care Licensing Standards	Head Start Standards
Washington	✓ (5)		
West Virginia	✓ (3)		
Wisconsin	✓ (4)		

1 Department of Education in cooperation with the Department of Health and Social Services certifies public and private pre-elementary schools that receive direct state or federal funding and that are primarily educational in nature.

2 Although programs are technically exempt from licensing, they must meet or exceed day care licensing standards.

3 There is also a voluntary registration or certification process for nonpublic school nursery and kindergarten programs.

4 The general school code applies to the permissive program; there are no additional prekindergarten program standards.

5 New Jersey's grant program is regulated through the Department of Human Services; the Washington program is regulated through the Department of Community Development.

state-funded child care and prekindergarten. All child care, pre-kindergarten, and early education programs, including public school-operated programs, are licensed by the Department of Social Services. State funds for these programs are administered by the Department of Education's Office of Child Development. Any programs which receive state funds must meet the additional staffing and curriculum requirements of the Department of Education's *Funding Terms and Conditions*. Fiscal and program compliance is monitored by DOE every three years; the department provides programs with technical assistance in both areas. Programs are expected to conduct an annual self-review using the *Program Quality Review Instrument*, which also provides the DOE's Office of Child Development with a method of monitoring and rating program quality. This self-monitoring instrument covers administration, developmental program, staffing, support services, and family and community involvement. Each component contains subsections scored on a five-level scale, with level 3 being the minimum, or compliance, level and 5 the highest level.

DSS day care licensing and DOE program regulations differ in staff–child ratios, which, under licensing, are not age specific but may not exceed 1:12 with one teacher or 1:15 with one teacher and one aide. Programs funded and regulated by DOE are required to maintain staff–child ratios of 1:8 for children ages three to six. Teaching staff requirements also differ considerably. Day care licensing requires only 12 postsecondary units in early childhood education or child development and six months work experience in a licensed child care setting. DOE requires a Children's Center Permit which, at a minimum, requires an associate degree or a passing score on the California Basic Skills Test, 24 semester hours of course work in early childhood education or child development, and field course work with two full years of instructional experience or its equivalent.

Like California, Michigan requires its state-funded prekindergarten programs to be licensed by the Department of Social Services as child care centers, as well as to comply with State Board of Education program guidelines. Health, safety, and facility/space requirements are similar under both sets of regulations, while some teacher certification and curriculum requirements differ. Staff–child ratios and class sizes are more favorable under the DOE's Standards of Quality (1:8 for four-year-olds with a maximum class size of 18) than under day care licensing (1:12 with no specified class size). The minimum staff qualification accepted under both sets of standards is a Child Development Associate (CDA) credential;[4] however, the day care licensing requirements also mandate at least 12 semester hours in child development or a related field. The DOE requires only the CDA credential, although it encourages an endorsement for prekindergarten and kindergarten certification, which requires the completion of 18 hours in early childhood education at an approved college or university.

Thoughtful combination of day care standards and state-defined prekindergarten program standards places the prekindergarten programs within the early childhood community—governed by similar (if not identical) standards. If the prekindergarten regulations cover teacher qualifications, some overlap among teacher certification and child care licensing standards is likely to occur, broadening the range of qualifications considered acceptable for prekindergarten teachers. This is a positive development; it both opens the way for community agencies (which generally are not staffed by certified teachers) to operate state-funded prekindergarten programs and encourages noncertified (but otherwise well-qualified) staff to work in public school prekindergartens.

Using the Day Care Code

Vermont, with one of the newest state-funded prekindergartens, requires that all these programs (both those operated by public schools and those operated by community agencies) be licensed by the Agency for Human Services, either as a preschool or as a day care center, depending on the length of the program day. At present, very few public school-based prekindergartens in Vermont have been licensed, and it is unclear whether public school programs will require teachers to have early childhood certification in addition to meeting the education and training requirements under day care licensing, although it is a likely possibility.

Using the day care code to regulate new prekindergarten programs is certainly efficient. Rather than creating one more set of regulations, an existing system is expanded to cover the new programs. Assuming that monitoring and enforcement are already functioning well in the system and that the number of new programs to be monitored will not create a burden on the licensing agency's staff, it is a very effective regulatory choice. If the new prekindergarten program permits either subcontracting (or direct contracting) with local agencies other than public schools, this regulatory choice will facilitate the participation of those agencies (which probably are already licensed) in the prekindergarten program.

However, turf barriers among state agencies may undermine the choice. The state DOE may resist what it perceives as intrusion by another state agency onto its turf. Further, if the state's day care code requires smaller group sizes and/or higher numbers of staff per child than DOE permits, the cost of meeting these staffing requirements might create opposition to use of day care regulations. If the state's day care regulations are poor ones, this choice would be inappropriate for ensuring a reasonable level of quality in the new program.

Overlapping Standards

Prekindergarten legislation in the state of Florida provides an interesting example of overlapping regulations, blending from day care licensing and state Department of Public Instruction (DPI) requirements. Day care is licensed by the Department of Health and Rehabilitative Services (DHRS) with additional POS standards for day care programs receiving public funds. Public school programs are technically exempt from day care licensing requirements, although state-funded prekindergarten programs that are not provided in the public schools (districts may subcontract to private agencies) must meet all state and local day care licensing requirements for child care facilities. Staff education and ongoing training requirements overlap among the various state-funded programs (prekindergarten, migrant, and day care) as well as between teaching and administrative staff. The DPI requires all staff in the state-funded prekindergarten program (as distinct from the state-funded migrant prekindergarten program) to complete the 20-hour introductory child care training course or its equivalent that is required for child care workers by the state day care licensing agency (DHRS); the migrant prekindergarten program does not require its teachers, who must be state-certified, to have this preservice training. The project director in a Chapter 228 state-funded prekindergarten program must have a college degree in early childhood or its equivalent, which is the degree DPI requires for teacher certification in early childhood education, while prekindergarten teachers (referred to as supervisory personnel) must have a CDA or the equivalent, which is also one of three options for being qualified as a teacher under day care licensing. Recognizing teaching qualifications as part of administrative qualifications is commendable because it offers a professional career ladder of sorts within each system. These two ladders, one under DPI and the other under DHRS, intersect only on the one element of teacher qualifications common to both Chapter 228 prekindergartens and child care.

Just as the DPI's personnel requirements for Chapter 228 prekindergartens and migrant prekindergarten programs are more stringent than the general school code, the DHRS Purchase of Service Standards for Title XX/SSBG-funded programs are more stringent than those of day care licensing. The training requirements during the first year of employment (40 hours) are more than twice what day care licensing requires. Staff–child ratios under the purchase-of-service standards are 1:10 for two- to five-year-olds; licensing requires 1:15 for three-year-olds, 1:20 for four-year-olds, and 1:25 for five-year-olds. Florida's day care POS standards require the same ratios as the state prekindergarten and migrant programs. The state migrant education program maintains a staff–child ratio of approximately 1:10, the same as that recommended for the state prekindergarten program, and class size is limited to between 17 and 20 children with one teacher and one aide. Class size is not regulated under day care licensing.

Florida's funding standards for DPI programs (prekindergarten and migrant) and for DHRS (day care) programs are similar to one another on ratios, are both higher than day care licensing in terms of ongoing training requirements, and offer two disconnected career ladders. The fact that standards for the newer Chapter 228 prekindergarten program incorporated day care licensing requirements (such as the 20-hour training requirement) reflects the influence of the child care community and the legislated inter-agency coordination between DPI and DHRS that has been man-datory since 1974. Florida has taken the first steps toward recon-ciling regulatory differences.

The state of Illinois offers a different perspective on reconciling regulatory differences. The state includes staff qualification re-quirements from the day care code in the standards for the prekindergarten program. Like many states, Illinois exempts pro-grams operated by public schools and private elementary schools from licensure by its Department of Children and Family Services (DCFS). However, the Illinois Board of Education standards for its state-funded prekindergarten program permit teachers to meet qualification requirements *either* by holding an early childhood teaching certificate issued under the school code *or* by meeting the standards set under day care licensing for a day care center supervisor. These two sets of requirements differ significantly. Early childhood certification requires a bachelor's degree with at least 22 hours in professional education and early childhood edu-cation courses, plus a preschool practicum. The minimum require-ment for a day care director under state day care licensing is a CDA credential, 12 semester hours of course work in child care or child development, and two years of teaching experience in a nursery school, kindergarten, or licensed day care center.

Even though the skills and abilities possessed by (day care) directors and (public school) teachers are presumably not equiva-lent (administration and teaching require different skills), and the minimum requirements are different for certified early childhood teachers and day care directors, this connection between the day care and public school prekindergarten regulatory systems in Illinois opens the way for an integrated professional career ladder.

The promise is real, but putting it into practice presents some real issues for resolution. In addition to two state agencies (BOE and DCFS), two different levels of regulatory compliance are involved: individuals versus program sites. Individuals are certified by the Illinois BOE as credentialed teachers. Day care directors (supervisors) are not individually credentialed, although their qual-ifications are evaluated by the DCFS in the process of licensing the day care program they direct. Clearly, this is an opportunity for interagency collaboration.

Combining Funding Standards from Day Care and Head Start

Under New Jersey's permissive prekindergarten legislation, which has been part of the school code since 1903, its program for four-year-olds is exempt from all day care regulations and is subject only to the regulations that apply to all public school programs. (Certain options for head teacher qualifications under day care licensing requirements are equivalent to teacher certification under DOE.) The new early education effort funded in FY 1988 for a comprehensive child development program (similar to Head Start) for at-risk three- to five-year-olds is administered by the Department of Human Services (DHS), Division of Youth and Family Services (DYFS), rather than by DOE. In contrast to the DOE permissive program, new programs will have to meet Head Start standards and state purchase-of-service standards for state-subsidized child care, both of which are more stringent than day care licensing standards.

The intertwined effects of purpose and turf are evident. In the state with the oldest permissive (not targeted, in public schools only) prekindergarten program, a new program drawn from the comprehensive education/social service model of Head Start was not on DOE turf. A program for at-risk preschoolers based on this model fits better with the mission (and turf) of DHS. Because DYFS already administers the state's day care purchase-of-service program and its POS standards, having the new prekindergarten program meet these standards is consistent with its administrative home (DYFS of DHS).

Using the Day Care Code to Create Prekindergarten Program Standards

Massachusetts, like most states, normally exempts from licensing those programs for young children that are part of a public school system or of a private organized educational system, unless the system is limited to kindergarten, nursery, or related preschool services. Nonetheless, prior to the 1987–1988 school year, public school-operated prekindergarten programs funded under the state education reform legislation (Chapter 188) were required at a minimum to meet Office for Children (OFC) day care licensing standards for center-based care. Beginning with the 1987–1988 school year, public school-operated prekindergarten programs under Chapter 188 must continue to meet day care licensing standards plus the new DOE program standards. Nonpublic school programs funded under subcontract will continue to meet OFC standards.

The newly developed Early Education Program standards are closely aligned with those included in the National Academy of Early Childhood Programs accreditation standards.[5] As in the

California DOE standards, a goal is stated and the standards necessary to meet that goal are spelled out.[6] Standards cover 11 program features: curriculum; physical environment; interactions among staff and children; interactions among children and peers; family involvement; staff qualifications; staff development; staffing; health and safety; administration; and evaluation. The standards also call for initial and continued developmental screening and classroom observation to measure individual children's progress and for sharing this information with parents on a regular basis. At least annually, grantees are required to evaluate the program's degree of compliance with the Early Education Program standards, as well as the program's effectiveness in meeting its own stated goals. Members of a local advisory council (mandated by law), as well as others in the community, are to be involved in the evaluation process, using locally designed or selected evaluation instruments and methods.

To increase the likelihood that children in need of special education services can be served in mainstream programs, the revised requirements for staff and staffing patterns link the Nursery through Grade 3 Certificate requirements with those for the Young Children with Special Needs Certificate (ages three to seven). Until the revised requirements go into effect, public school teachers of three- and four-year-old children must, at a minimum, hold a bachelor's degree in early childhood education (or a related field) or a K–3, K–8, or Teacher of Young Children with Special Needs certificate. All teachers must have a minimum of three months half-time experience with three- through five-year-olds in a group program, two months of which must be at the preschool level; four postsecondary courses in early childhood education; and 24 hours inservice training per year. Preschool group size may not exceed 15, and each classroom must have, at a minimum, a teacher and an aide who meet the new staff qualifications. (In contrast, under day care licensing, head teachers must have at a minimum a high school diploma or its equivalent, four postsecondary courses in early childhood education, and 36 months of half-time experience with preschool children in a day care center.) All teaching staff are required to have 24 hours inservice training per year. Staff–child ratios are 1:10 for three- and four-year-olds for full-day; 1:12 for part-day. Group size is twice the staff–child ratio.

Day care licensing regulations were drawn on heavily in the formulation of standards for the Chapter 188 prekindergarten programs; those standards are now, in turn, affecting day care licensing. Within the last year, an extensive review of staff qualifications for group day care was undertaken, and the regulations were revised to bring them into closer compliance with DOE's new (N–3) teacher certification standards. Both sets of new standards are in the process of implementation.

Regulatory Issues and Problems in Regard to Young Children

Because school codes were developed with older children in mind, in many respects they are neither appropriate nor adequate for younger children. Take the case of fire safety standards, including building materials and design and placement of exits. The local building code may adequately safeguard older children, but it may not be stringent enough for younger children, who are not able to move as quickly or negotiate stairways and may require more adult assistance.

Building codes that govern programs operated by public school districts may not include certain items necessary for younger children. For example, easy access to toilets is essential for young children. Most child care licensing codes specify either that toilets be child height or that steps be provided. The location of bathrooms is also important. Young children, obviously, have less control of their toileting than older children and need to be nearer a toilet, preferably in their classroom. Frequent handwashing is critical in stopping the spread of diseases and is more important for younger children, who are more likely to be in need of handwashing and less able to go down the hall or to another floor to do it. In one-quarter of the classrooms observed in the case study sites, bathrooms were located outside children's classrooms (down the hall on the same floor). Attention to details such as these is fairly typical of building regulations for day care facilities but is unlikely to be addressed in the local building codes applicable to public schools.

Another area in which specific school code standards must be developed for younger children is class size. Although more attention is being paid to lowering class size at the elementary level, these improvements define what is acceptable for older school-aged children (age six and older) but do not represent acceptable practice for younger children (ages five and under). It is well known that group size as well as staff–child ratio—both aspects of early childhood programs which can be regulated—are strongly related to the quality of a program for young children. Smaller groups and more staff per child are best. The relationship between these aspects (especially group size) and program quality is very strong for young children and has been well documented.[7] Class size for four-year-olds should not exceed 20 children, and 2 adults should be available at all times. This level of adult attention stands in clear contrast to the typical kindergarten classroom of 25 children and 1 teacher.

Problems with Exemptions from Regulation

Most nonpublic school early childhood programs are subject to state or local government regulations governing child care services and must be licensed. As discussed earlier, public school-operated programs are nearly always exempt from this process. It is unclear what standards the majority of public school-operated programs (except state-funded prekindergartens with clear regulations) are subject to and how they are monitored for compliance. In those rare instances where programs operated by public schools are required by law to meet child care regulatory standards, they may not be monitored for compliance by the same agency which monitors nonpublic programs.

In our survey of school districts, we found that the vast majority of programs operated by the public schools are indeed exempt from child care licensing—except for subsidized child care programs, which generally must be licensed and/or meet funding standards to qualify for public child care funding. The District Survey found that, in general, while most full-working-day programs are licensed (85 percent of parent fee child care and 92 percent of subsidized child care), all types of part-day programs are not. A few part-day programs reported that they were exempt from child care licensing but were subject to regulation by the state education department, which they believed imposed stricter standards. Strictness is a relative concept. While the DOE standards clearly impose higher minimum educational requirements for teachers than day care licensing standards do, the range of program aspects regulated in school codes is narrow and the enforcement of school codes is certainly not stricter. A small number of programs (4 percent) reported that they chose to acquire a license even though they were not required to (21 percent of teen/parent child care and 16 percent of parent education programs). Many child care programs for teen parents do receive some public funds and therefore probably are licensed for that reason. The case study interviews offer some explanation for this action on the part of districts operating child care programs funded by parent fees. A school district is more likely to obtain licensing for an exempt program if it regards the program as being part of the larger (nonpublic) community of other early childhood programs. It is unlikely to consider obtaining a license if it regards its program as being firmly on public education turf and therefore inherently different from (and in some cases, superior to) the rest of the community, and/or if there are cost implications of licensing such as higher staffing costs. Becoming licensed establishes the district's child care program as a peer on equal footing with other early childhood programs.

The Consequences of Exemption

Allowing public school programs to elect whether to seek a license can have significant economic implications for families and safety implications for children. One public school-operated child care program that we visited had previously been licensed in order to be eligible for state-subsidized child care funding. Licensing enabled lower-income families to use the program, which is supported mainly by parent-paid tuitions. However, the licensing regulations required the school to install an expensive fire alarm system. After weighing the cost of the fire alarm against the loss of the publicly subsidized families, this school district decided that rather than comply, their program would give up its license. There were two consequences of this action. The first was that lower-income families were forced to locate other child care arrangements—the district's commitment to serving them was outweighed by the cost of the fire alarm. The second consequence concerns safety: If the safety of the children demanded the fire alarm system while the program was licensed, surely their safety required it when the program was not licensed. The safety of the remaining children may have been compromised by the district's action. If this program had been operated by a community agency *in the same location*, the choice would not have been available: The program would have been closed if the fire alarm had not been installed. It is unacceptable that the protection of children can vary according to which agency operates the program.

Generally, when public funds are expended on programs for children, standards are set to ensure that the funds are being used appropriately and equitably, that is, that a specified level of service is being provided to all those eligible. These funding standards may or may not conform to child care licensing requirements. In the state where the district discussed above is located, the POS or funding standards *are* the state's basic day care licensing standards. The issue is not whether public schools must be licensed through the same system as nonpublic programs, but whether the public school programs are being held to a standard that is the same as that for all other programs.

The rationale for exemption of public school programs from day care licensing—that because a state agency (education) is already responsible for them, the licensing agency doesn't need to be— doesn't hold up well in practice. Generally, two erroneous assumptions support this argument. First, it is assumed that exemption of educational programs from child care regulations means exemption only from licensing, not exemption from meeting some set of standards—presumably either the standards of the state education agency (which are generally assumed to be stricter than day care codes) or the standards of the day care code itself. It is further assumed that public school programs meeting these "stricter DOE standards" will at least meet, if not exceed, day care codes and that these local schools will be monitored by local districts or the state DOE. But unless specifically directed to do so, the DOE will not conform its standards to the day care code or monitor local school districts for compliance with the state day care code.

As they stand now, school codes don't include specific requirements for younger children. Further, even if the codes were age-specific, the relationship between a state education agency and a local education agency is not conducive to strict enforcement. Modifying school codes to conform to child care licensing standards and strictly enforcing the school codes is one way to ensure that minimum standards are being met without imposing a second regulatory system on public schools.

Problems with the Proliferation of Regulatory Systems

Viewing the regulation of all early childhood programs—both nonpublic and public school-operated—from a state policymaking perspective is at best confusing and at worst chaotic. There are program standards for state-funded prekindergartens, school codes for others, apparently no specific regulations for locally funded public school prekindergartens, day care licensing for most (but not all) child care programs, voluntary registration for nursery schools, day care funding standards for publicly subsidized child care, exemption from day care licensing for public school-operated child care, federal performance standards for Head Start, Chapter I/migrant program guidelines, and more. One large school district operating Head Start, Chapter I prekindergarten, state-funded prekindergarten, and subsidized child care programs could keep a large staff busy just meeting all the different regulatory system requirements.

The simple (-minded) answer to such regulatory chaos is to "just say no" to more regulatory systems. Consolidate the chaos—just pick one set of standards and use it for everyone. After all, children are children are children; they have the same needs for a quality program no matter who runs the program (or funds it or houses it). It sounds sensible for every program operator to meet the same standards—consistent levels of quality, uniform accountability. Obviously, it's not that simple.

If it were possible for a state to adopt a single regulatory system for all early childhood programs, the process of doing so would be full of difficult issues. Which of the many contenders should be selected? A federal system (Head Start, for example) because it would be the most difficult to change (not being under direct state control)? The state day care code because it has been in place longer and can be enforced? The prekindergarten standards because they specify higher quality? What about interagency turf battles—will the licensing agency give up its staff to DOE for monitoring? Will the DOE permit licensing agency staff into the public schools? Should the choice be the system with the highest quality standards or the one that establishes a minimum floor of quality? What are the fiscal consequences of either choice? Raising standards will improve quality and may raise costs; but lowering standards will surely compromise the quality that has been achieved and may jeopardize funding (from federal or other sources with program standards).

Rather than simple-minded solutions to regulatory chaos, states' experiences with regulating prekindergarten programs offer policymakers some guiding principles and directions for future action. First, it is true that all children deserve a minimum guarantee of a reasonably good program, no matter what the funding source, auspice, or location. Exemptions from regulation should be carefully considered (and current exemptions reexamined) to ensure that there is an acceptable alternative regulatory system in place before the exemption is granted. Second, the aim of state regulatory policy across early childhood programs should be to reduce confusion for the local program operator. Examine the regulatory situation from the perspective of the school district operating four separately regulated programs—or from the perspective of the local children's services agency that is a Head Start grantee, participates in the state child care purchase-of-service system, and has a direct contract to operate the state-funded prekindergarten. Significant input from a variety of local program operators—both public and nonpublic—can inform the drafting or revision of regulations.

Third, move slowly toward conformity among the regulatory systems that apply to children's programs, taking whatever opportunities for reform are available. There are several natural points for examining the whole array of regulatory systems. One is whenever any one of the regulatory systems is being reviewed and/ or revised. Day care regulations are reviewed more often than other systems and so may offer the first opportunity. New federal child care legislation/appropriations—for example, the newly passed welfare reform legislation (Family Support Act of 1988)— may offer an opportunity to examine state day care regulations. The creation phase of a new prekindergarten program presents another opportunity to create conforming regulations or even to use an existing system such as the federal Head Start standards or the state's day care funding standards, if it is appropriate to the new program's goals.

The focus of the review/revision process can be expanded to review simultaneously other existing regulatory systems that apply to young children and to make recommendations for revisions of these systems. The review should focus on reconciliation of differences among systems and move toward conformity, not only in the standards themselves but in their enforcement procedures as well. State uniform building codes should be included in the review. The purview of a state regulatory review committee may be the state's portion of early childhood program regulation; the locally determined portions of the system should also be reviewed. The differences in local building codes regarding day care and school requirements should be reviewed with the needs of young children in mind.

While some state regulatory systems illustrate the lack of uniformity and congruence in standards across the early education and day care domains that lead to redundancy and confusion, the study did note an increased effort in some states to work toward uniformity in regulatory language across domains in order to create a more orderly process. Many states are making greater efforts to increase congruity in staffing requirements across regulated domains. Unfortunately, turf issues—including the question of professional standards for staff qualifications—often impede the process. On one hand, stringent staff education requirements may serve to exclude programs such as Head Start from applying for state-funded prekindergarten funds. On the other hand, accepting the CDA (as a few states do in their prekindergarten program regulations) may threaten staff retention in Head Start and child care programs by encouraging teachers to move to better-paying public school positions.

One of the purposes of regulation is to set the floor of quality below which no program should fall. It is possible for regulatory systems to promote levels of quality above the floor, as purchase-of-service standards do. In most states there is a wide range of quality in practice among all (public and nonpublic) programs for young children. The range is not hypothetical—that is, between what exists and what is ideal—but rather it is real and part of the range is below the floor. The minimum acceptable level of quality that most programs practice is very far from what has been achieved by a few programs (given sufficient vision, inclination, and resources). Voluntary accreditation systems, such as the state of Missouri's or the National Academy of Early Childhood Programs, offer policymakers a significant lever to move practice toward higher quality when the voluntary system is combined with a solid mandatory regulatory system that establishes and enforces the minimum acceptable level of quality.

Taking a broad perspective on regulatory policy, working carefully to reconcile differences, and moving toward conformity among systems will lead to a more coherent (and less confusing) regulatory system in the future. The choices that states have made in regulating their prekindergarten programs illustrate promising approaches toward reconciliation.

Recommendations

- Ideally, all programs for young children should be covered by one regulatory system that promotes quality—both in the provision of service to children and in monitoring and enforcing the regulations.
- At minimum, in regard to basic health, safety, and building code regulations (bathroom location, fire safety, square footage, food services), conflicting requirements among regulatory systems should be reconciled.
- Requirements for day care licensing and for programs regulated through the department of education (and other state agencies) should be reviewed for inconsistencies and differences and reconciled toward conformity between and among systems wherever possible. Such a reconciliation process should promote higher quality—not a least-common-denominator lowering of standards.
- Existing interagency day care regulatory committees or task

forces at the state level should undertake the joint development of standards for all early childhood programs.
- Ideally, a single monitoring system should be developed that
  is jointly operated between the departments of education and
  human services (or, if more than these state agencies are
  involved in programs for young children, among all involved
  agencies).
- If a joint system cannot be developed, then the existing
  regulatory systems, including monitoring, should be moved to
  a neutral state office, such as the office of the inspector
  general.
- Teacher qualifications should be reconciled among the regulatory systems so that a smooth continuum among all regulated
  programs results, beginning with paraprofessional and pro-
  gressing up the career ladder through teacher, master teacher,
  and program supervisor.
- A reasonable range of qualifications should be assigned to each
  step on the career ladder, including both credentials (such as
  Child Development Associate; associate, bachelor, and mas-
  ters degrees) and experience working with young children.
- Inservice training programs for staff at all levels on the career
  ladder should be conducted jointly under the auspices of all
  state (and federal) agencies funding local programs.
- The voluntary registration systems in place in some states offer
  one model for achieving higher uniform standards of practice
  in early childhood programs operated under a variety of
  auspices. These voluntary efforts must be built on the firm
  foundation of a mandatory regulatory system.
- Similarly, voluntary accreditation via the National Academy of
  Early Childhood Programs (NAECP) offers another model for
  program improvement. The Maryland DOE provides modest
  financial support and technical assistance to public school
  programs seeking accreditation through the NAECP. Efforts
  such as this should be supported financially and extended
  beyond public schools.
- To move toward greater equity among the states, the federal
  government should establish guidelines defining the scope
  and content of state regulatory standards governing services
  for young children.

Endnotes

1. Morgan, Gwen (1987). *The national state of child care regulation 1986.*
   Watertown, Mass.: Work/Family Directions.

2. Telephone interview with Catherine Sonnier of the National Conference of State Legislatures, October 26, 1988.
3. Morgan, pages 3–7.
4. The Child Development Associate is a nationally available competency-based credentialing system for persons working in center-based programs with children aged three to five or with infants and toddlers, or in home-based programs as home visitors or in family day care programs. To be awarded the CDA credential, candidates must demonstrate their competence across 13 functional areas of work with young children and their families. The observations of parents, the candidate's supervisor, and a representative of the larger early childhood community are necessary components of the process as well. The CDA is a recognized credential in the day care licensing regulations of 34 states.
5. National Academy of Early Childhood Programs (1985). *Guide to accreditation*. Washington, D.C.: National Association for the Education of Young Children.
6. Unlike California, the Massachusetts standards apply only to state-funded prekindergarten programs administered by the DOE—not to all programs for young children that receive any state funds.
7. Ruopp, R., W.L. Basche, C. O'Neil, and J. Singer (1979). *Children at the center: Final results of the National Day Care Study*. Cambridge, Mass.: Abt Associates.

Phillips, D.A. (Ed.) (1987). *Quality in child care: What does research tell us?* Washington, D.C.: National Association for the Education of Young Children.

Bruner, J. (1980). *Under five in Britain*. Ypsilanti, Mich.: High/Scope.

Clarke-Stewart, A. and C. Gruber (1984). Daycare forms and features. In R.C. Ainslie (Ed.). *Quality variations in daycare*. New York: Praeger.

Chapter 6

ELIGIBILITY CRITERIA AND THE ISSUE OF UNIVERSALITY

No educational program for young children, with the exception of compulsory schooling, is universally available. The issue of universally available programs for four-year-olds has been raised in the continuing public debate over prekindergarten; universality is now a stated goal in some state (and local) preschool efforts, but it is not a reality in any locale. The fact remains that the vast majority of public school prekindergarten programs—indeed *all* publicly funded programs for children under five whether in public schools or not—are restricted to a specific category of children.

First Grade and Beyond—A Universal Service

It is a basic tenet of the American social contract that all children are entitled to a free and appropriate education in the public school system. Every state has a state education agency; every community is served by a local education agency—the public school district. Typically, the only limitation on entry to the public education system is the age of the child, with residence determining which school district (and often which school building) the child will attend. Every child is entitled to an education and, after a certain age, must attend school (either in the public system or in one of the private ones, either parochial or independent). The compulsory attendance *age* for beginning school, at whatever *grade level* is appropriate, varies among the states from age six (in 26 states), to age seven (in 21 states), to age eight (in 3 states). Whether attendance is compulsory, the fact is that from first grade on public education is universal. That is, every child is entitled to attend first grade in a public school and every public school offers first grade classes in sufficient quantity to satisfy all comers. Over 3.5 million children are enrolled in first grade, roughly 88 percent of them in public schools.[1]

Kindergarten—Nearly Universal

In a sense, public kindergarten has become virtually universal (offered in all communities in sufficient quantity to satisfy all children of eligible age). With the recent enactment of legislation permitting kindergarten in Mississippi, all states now permit districts to offer kindergarten. Nearly three-quarters mandate that local school districts provide kindergarten. Although state statutes on compulsory attendance ages do not reflect the fact, kindergarten attendance is compulsory in six states (Delaware, Florida, Kentucky, Louisiana, South Carolina, and West Virginia). Although not all public school districts are required to provide kindergarten, the vast majority do offer programs and most children attend kindergarten. According to the National Center for Education Statistics, about 3.5 million children are enrolled in kindergarten, with 85 percent attending public schools.[2]

While kindergarten has achieved a de facto universality, class composition is changing. Eligible age is a mutable concept. Although it is common to think of five-year-olds as synonymous with kindergartners, there is a trend toward raising kindergarten entry age, thereby denying access to public school to some five-year-olds who a generation ago would have been among the younger, or even "middle-aged," kindergartners.[3] Another trend in current kindergarten practices is the increasing use of entry testing to determine which children are "ready" for kindergarten.

These trends might seem positive given the perception that kindergarten has "gotten harder" over the years; the ideas of raising the entry age and testing to select children who appear more likely to succeed at kindergarten sound like good ones. However, there are regrettable consequences as entry ages are shifted to ensure older children in kindergarten classes and as testing is increasingly used to sort children into supposedly homogeneous groupings. The population of children in kindergarten is changing and is dramatically different from the population of three- to five-year-olds who attended when kindergarten was originally incorporated into the public school system. Younger children are now eliminated by their birthdates. Those who are most likely to be denied entry by testing are boys who are chronologically (and developmentally) younger, children who are black or Hispanic, and children who are poor. These consequences are particularly ironic given the historical arguments for placing kindergarten in public schools: that the more disadvantaged children would be assured access.

Early Childhood Programs Before Kindergarten

For children younger than kindergarten entry age, the availability of and eligibility criteria for early childhood programs are quite different from those of kindergarten or first grade programs. The early childhood system, as noted in earlier chapters, includes many forms of early childhood programs. These programs are offered in homes, centers, schools (both public and private), religious organizations, and many other settings under various auspices—public, private, nonprofit, and for-profit. Some are called school, as in *preschool* or *nursery school*; others are called *child care* or *day care*. This early childhood ecosystem offers a wide variety of educational opportunities for children younger than five, most of which are not operated by the public school system.

Unlike the consensus for a universal system of education for older children and the public responsibility to provide it, there is no public agreement about prekindergarten education. The shared public responsibility to provide education for *all* children begins, in the view of the general public, probably at age five (given the nearly universal nature of public kindergarten) and definitely at age six. Opinions about whether (and at what age) education is desirable for children younger than age five tend to be based on beliefs about whether mothers should work or stay home to care for and educate children. These conflicting beliefs appear to many to be irresolvable; therefore, the public generally regards prekindergarten education as a private decision that each family' can choose (or not) for its own children. As a result, there is no consensus on the question of whether providing prekindergarten education for *all* children is a public responsibility.

The history of public investment in prekindergarten programs clearly illustrates that, barring a compelling social problem that is presumed solvable through an early childhood program for some identifiable group of young children (poor children or abused children) or for certain of their parents (mothers receiving welfare), the issue is left to families. For example, during World War II, when the nation's war industry needed women to work, the Lanham Act created and funded child care centers. A major rationale for Head Start was that the negative effects of poverty could be ameliorated through early education. Some amount of child care for children at risk of abuse and/or neglect is provided with public funds in every state. Although each program certainly offers an educational opportunity for young children, the rationale for public investment in them is not argued on educational grounds but as a solution for social problems.

No publicly funded program for children younger than five has ever been universal, or available to *all* children. Whenever public funds are expended on children, only those children are eligible whose poverty or obvious family or social circumstances make them the targets of public policy. Even those programs targeted to a particular population often fail to serve all eligible children. In many cases, this failure is a direct result of inadequate funding (Head Start) or the withdrawal of funds once the perceived problem had disappeared (Lanham Act programs). After 20 years of demonstrated success, limited federal funding for the Head Start program nationwide permits it to serve less than 20 percent of all eligible children. Publicly subsidized child care programs probably serve less than one-third of all eligible children, judging from the number of applicants on waiting lists for openings in such programs. Chapter I programs reportedly serve 50 percent of eligible children across all grade levels (prekindergarten through high school); because only a small fraction of these funds is expended on services for children below kindergarten level, the proportion of eligible prekindergartners reached is probably very small.

Public ambivalence toward working mothers (unless they are welfare mothers), combined with resistance to the higher taxes that would certainly be required to fund universal public prekindergarten, will likely continue to restrict public investment in prekindergarten to programs targeted to a limited population of children defined as disadvantaged or most needy.

Factors Relating to Prekindergarten Enrollment

Two sources of information can be used to determine the number of prekindergarten-aged children enrolled in the various forms of early childhood programs: preschool enrollment data (from the annual *School Enrollment Supplement* to the Census Bureau's *Current Population Survey* [CPS][4]) and child care arrangements data (from the Census Bureau's *1984–1985 Survey of Income and Program Participation* [SIPP][5]).[6]

Today, according to the CPS, 49 percent of all four-year-olds and 29 percent of all three-year-olds are enrolled in some program their parents view as school. *School*, in this context, probably represents a wide variety of settings (both public and private), in that the parent's opinion determined whether the setting constituted a school. Parents were asked: Is your child attending or enrolled in nursery school or kindergarten (this year)? Some parents may have considered a wide range of settings (such as child care centers) and activities as school, while others may have considered only formal instructional programs in settings labeled schools to be school. Overall, only about 15 percent of these programs were identified as public schools.

Preschool enrollment is related to family income—the higher the income, the more likely that the child is enrolled in preschool and that the preschool is a private one. This correlation is not surprising, given that there are many more private early childhood programs than public ones and that all private programs charge fees. A higher family income means that more money is available to purchase preschool programs. Moreover, children from higher income families are likely to be in private programs because public programs are nearly always limited to children from low-income families. By contrast, for four-year-olds from low-income households who are enrolled in preschool, twice as many white children and nearly four times as many black children are enrolled in public programs than in private ones.

Parental desire for earlier education is also a factor influencing preschool enrollment. Although it is probably a factor for families at all income levels and with all working patterns, an increased desire for early education is more easily satisfied through part-day programs. It is clearly evident in the preschool enrollment rates for four-year-olds whose mothers do not work. Preschool enrollment rates for these children increased from 37 percent in 1975 to 48 percent in 1984. (This increase was the only statistically significant change found by the CPS during this period.)

Another issue affecting preschool enrollment is whether a mother works outside the home. The CPS reported that children whose mothers don't work or work part time are more likely to be enrolled in preschool than children whose mothers work full time. This finding is explained by the fact that most preschool programs are part time; while these programs' hours may coincide with a part-time worker's hours, they create difficulties or gaps for full-time workers. In fact, the preschool enrollment rate for children with single mothers who worked full time actually *decreased* between 1975 and 1984 (from 43 percent to 36 percent), while the overall rate for all three- and four-year-olds regardless of their mother's work status *increased* from 32 percent to 39 percent in the same period.[7]

Although less than half of all three- and four-year-olds are reported to be enrolled in school, prekindergarten enrollment can also be viewed from the perspective of child care arrangements—many of which are in settings that would be included as *school* in the CPS. Nearly all of the more than 8 million children under age five whose mothers work receive some form of child care. The SIPP asked custodial parents/guardians: What was your child usually doing, or how was your child usually cared for, during most of the hours that you worked last month? These children are in what the SIPP referred to as *organized facilities* (such as child care centers or preschools) or in *homes* (their own and others'). About 3.5 million three- and four-year-olds have mothers who work. While their mothers work, 32 percent are in organized facilities (1.1 million children). The majority (58 percent) are in homes or are cared for by their mother while she works.[8]

Although the education system does not always acknowledge its custodial role, the SIPP recognized that school is a child care arrangement. For the vast majority (75 percent) of children over age five, school is the most common child care arrangement used while their mothers work. In contrast, less than 2 percent of three- and four-year-old children are reported to be in elementary schools while their mothers work. Unfortunately, no conclusions can be drawn about the proportion of children enrolled in publicly supported programs, because the SIPP did not distinguish the auspices, public or private, of the organized facilities (day care centers and nursery schools) or of the elementary schools.

Children whose mothers were in higher-income occupations (managerial versus service) were more likely to be in centers or schools than in homes. Higher incomes allow mothers to purchase organized programs, which usually cost more than home-based care. Also, children whose mothers had more education (completing four years of college versus not completing high school) were more than twice as likely to be in centers or schools than in homes.[9]

Taking child care arrangements data from the SIPP (which include some preschool enrollment) and preschool enrollment data from the CPS together, about one-third of all three- and four-year-old children, particularly those from higher-income families and those with more highly educated mothers, participate in organized prekindergarten programs of various types. The majority of these children are enrolled in private, rather than public, programs. The most local form of control—that is, parental choice—to a large degree determines prekindergarten attendance.

Is There a Trend Toward Universal Prekindergarten?

The recent expansion of prekindergarten programs in public schools appears to resemble the movement of kindergarten from primarily private auspices early in this century into the public school system by mid-century.

The Nineteenth-Century Kindergarten Movement and Prekindergarten Today

The early proponents of kindergarten firmly believed that the play-based, child-centered education they practiced and advocated was beneficial to children, especially disadvantaged children living in urban ghettos where many of the early kindergartens were. Kindergarten proponents worked diligently to have the public schools adopt kindergarten. They believed that kindergarten should be in the public school system for two primary reasons. First, they reasoned that the progressive manner in which kindergarten was practiced outside public schools would be a force capable of changing what they regarded as the inappropriate practices of public schools in regard to young elementary-aged children (sitting at desks all day, rote memorization, no opportunity for play). Second, public auspices (and the public funding thus guaranteed) would ensure that more needy children could attend and benefit from kindergarten. Those arguments sound familiar to us today.

Some of the language of debate may sound familiar, but in fact, there are few similarities between the early kindergarten movement and the prekindergarten situation today. While there clearly is renewed and intense interest in prekindergarten education today, there is no unified "movement" as there was with kindergarten.

The early childhood system is vastly larger and more diverse, both in terms of delivery systems and opinions, than it was early in the century. Tremendous growth has occurred in early childhood services generally and child care particularly—especially services for three- and four-year-olds. The strictly public sector portion of the system (publicly operated child care centers, public school-operated prekindergarten programs) is relatively small—

perhaps 2–3 percent of the whole early childhood system, which has been estimated to be a $15–$20 billion market of close to 100,000 center-based and over 300,000 home-based settings.[10] The vast majority of the early childhood system is privately sponsored and financed. The most strictly private part of the system—the for-profit sector (like individually owned centers, smaller local chains, and large national ones)—is growing.

Early on, during the kindergarten movement, pressure began to build, from the public and from kindergarten practitioners alike, toward public responsibility for kindergarten. Today, early childhood advocates and practitioners express a wide range of opinion about public school involvement in prekindergarten—from strong opposition, to grudging acceptance of an inevitable move, to guarded support. Much of the private for-profit sector of the early childhood community strongly opposes what it regards as unfair competition from public schools.

Other sectors feel that greater public school provision of prekindergarten would be good for much the same reasons that public kindergarten was promoted. That is, good early childhood practices in prekindergarten will influence the elementary school curriculum, transforming kindergarten and the early grades to a more child-centered orientation, and public provision of prekindergarten will ensure opportunities for needy young children. Recognizing that the kindergarten movement failed in the first regard, proponents of public prekindergarten today are actively and explicitly promoting good practices, rather than assuming that transformation of the elementary grades and kindergarten will occur by osmosis.

Unlike the push for universally available kindergarten in a single delivery system—the public schools—today the rallying point for proponents of public funding of early childhood services is universal access to a diversity of prekindergarten programs across the ecosystem.

Attempts at Universal Prekindergarten

Two cities, using different approaches, have initiated prekindergarten programs for four-year-olds that aim at universality. Those in the District of Columbia come close to being universal in that each of the District's elementary schools has at least one classroom of four-year-olds. More than 60 percent of the four-year-old population in the District is being served according to the latest enrollment figures. The District completely absorbed the expense of prekindergarten programs for four-year-olds into the general education budget as a line item, making this program free to parents. Originally, these classrooms were funded through Chapter I, which restricted access to children at educational risk, but community pressure influenced the Board of Education to integrate the programs into every school. Now, eligibility is determined by the child's age and residence in the district; a physical examination and necessary immunizations are also required.

In New York City, the creators of Project Giant Step (PGS) intended it to fill the gap between the total demand for prekindergarten services and the capacity of the existing supply of prekindergarten services. They assumed that families who could afford to pay for prekindergarten services would continue to use the private system of schools and centers for their children. Low-income families would continue to use publicly funded services (Head Start, publicly funded child care centers, and the public school system). PGS was not intended to replace the existing system of public and private services with a new one. Instead, the goal was to sufficiently expand the supply of early childhood services in all the publicly funded delivery systems to ensure that prekindergarten would be available to all four-year-olds throughout New York City. When the city introduced Project Giant Step, the plan for universal service to all four-year-olds was to be phased in over four years. Two years into the program, Giant Step has been well funded by the city but not at the level needed to meet the goal of universal service on schedule. According to 1988 figures provided by the Mayor's Office of Early Childhood Education, nearly 40 percent of the city's four-year-old population is being served through the publicly funded delivery systems.[11] And contrary to the District of Columbia's move, this year those PGS classrooms operated by the NYC Board of Education are funded with Chapter I monies—a pragmatic fiscal decision which appears to conflict with the ultimate goal of universal service.

Similarly, Missouri's Parents as Teachers Program (PAT) and Minnesota's Early Childhood Family Education Program (ECFE), which focus on parent education, ultimately aim to provide access to such education in all school districts statewide. Both are close to reaching that goal. The Council of Chief State School Officers recently issued a statement calling for universally available high-quality early childhood services for all children, targeting *public* resources to children at risk. The current council president wrote: "Our concern is children—their health and nutrition, well-being, care, safety, housing, and when these needs are met, their education."[12] The council recognized that access and availability of services are the basic issues and saw an expanded, but not exclusive, role for public schools in providing early childhood services.

Eligibility and Access in the Early Childhood Ecosystem

Although prekindergarten is not a publicly provided, universal service, well over half of all four-year-olds do attend some kind of early childhood program before entering kindergarten. Recognizing that consumer factors (such as parental desire for educating their young children, need for child care, and family resources) influence enrollment, what factors from the provider (or supply side) determine which children attend prekindergarten? Access to *any* prekindergarten program (public or private) is restricted through the use of eligibility criteria, which are usually based on child (and family) characteristics. All prekindergarten programs, of course, restrict their services to a specific age (or range of ages) of children; the child's age may be the only stated criterion for entry to a prekindergarten program.

Prekindergarten programs supported with public funds (Head Start, subsidized child care, state-funded prekindergarten programs) nearly always limit eligibility in some clearly specified way beyond the child's age. The criteria used may be family income, parents' employment status, some child characteristic such as risk for abuse or special educational needs, or some combination of child and family characteristics. These eligibility criteria are *explicit*—they are stated, and they determine access to the program.

More subtle factors also influence access to prekindergarten programs, or what might be called *implicit* eligibility criteria. Ability to pay is one of these. The majority of programs for young children charge fees to parents; only those families who can afford the program's fees are eligible to attend. Publicly funded programs, operating with scant resources and overwhelmed with more eligible applicants than they can enroll, may further limit eligibility to the "neediest of the needy" to ease pressures caused by the imbalance of supply and demand. The location of a program further determines who can attend. If the program does not provide transportation, is not within walking distance, and is inaccessible via public transportation, only those families who can provide their own transportation can enroll their children. Enrollment is also influenced by the program's hours of operation. Full-time workers may find that part-time programs do not meet their child care needs and therefore may not enroll their children in such programs. Parents who do not speak English may have difficulty even finding out about prekindergarten programs unless recruitment materials are available in languages other than English. These are all examples of practices that *implicitly* restrict eligibility.

Eligibility and Access to Public School-Operated Prekindergarten Programs

Many of the characteristics of prekindergarten programs in the wider early childhood ecosystem described earlier hold true for prekindergarten programs operated by public schools. No public school-operated prekindergarten program is as widely available as kindergarten in a given school district. And not all public school-operated programs are publicly funded. About one in ten is a privately (parent-) funded program. Eligibility for all public school-operated prekindergarten programs is limited both explicitly and implicitly.

Public schools participate in many of the same publicly funded programs that nonpublic community agencies do (like subsidized child care or Head Start) and must use the same criteria to restrict eligibility. In addition, public schools operate other publicly funded programs such as Chapter I prekindergartens and pre-school special education. Each has its own quite specific criteria for eligibility determination. In contrast, the privately funded programs operated by public schools—the nursery or child care programs supported by parent fees—often seem to have no eligibility restrictions and are regarded as equally available to all families living in the school district. In reality, access is limited to those families who can afford the fees and provide their own transportation.

Only the so-called permissive prekindergarten programs appear to have characteristics of universality associated with public kindergarten—that is, free and available to any child of eligible age. But the resemblance is misleading. In fact, these are very small-scale programs offered in relatively few districts in the states (New Jersey, Pennsylvania, Wisconsin, and Maine) that permit public school districts to offer prekindergarten in this manner. Further, local districts may apply entry criteria (beyond the child's age), such as meeting Chapter I eligibility requirements, or districts may charge fees to make up the difference between operating costs and state reimbursement.

Although it is clear that in some states and communities there is considerable interest in expanding services to increase the number

of children who have access to prekindergarten programs, nowhere
has universal service been realized. Despite discussions of universality, the question of wisely targeting scarce public funds remains:
Which children are most in need and will benefit most from early
childhood programs? The answer is usually that the most disadvantaged children will benefit the most—those who are poorest, those
whose mothers are least educated, those who have the fewest
options for participation in existing programs. Explicit eligibility
criteria are designed to target public funds effectively.

Public schools as a whole are currently engaged in providing a
wide variety of publicly funded programs and, at the same time, a
limited number of privately financed programs. As a result, local
school districts have adopted explicit criteria (usually defined by
the program's funding source) and implicit criteria. The use of
such criteria has significantly affected the recruitment and enrollment procedures used in districts. It is, perhaps, not surprising
that there are differences in district practices between publicly
funded and privately financed programs.

Privately Financed Programs

The District Survey found that only privately financed, public
school-operated prekindergarten programs—those child care and
nursery school programs funded by parent tuitions—reported no
explicit limits on eligibility except for the child's age and sometimes residence in the district. The decision to enroll a child in
these programs is more like a private transaction than a public
one. It is governed by the demands (and means) of the parent/
consumer and by the enrollment capacity of the provider school.
The obvious implicit criterion—ability to pay—does limit access to
these programs. Only children whose parents can afford the program, and transport them to it, are eligible.

Parent-tuition-supported programs are usually found in modest-
sized, relatively wealthy suburban school districts with declining
K–12 enrollments (and, therefore, available school space). These
districts tend to offer a variety of services in response to consumer/
parent demands that include, at a minimum, both part-day and
full-working-day hours. Often, the range of available services is
quite broad. For example, the Affton-Lindbergh Early Childhood
Education (St. Louis, Missouri) offers everything from a drop-in
mother's day out service to full-time, full-year programs with
mainstreamed early childhood special education services.

In general, tuitions for privately financed programs are on a par
with those of most other child care centers or nursery schools in

the community. Families who cannot afford the tuition might be served if these programs would accept state reimbursement for child care; most do not accept these subsidies. Those districts we visited did not accept state child care subsidy for a variety of reasons: because the amount reimbursed was too low (Missouri), because licensing was a prerequisite for reimbursement eligibility (Washington), because districts were unaware of the existence of such reimbursement options (Nebraska), or because no child currently in a district program appeared to be eligible, even though the district was willing to accept state reimbursement (Michigan).

Programs housed in public schools operate in the local child care market and must walk a fine line between fair and unfair competition. Respondents in some states mentioned that private programs perceive universal public preschool for three- and four-year-olds as a threat to their continued existence. The public school district in Northville, Michigan, encountered organized community resistance when it decided to re-open an elementary school as an early childhood center. The chamber of commerce became involved at the urging of local proprietary child care providers, who believed the public school district was unfairly competing with private business. An agreement was eventually reached which included three main points: tuition in the public school-operated center would be set based on the local average tuition and would never be lower than that average, no direct local tax support would go to the program, and the program would be open for inspection by the community.

Because they are tuition-supported, these programs must attract families in much the same way any proprietary program does: by offering services that are in demand and by maintaining a good reputation so that word of mouth will bring families to them. To stimulate enrollment, school districts can be very creative in their recruitment strategies. (In suburban Omaha, all three-year-olds who live in the Westside Community School District receive a birthday card from the district's early childhood program.) However, simply being part of the school district is a draw to most parents, who respect local schools as institutions that are "here to stay" and can be trusted.

Typically, districts limit the number of sites for a given program. Our survey of districts found that 80 percent of districts operating tuition-funded programs operated only one site. In those districts we visited that offered such programs, Northville, Michigan; Seattle, Washington; and St. Louis, Missouri, operated in one site; Omaha, Nebraska, was at the other end of the spectrum, operating in six sites. Enrollment procedures in these programs are usually school-based. In single-site programs interested parents go to that school building to find out about the services and enroll their child. This may implicitly limit eligibility, depending on the nature of the public transportation system and the private transportation resources of families. However, school-based enrollment can make the enrollment process easier for families, as long as recruitment is vigorous and widespread throughout the community, so that all families know about the program. Centralized intake procedures, such as enrollment at the district office, could limit eligibility (depending on transportation resources) and would be more costly and overly bureaucratic for these smaller districts. In the district we visited with multisite programs, Westside Community Schools (Omaha, Nebraska), enrollment is also school-based rather than centralized. In suburban Omaha, parents go to whichever site is most convenient; if one site is oversubscribed, parents are directed to other sites which have openings.

Publicly Funded Programs: State Prekindergarten Programs

Generally, state-funded prekindergarten programs are designed for four-year-old children at risk of school failure. The programs are typically half-day for the school year prior to kindergarten entry. The legislative intent of most programs is to facilitate later school success; by and large, the purpose of these programs is early intervention to prevent school failure. States define as risk factors lack of school readiness, limited English proficiency, low developmental level, handicapping conditions, low family income, having a teenaged parent, delinquency of a teen sibling, mental illness or psychological needs of a parent, abuse and/or neglect of the child, crowded living conditions, frequent changes in the family unit, migrant, or in rare cases, having working parents (New York). Of all these explicit eligibility criteria, family income is the most common. Implicit criteria that may restrict eligibility are not apparent at the state level, except for state transportation policies. Implicit eligibility limitations appear in local district practices.

In a few states family income and age of child are the only eligibility criteria imposed (California, Massachusetts, and Washington). In Massachusetts 75 percent of the funds allocated must go to low-income school districts, as determined by the number of children ages 5 to 17 living in families receiving AFDC. First priority is given to school districts where more than 10 percent of the enrollment is low income. Second priority is given to individual schools which qualify under Chapter I. The remaining 25 percent may go to schools or districts which do not meet the low-income criteria but which offer innovative models. No screening procedures for individual program participants are required, but local programs may exercise discretion in giving priority to lower-income children.

The state of Washington uses a two-tiered eligibility approach. Priority for program funds is given to counties with a high percentage of families below 100 percent of the federal poverty level who are not being served by existing intervention programs. Sixty percent of available funds are to be set aside for counties where 20 percent or fewer eligible children are served by Head Start. The remaining 40 percent of allocated funds are available to counties in which more than 20 percent of eligible children are already being served. A recent policy change set aside a minimum of two hundred slots for migrant or Indian children. At the program level, individual children are accepted on the basis of age (four years old) and family income (federal Head Start poverty-level guidelines).

In some states, defining the population to be served is a local district option. In New Jersey many of the schools providing four-year-old programs (called kindergarten) are also Chapter I eligible; they combine both programs, screening all children according to Chapter I criteria. Pilot programs in Delaware were originally targeted for the "educationally disadvantaged," but opposition from several sectors led to the expansion of services to children representative of the participating school district's population. There has been debate in Delaware about establishing specific programs for four-year-olds versus setting an earlier kindergarten entry age as the permissive prekindergarten programs in Maine, New Jersey, and Pennsylvania do (kindergarten is defined to include two years of service for which both four- and five-year-olds are eligible).

Our survey of districts showed that the eligibility criteria most often used in state prekindergarten programs are low family income and speaking a language other than English. In Texas three criteria determine whether a district must offer the state prekindergarten program and which children will be served: age, family income, and language. If there are 15 four-year-olds residing in the district whose family income qualifies the child for free or reduced-price lunch (USDA guidelines), or who cannot speak or comprehend the English language, then a program must be offered. In Dallas recruitment efforts are centrally managed and include distribution of leaflets and placement of newspaper notices during summer "round-ups." The enrollment procedures during "round-ups" are school based, and children must reside in the attendance area of the school. Parents bring children to the school, where an informal oral language inventory is done and/or family income is assessed. Once one of these eligibility criteria is met, enrollment is first-come, first-served.

Although the stated goal of many state-funded prekindergarten programs is early intervention to prevent school failure, or to address children at educational risk, few programs rely solely on tests of educational risk or assessments of potential school failure. Although two of the four districts we visited that offered state prekindergarten programs used a test to determine eligibility (in Illinois and South Carolina), such tests are not the sole criterion for entry. This is fortunate, given that the tests commonly used are not reliable enough to categorize children and should only be used as one element of a multifaceted assessment.

The South Carolina DOE recommends use of the Dial-R screening instrument in its state prekindergarten, but family and environmental factors (such as the parent's age, the number of parents, the educational level of the parent(s), whether the child was referred by a community agency, and whether the referral involved child abuse/neglect) are considered by districts in selecting children.

In Illinois districts select their own screening instrument; neither the state Board of Education nor the legislation mandates the use of any specific test. However, if tests are used, they must be both "reliable and valid" and based on state Board of Education criteria. Parental interviews and permission for the screening are also required. A list of suggested screening instruments and comprehensive screening programs is available to districts from the state Board of Education. The Chicago Public Schools have developed, originally for use in their Chapter I prekindergarten programs, their own battery of tests (Chicago EARLY) to determine risk. The Chicago EARLY includes subtests for language, visual discrimination, memory, and fine and gross motor skills; the subtests are weighted so that language is the largest factor in the child's score. Social skills are also assessed during the testing process, and points are given for poorly developed skills. Hearing and vision tests are also conducted. Children who fail either of these tests are automatically enrolled. Those children with the most points are judged most "academically at risk."

While the child is being tested, the parent is interviewed, using the Child/Family Assessment (a locally developed instrument) to determine family and environmental factors. These data are used to select among children who have all scored "academically at risk" on the EARLY. Factors considered are low birth weight, lack of prenatal care, substance abuse by the mother, high-risk birth, low family income, and limited proficiency in English. Screening is done by an itinerant team which travels from school to school and includes teachers, a nurse, a health aide, a vision technician, a hearing technician, and a speech teacher.

In the magnet Early Childhood Centers in Buffalo, New York, selection is by lottery. (The centers were created in response to a 1976 desegregation order after a year of busing. They are schools with prekindergarten through grade 2, located in minority neighborhoods, which are linked to "academy" schools, including grades 3–8, located in majority neighborhoods.) Eligibility for these prekindergarten programs is open to any resident of the Buffalo school district. Enrollment is centralized, and each classroom is balanced in terms of race and gender. While a citywide lottery is cumbersome to conduct, it is probably the only way to ensure the necessary racial balance. Children who are not selected are informed of other prekindergarten programs operated by the district for which they might be eligible (the Chapter I "Early Push" and NYS prekindergarten program). Making information about other programs available to parents is one benefit of this centralized enrollment system.

Publicly Funded Programs: Subsidized Child Care

In states where permissible, some school districts offer subsidized child care programs. We visited four such districts in the states of California, Florida, Pennsylvania, and South Carolina. Typically, the explicit eligibility criteria used are defined by the state agency administering the subsidized child care program and are similar across states. Although explicit criteria are similar, these districts offer insight into the effects of implicit criteria.

These programs operate under state regulations governing subsidized child care, as well as under district policies. The programs are designed to serve two categories of children: those from low-income working families and those at risk of abuse and/or neglect. Children eligible under child abuse and neglect rules generally have priority over children from working families. To be eligible, children must be in the age range that the program serves, their parents must be working or in an employment training program, and family income must be low (usually judged in relation to the state median income or official poverty level). In California family income must be at or below 84 percent of the state median. In South Carolina the family must be receiving AFDC (and nonworking) or working and earning not more than 80 percent of the state's official poverty level.

The Pomona Unified School District in California offers a wide variety of services through California's subsidized child care program (Children's Centers) as well as both the California state-funded prekindergarten and Head Start. Family income is a criterion for all programs, but the specific level varies with the program. Head Start and state-funded prekindergarten require income below the state poverty level; the Children's Center programs require income at or below 84 percent of the state median income (about $1,300/month for a family of two). Because the decision rule required by the state mandates lowest per capita income first and because so many families apply for Children's Center programs, only those with the lowest incomes are enrolled. This rule makes de facto eligibility more restrictive than the stated income criteria indicate.

The enrollment procedure is centralized but not overly bureaucratic—that is, it is efficient and responsive to each family's individual needs. Parents who want to enroll their children in any of the Pomona USD's programs come to the district's Child Development Office. The counselor informs parents about each of the programs and helps them apply for the program that best meets their child's (and parents') needs. For example, Head Start offers somewhat more comprehensive services than the state prekindergarten program and also provides special education. Families who need a program with longer hours apply for the Children's Centers. The personalized attention of the counselor and the location of program sites throughout the district on public transportation routes ensures that those children who are admitted are served in the program most appropriate for the child and the family.

The School District of Greenville County (South Carolina) has operated two Title XX/SSBG (state-subsidized) centers since 1972. Word of mouth is sufficient to ensure full enrollment and a waiting list at both sites. South Carolina is changing the eligibility regulations for this program. Formerly, all children who were low-income (defined as receiving AFDC) and had a need for "child development services" were eligible, including children of low-income working parents. Although no currently enrolled children who do not meet the new criteria will be dropped, the shift is toward serving mainly children of low-income parents who are working or in employment training programs. The state-funded prekindergarten program (also offered by the district in many elementary schools) will presumably serve those children who do not require full-day services. There is some concern in the wider Greenville community that these newer programs will not reach the eligible four-year-olds because of the location of the programs, the complexity of the enrollment process, and the lack of transportation.

The School District of Philadelphia operates two subsidized child care programs: One is state subsidized; the other uses local funds and serves families with a wider range of incomes. Explicitly, eligibility is similar for both programs: parents must be employed and have low incomes. Both have sliding fee scales, but the state subsidized program is more restrictive. A family of two earning more than $275 per week is ineligible for the state-subsidized program but remains eligible for the local program even as income rises. Fees are on a sliding scale that rises gradually to $70 per week when weekly income exceeds $750. The enrollment process is school-based and is conducted by a social worker on site. Although the school district offers two child care programs, federally funded Head Start, and the Parent Cooperative Nursery Schools (a locally funded part-day program), no centralized recruitment efforts are made. Parents find out about each program by word of mouth. All four programs are spread more or less uniformly throughout the entire district, and parents are on their own in finding out about which program is available in their area. When demand for a program far exceeds supply, recruitment efforts can be counterproductive—only raising expectations that cannot be met. In contrast, if recruitment is not vigilant, the neediest children are less likely to be served than are the children with the most resourceful parents.

The School Board of Palm Beach County (Florida) also offers two forms of child care: the Chapter I/Migrant Early Childhood Program and state-subsidized child care through both Title XX/SSBG and the Job Training Partnership Act. The migrant program is offered throughout the district and enrollment is school-based. A community resource coordinator, assigned to each school with a migrant early childhood program, recruits and enrolls children. Children who are three or four years old and are "currently migrant" are eligible. "Currently migrant" children are defined as having moved at least once during the last 12 months because their parents are employed in the agricultural or fishing industry. First priority is given to children who have older brothers and sisters in school whose education has been interrupted due to the migration of their family. The next priority is to children who have been enrolled in a migrant preschool program outside the county (in any state). Recruitment is done with the growers and with fishing industry employers as well as directly with families employed in these sites. Family income is not a criterion for enrollment. Transportation is provided by the district. Although the explicit criteria are complex, recruitment practices and transportation reduce the implicit restrictions and increase access for eligible children.

To be eligible for the Palm Beach County School Board's subsidized child care programs, a child must be at risk of abuse or neglect, from a family receiving AFDC, or from a low-income working family. Enrollment is center-based and conducted by social workers assigned to each center. Parent fees for working parents are on a sliding scale based on income. The highest fee is $28 per week for a family of two with an annual gross income of about $10,000. Transportation is not provided, and less vigorous recruitment efforts are made for this program than for the migrant program.

Publicly Funded Programs: Parent Education

Publicly funded parent education programs are aimed at the parents of young children. They are usually designed to provide parents with child development information and to support them in their role as parents. Minnesota and Missouri are the two states which currently have such programs operating statewide through public school districts. These programs are free (or inexpensive) and available to all parents who are district residents. The only criteria are a child in the age range served and a parent who will participate with the child. In Missouri the Parents as Teachers (PAT) program is aimed at parents of children from birth through age three and is free. In Minnesota parents of children from birth through age five are eligible; small tuition fees are charged after one free term but are waived for those unable to pay. Minnesota districts which choose to offer Early Childhood Family Education (ECFE) must provide sufficient services throughout the district to ensure access to all families.

The Affton-Lindbergh (St. Louis, Missouri) Parents as Teachers program recruits families by placing ads in newspapers, by word of mouth, and by sending a notice to each eligible family in the two districts. Parents who want to participate call the school to schedule the first home visit at their convenience. Five home visits constitute the mandatory program, but Affton-Lindbergh also offers a mothers and toddlers playgroup on a monthly basis and other events for families throughout the year. Special efforts are made to serve working parents through evening home visits.

The Duluth, Minnesota, Early Childhood Family Education (ECFE) program has developed entrepreneurial recruitment strategies, although word of mouth is strong because the program has existed for over ten years. New parents are told about the program during prenatal classes at local hospitals; a working parents resource center holds brown bag lunches downtown; community early childhood programs such as Head Start and child care centers publicize the program to their parents; and ECFE program staff speak at various community events, clubs, and organizations. As one parent said during a discussion of how parents find out about ECFE, "You'd have to live in a hole *not* to know about it." Parents who want to participate sign up for a 14-week discussion group which includes a time with parents and children and a period of parent discussion with a facilitator/parent educator. Most implicit eligibility limitations are eliminated by the extensive recruitment efforts, combined with not only a willingness but enthusiasm for offering the program on varying schedules and in different locations in order to serve parents who may not be able to come to a school during day-time hours.

Conclusion

The major reason for limiting children's eligibility for prekindergarten programs is insufficient public funds to support the programs. The resulting eligibility criteria that children must meet to be enrolled are complex and vary among program types.

Explicit Criteria

Research indicates that the most disadvantaged children benefit most from a high-quality prekindergarten experience. However, tests of "educational disadvantage" or "at-risk" status are far from precise. As a proxy, the most commonly used criterion is family income. (Head Start, subsidized child care, and state-funded prekindergarten programs use family income, while Chapter I programs test for "educational risk" without regard to family income.)

Locally funded prekindergartens and parent-tuition-funded child care programs do not limit eligibility explicitly beyond the child's age, although a family's ability to afford the program is an implicit criterion which denies access to poor children. Parent education programs are typically open to any family; if fees are charged, they are so low that no family is denied access.

Implicit Criteria

Explicit eligibility criteria aside, a number of implicit eligibility criteria determine which children will be enrolled in a particular program: recruitment and enrollment procedures, tuition, hours, location, and access to transportation. How recruitment campaigns are conducted can affect which families know about a program. Whether written materials are distributed in the community, where the materials are available, the language in which they are written, and the ability of parents to read and understand them all have an effect on enrollment. If parents must come to a particular location at a particular time to enroll their children, the distance from home, whether transportation is available, and whether the parent is working are factors limiting enrollment.

A program's hours of operation strongly affect which children will be enrolled. If the program is part-day (as most are) and the child's parent(s) work, it is likely that only those parents who can arrange additional child care can enroll their children. On-site before-school and after-school care for children younger than five is not readily available in many locales, so most working parents must arrange for relatives or neighbors to drop off, pick up, and, often, care for their children. Eligible children of working parents may effectively be denied access.

Full-school-day programs are somewhat better suited to the needs of working parents than are part-day programs. The longer hours and the fact that the public school program is usually free are attractive features. However, many of these programs use family income and/or low test scores as entrance criteria. Two-worker families may not have incomes low enough to qualify, although single working parents may. In one large urban school system with a full-school-day Chapter I program, some parents desperate for affordable child care had apparently coached their children to fail the entrance test (a disturbing message for the child) in order to qualify for the free public school program. If no transportation is provided (which is the typical situation), then only those families who live nearby, can use public transportation, or can otherwise arrange for transportation will be likely to enroll their children.

Universal Prekindergarten

Consumer demand for prekindergarten programs comes from families at all income levels who are seeking to satisfy needs for programs that offer good education and socialization for their children and child care while they work, at a price that is within the limits of their resources. These demands cannot be satisfied on a universal basis relying only on the public school system. The public school system is one part of the early childhood ecosystem.

Universality will develop slowly, not by following blueprints from the past (such as the kindergarten movement), but by careful analysis of the strengths than can be built upon and the weaknesses to be corrected throughout the existing early childhood ecosystem. Universal access to prekindergarten services that are good for children and for parents can be achieved through a combination of supply building across the early childhood system and greater commitments of public funds—not only from education sources but from social service sources, the private sector, and the income tax code—to support those families who cannot otherwise afford prekindergarten.

Publicly funded prekindergarten programs operate within the larger early childhood ecosystem. Competition for children eligible for more than one publicly funded program creates problems. For example, Texas requires districts identifying 15 poor or limited English proficient four-year-olds to provide prekindergarten programs. Because all programs provided by school districts must be located in school buildings, some local Head Start programs have had to relinquish public school space and have also lost teacher aides to the better-paid public school programs. Many of the children served by the new state program were eligible for or already participating in Head Start, and the loss of space and staff experienced by Head Start actually resulted in a net reduction in the number of children served. Many other state-funded prekindergarten programs offer examples of overlapping eligibility—similar populations eligible for both Head Start and the state-funded preschool program. Such overlapping produces competition for space, staff, and children. Public funds should be used to increase access to prekindergarten programs by expanding the supply, not by supplanting existing programs. The goal is increased access for needy children first, which will ultimately result in increased access for all children.

Recommendations

- School district early childhood programs should be included in databanks maintained by community-based child care resource and referral agencies to increase parental access to information about all programs for which their children may be eligible.
- School districts which offer more than one type of early childhood program should inform applicants about all district programs for which their children may be eligible.

- Recruitment materials should be available in languages commonly spoken by parents, as well as in English.
- Enrollment procedures should be neighborhood-based (or school-based) whenever possible.
- Tests for educational risk are imprecise at best and should not be used for placement. Other more easily determined factors, such as family income or eligibility for school lunch programs, should be used.
- Among programs targeted to the same population over which the state has jurisdiction (subsidized child care for AFDC recipients, state prekindergarten), eligibility requirements should be made as similar as possible and any conflicting requirements reconciled.
- Expansion of publicly funded programs should be planned within the existing framework of early childhood programs in a given community, so that public funds are used to support those children most in need and to fill gaps in services, not supplant existing services.

Endnotes

1. Westat, Inc. (1987). *Private schools and private school teachers: Final report of the 1985–86 Private School Study*. Washington, D.C.: U.S. Department of Education, Office of Educational Research and Improvement.
2. National Center for Education Statistics (1987). *Condition of Education*. Washington, D.C.: U.S. Department of Education, Center for Education Statistics.
3. Shepard, L.A., and M.L. Smith (1986). Synthesis of research on school readiness and kindergarten retention. *Education Leadership* 44 (3):78–86.
4. U.S. Bureau of the Census (1985). *Current population survey: School enrollment supplement*. Washington, D.C.: U.S. Government Printing Office.
5. U.S. Bureau of the Census (1987). *Who's minding the kids? Child care arrangements, Winter 1984–1985* (Series p–70, No. 9). Washington, D.C.: U.S. Government Printing Office.
6. These data sets overlap. The CPS sample includes all parents (including working mothers) but is limited to three- and four-year-old children who were reportedly in school; the SIPP sample included only working mothers (and their children under age fifteen) but used a broad definition of program participation—any care arrangement. Unfortunately, it is impossible to eliminate the duplication and arrive at a true estimate of the program participation of *all* preschoolers.
7. National Center for Education Statistics (1986). Preschool enrollment: Trends and implications (065-000-002761-1). Report reprinted from *The condition of education*. Washington, D.C.: U.S. Government Printing Office, U.S. Department of Education.

8. The National Day Care Study (1977–1978) found that while child care centers enrolled children from infancy through about age ten, 75 percent of the enrolled children were either three- or four-year-olds. The pattern that emerged from SIPP is that about 60 percent of center enrollments are three- or four-year-olds, which attests to the growth during the 1980s of center-based care for infants and toddlers.

9. U.S. Bureau of the Census (1987). *Who's minding the kids? Child care arrangements, Winter 1984–1985* (Series p-70, No. 9). Washington, D.C.: U.S. Government Printing Office.

10. Wilson, M. (1988). *A strategic overview of the early childhood market*. Los Angeles, Calif.: Mike Wilson List Council, Inc.

11. Telephone conversation with Maryann Marrapodi, director of the Mayor's Office of Early Childhood Education, March 17, 1989.

12. Council of Chief State School Officers. (1988). *A guide for state action: Early childhood and family education* (Preface). Washington, D.C.: Author.

Chapter 7

COORDINATION

When most of the older early childhood programs began in the 1960s and 1970s, the early childhood climate was very different from that of today: Head Start had just begun, publicly subsidized day care was seen as strictly a social welfare service; state-funded prekindergarten programs were relatively rare; and family support and parent education programs were practically unknown. Each was viewed as a separate program; there was little perceived commonality of purpose or clientele. In general, there was little incentive to develop coordination mechanisms; indeed, in states with long-established prekindergarten programs, such as California and New York, the question of coordination did not even surface until fairly recently. When these programs were started, they were seen as clearly a part of the education bureaucracy and quite distinct from any child care or Head Start programs in the state. Even though New York and California modeled their programs on Head Start and created them at about the same time as Head Start, there were no direct links with the federal program. By the early 1980s, the early childhood climate had changed considerably. Many more families are using early childhood services; many new programs have been created and existing ones expanded. New constituencies concerned about early childhood have emerged. Along with public officials, business leaders have taken a strong stand in support of expanded early childhood services coupled with calls for coordination. As noted by the Committee for Economic Development in *Children in Need:*[1]

> *We have to have a workable plan for greater coordination and cooperation among the dizzying number of current and potential actors: federal, state, and local governments; education, training, welfare, and economic development systems; public and private sectors; and the various levels of schooling.*

162

As states have created new prekindergarten programs in this decade, some have been aware that they were entering an existing system and have paid attention to the players in it. Others appeared to believe they were starting a completely new service.

During the past few years there has been a significant increase in the number of programs and services for young children that states fund, regulate, and operate. In some states more than a dozen distinct programs may be offered to eligible populations of children and families, including state-funded prekindergarten programs, various forms of subsidized child care, Head Start, Chapter I prekindergarten, migrant prekindergarten, and special education preschool. Agencies charged with managing or overseeing these services include departments of education, departments of social services or welfare, departments of public health, Head Start, day care licensing, offices for children, and employment and training departments. In short, although different state agencies manage *different* programs with *different* funding sources and administrative auspices, there may be considerable duplication among program purposes and the populations targeted for service. Even *within* one department, programs are often not coordinated. For example, state departments of education may operate several different prekindergarten programs (special education, Chapter I, state-funded prekindergarten) with no formal mechanism for communication among the programs. Some states even have trouble identifying who is administratively responsible for the various programs lodged in different divisions under the aegis of the same department.

As more states enact more legislation targeted to serve young children's care and educational needs, we can expect to see a continuing proliferation of separate programs. Each new program is usually designed to meet one specific need of targeted children or families. However, children's needs are integrated and sometimes inseparable from each other and from their families' needs. The challenge is to ensure that the multiple needs of child and family are all met through careful coordination across programs and agencies.

Failure to coordinate services will result not only in wasting resources but, more importantly, in less successful outcomes for children and their families. Because so many programs are separately funded, under separate auspices, there is a serious risk of inefficiency and overlapping services. The consequence of such overlapping is confusion at the local level, where the services are delivered. For example, a four-year-old child eligible to attend a state-funded prekindergarten program is usually eligible because of poverty or because she or he meets other risk criteria. At-risk children have an array of needs that are likely to call for health services, and/or family social services, or possibly special education programs. If the child's parents are working, the child will probably need extended care beyond the prekindergarten program closing time. The comprehensive services a child needs are often delivered by a number of different service providers. For the child to benefit from the services, they must reinforce and complement, not contradict and collide with, each other. The delivery of these services must be coordinated—for efficiency's sake and for the child's sake.

The child, appropriately, is the epicenter of targeted prekindergarten programs. However, parents (especially young, single mothers) can benefit from other programs aimed at them if the special services their children receive also include attention to their own needs. Prekindergarten programs ideally include support to parents, helping them strive for better jobs and higher incomes. Most programs do not. A recent study of 75 poor women whose children attend half-day prekindergarten programs in New York City provides a poignant illustration. Ninety percent of these women were not working. They were reported to be waiting for their children to enter full-day school before pursuing their own education and training. The programs their children attended provided no information on education, training, or child care options.[2]

A compelling example of why coordination is necessary is the paradox created by the increasing number of part-day educational programs for young children from poor and high-risk families. These are the very families targeted for training and employment programs by recently enacted welfare reform legislation (the Family Support Act of 1988) which requires work in order to receive AFDC payments. Parents are required to participate in full-day work and training programs, while their children are offered half-day early childhood programs as preventive educational strategies. This is a prime example of the need for better coordination: Proper provision of adequate child care under the Family Support Act must incorporate targeted prekindergarten programs because it will then simultaneously reach precisely the at-risk children who will most benefit from high-quality early childhood programs *and* support the job training and employment efforts geared to their parents' needs.

Examples of policies that are on a collision course include lack of coordination between providers of various services needed by at-risk children, lack of attention to parents' needs by their children's programs, and the competing purposes of programs aimed at children and those aimed at their parents. Programs with similar purposes aimed only at children may also collide. The recent extension of ECIA expanded eligibility for Chapter I/migrant programs to include three- and four-year-olds; a portion of Head Start funds is already targeted to migrant young children. Coordination of Chapter I/migrant programs with Head Start migrant programs is not mentioned in the legislation. These potential collisions will occur at the community level, with little hope for state intervention, because both Chapter I and Head Start are federal-local programs. More generally, the proliferation of various programs aimed at the same population of children (Head Start, targeted state-funded prekindergarten programs) could collide with the good intentions of federal policymakers as they move forward with major legislation aimed at young at-risk children (Smart Start, Even Start). Ideally, each of these programs is complementary—one part of a larger, coherent effort to increase the number of young children reached by quality early childhood programs. Collisions can be avoided, or at least made less serious, through coordination.

Programs are almost always funded by separate funding streams. No state has yet moved to coordinate funding of early childhood programs across state agencies. Localities, reflecting state and federal policies, rarely coordinate these separate streams (although there are some significant exceptions in some communities). Would a coordinated approach to funding be feasible in light of traditional agency turf issues and competition over resources? It may be not only feasible but necessary. At a time when resources are increasingly scarce and administrative (and service) duplication costly, it is widely acknowledged that an integrated approach would be both efficient and cost-effective when funding early childhood programs—including special education and child care—and work/training programs for parents of young children.

If collisions are to be avoided (among various providers of the array of comprehensive services, between half-day prekindergarten programs and full-day vocational programs for parents, between programs competing for the same children), coordination must guide policy initiatives directed at young children. Yet in state after state, agency administrators at the state and local level mention the lack of coordination of programs as a serious concern. New programs are put into place without systematic consideration of their impact on children, families, and service providers at the local level.

Although states are attempting to organize the plethora of programs and services targeted to young children, coordination is generally limited and remains pro forma in many instances rather than a methodical process leading to shared resources, cooperative planning, and joint action. In general, truly collaborative resource sharing occurs rarely among representatives of state agencies concerned with the provision and management of early childhood programs. When mutual benefit directly and overtly results from coordination, coordination is more likely to be valued and institutionalized. Resource sharing has been most successful when related programs (such as AFDC, WIN, and Title XX/SSBG) serve the same population. In such instances, the implementation of coordinating mechanisms among these programs at the state level has resulted in improvements in cost efficiency and delivery of services. In most states, cross-agency coordination of services and programs for young children is not institutionalized (except for special education) where coordination is federally mandated. Rather, coordination depends on the goodwill of individual administrators and on informal agreements.

Defining Coordination

What is *coordination*? What are the means or mechanisms of coordination? How likely is it that historically independent systems can join forces and share resources? What are states and localities doing to make sense of the many funding streams, administrative auspices, sets of regulations, and competing interests that cover separate programs serving essentially the same populations?

Both *coordination* and *collaboration* are used, sometimes interchangeably, to describe intentional interactions among the various parts of the early childhood community, across and within a state's various departments, and among programs at the local level. The purpose of these interactions is to share information, to establish lines of communication, to cooperate on defining problem areas and to work to solve those problems, and to collaborate to reach a shared goal. Goals can be far-reaching and broad, as is that of achieving comprehensiveness, which requires combining services from a variety of sources. Or goals for collaboration can be targeted to one specific task, such as participating on an interagency committee on day care regulations in an attempt to make the regulations more rational by eliminating some of the boundaries between service areas. Coordination can also be vertical; that is, the state can encourage, participate in, and direct local level coordination.

In the context of early childhood, coordination has several different meanings. First, coordination refers to the cooperative planning and implementation of new early childhood programs within the existing ecosystem of early childhood programs. New programs must respond to real needs, filling gaps in services or creating necessary new services, not merely supplanting existing programs by offering new ones under a different auspice or through a different funding stream.

Second, coordination refers to the means for offering comprehensive services. Many of the new state-funded prekindergarten programs are aimed specifically at at-risk children, and it is the responsibility of such programs to recognize and make every attempt to meet the children's varied needs, by combining services from a variety of existing sources and by providing directly those that are unavailable in a particular community. The best example of this kind of coordination, which aims to achieve comprehensive service, is the Head Start program, which includes specific program components to meet the education, health, nutrition, and social service needs of its students and their families. The Head Start agency is the facilitator of the delivery of these services and is responsible for providing them either directly or by referral to other agencies.

Third, coordination refers to the combining of services and/or funds from a variety of sources to meet families' needs for full-working-day child care. Three main approaches accomplish this goal. One encourages new programs in public schools to offer full-working-day services. Another approach expands the scope of eligible providers of a prekindergarten program to include agencies that already offer full-day services, such as community-based child care centers. A third way creates a form of before- and after-school care service that meshes with and surrounds the part-day public school program (hence the term *surround care*). And, last but not least, coordination refers to attempts to make the early child ecosystem more of a system—that is, to treat it as a whole and work for greater consistency among its parts in terms of quality of service provided, resources available, and so on.

Ideally, successful coordination requires a certain degree of equality among collaborators, in terms of power, authority, available resources (both human and fiscal), and ability to provide services. Respect for differing perspectives (and for each other as people) is also needed. To succeed, coordination requires a shared goal or at least a real dependence among the collaborators on each other's resources or abilities in order to reach their separate goals. States with well-designed early education programs and strong commitments to their child care systems will obviously be in a much better position to attempt and succeed at coordination. The ultimate goal of coordination is improved services for children (and their families). The call for coordination is being heard and efforts to coordinate have begun. How workable—and effective—these efforts will be is yet to be determined. No provisions have been made to evaluate coordination efforts.

Obstacles to Coordination

Serious obstacles to coordination exist, especially in regard to funding issues. Separate funding streams for separate programs not only produce duplication and inefficiency; they also riddle the early childhood system with inequalities in the allocation of resources. For example, some state-funded half-day prekindergarten programs receive proportionately more funds per child than some full-day child care programs. (The public education system is certainly better funded than the child care system and is likely to remain so.) These inequalities in resources, which reinforce inequality among the coordinators, are not easily overcome.

Different funding sources frequently dictate different administrative auspices for programs for children. Because different administrative units exist to meet different objectives, their program goals and educational philosophy may be very different. The particular focus of the administering state agency often determines program content, funding level, and regulation. For example, education departments characteristically have not emphasized serving families but have focused on the educational needs of children. Human services or welfare departments, on the other hand, have a social services perspective which considers the need for full-day programs and other family needs but which often places less emphasis on the educational content of a program. Because purposes and approaches are different, identifying a shared goal that transcends the differences will foster coordination.

The proliferation of programs with varying funding streams and administrative auspices has had serious repercussions at the local level. Fewer than one-third of states with prekindergarten programs have legislative or regulatory requirements regarding local-level coordination with existing programs. The absence of mandates for local coordination has resulted in competition for space in public schools, for qualified staff, and for eligible children in particular between state-funded public school prekindergarten programs and Head Start agencies. (By contrast, in the past Head Start often forged constructive working partnerships with other agencies around health screening, recruitment of eligible children, and use of public school space.)

Today, public school space is at a premium in many communities. School facilities are not flexible enough to house all the programs that would benefit from being in schools. In some areas schools are faced with increasing enrollments and decreasing capacity. As a result, prekindergarten programs and others—such as school-age child care programs or community arts programs or elder day care—are now vying for space.

In many localities the early childhood community faces a serious crisis in staffing. Credentialed staff are at a premium, and new state-funded programs have resulted in competition for such staff. Most often these new programs are administered by public education agencies. Public school salaries, nearly always higher than those in programs not in public schools, often exceed those salaries by as much as 100 percent. Funding for child care programs is always inadequate to pay salaries competitive with those in state-funded prekindergarten programs. Resentment from the programs losing staff (Head Start, child care centers) impedes coordination efforts at the local level.

Other examples of disjuncture are state and local regulations or licensing requirements that cover one program but not another—or that conflict with each other on the same program feature in different programs, even though those programs provide essentially the same or very similar services. Teacher qualifications and certification constitute still another example of the lack of coordinated policy across state and local agencies. Requiring comparable qualifications of teaching staff across early childhood domains with the goal of working toward equity in both professional certification and salaries requires a coordinated approach across the domains.

A further obstacle to coordination exists in the creation of more and more new programs without reference to those already in operation. The creation of new programs has been fueled not solely by the public good but also by political considerations—there is less interest in expanding or modifying existing programs than there is in creating new ones that can serve as highly visible "feathers" in political caps. While these new programs may serve legitimate needs, they may also exacerbate many of the problems cited above. Existing programs, especially those struggling with irregular or insufficient funding, need to be brought into the process of new program creation at both the planning stages and during implementation.

Coordination at the State Level

Policymakers in several states have gone on record with recommendations for new structures to solve these problems. Governor DiPrete of Rhode Island urged that a child policy coordinator should direct all state activities and programs affecting children. Indiana's secretary of state, Evan Bayh, proposed a six-point plan calling for the establishment of a state Division of Child Care Services to "streamline a patchwork of government agencies now dealing with child care."[3] The Bayh proposal would combine six different state agencies, resulting in "streamlining" and cost efficiency for taxpayers, child care providers, and the agencies themselves.

State coordinating mechanisms take four main forms; any of the forms can be mandated or optional, ongoing or short-term. *Interagency councils* (or task forces, committees, or commissions) generally include state agency heads and are usually appointed by governors, state boards of education, or state legislatures. *Advisory councils* (or committees) generally have broader membership and often include business and civic leaders as well as state agency heads, service providers, and consumers; advisory councils can be "free-standing" or appointed to advise the interagency council. A third form is state *offices of child care* (or *child development*) that are either in governors' offices or within state human service agencies. These offices tend to focus on the child care system and on coordination of the alphabet soup of funding streams that support it (such as WIN, AFDC, JTPA, Title XX/SSBG, Dependent Care Block Grants, and the various state funding streams). The fourth mechanism is not a body, but a more limited *interagency agreement* which covers the sharing of specific resources among state agencies and/or service providers. Many states have agreements between state health and social service departments regarding training, or between the department of education and local Head Start programs regarding recruitment and screening of handicapped preschoolers, or between health departments and Head Start for the provision of health services.

Coordination is much more common on the state level than on the local, probably because there are well-established precedents in every state for limited state-level coordination of early childhood services: All states have coordinating mechanisms or bodies focusing on day care regulations and/or special education.

The incentive for coordination on day care regulations is common sense. Because day care regulations often involve enforcement by various state and local entities and always affect a large number of child care providers throughout a state, wise state administrators involve the regulators and the regulated in the process of regulatory review. Statewide committees review day care regulations and recommend changes. These committees usually have broad representation from state agencies that participate in the regulatory process (buildings, fire, and health) and from "affected parties" (those who are regulated).

In the area of special education, the federal government has provided the states with several financial incentives for coordination. The first was multiyear state Planning Grants for Early Intervention Services. These grants require departments of education to conduct needs assessments and engage in a thorough planning process before implementing new services for handicapped preschoolers. The coordinating bodies created tend to be broadly representative, including many state agencies (education, health, mental health, social services), various program providers (including Head Start), and parents. The second incentive is the Special Education Early Childhood Incentive Grants, designed to encourage states to offer special education to preschoolers. This funding has been available for a number of years, but the appropriation levels increased dramatically in FY 1987 and FY 1988 to enable states to comply with Part H of the Education for the Handicapped Act (PL 99-457), which requires that all states serve handicapped preschoolers by 1990. These special education efforts are good examples of the importance of mandating coordination and of providing financial incentives for it.

Coordinated Planning

Coordination efforts at the state level begin with the planning stage. Governors, state legislatures, and departments of education play a major role in convening groups to participate in planning state initiatives. Participation by representative experts on state-level committees and on advisory committees, councils, and task forces is a first step to achieving the representation of ideas and information that can be crucial to the decision-making process. States that emphasize the importance of representation in this way have an opportunity to model the coordination process for the local communities.

In almost all states at least one, and often two or three state-level coordinating bodies, have responsibility for planning. These groups are composed of representatives from state agencies, and often private agencies, advocacy groups, and parents. The typical procedure is to organize a task force around a single issue: planning the state's new prekindergarten program, or expansion of subsidized day care slots, or special education for preschool children. In an effort to get away from the single-issue approach, Massachusetts has established a Day Care Policy Unit in the Executive Office of Human Services to coordinate the planning of many of these related programs.

A significant example of coordination in the planning process is New Jersey's new (1988) Urban Prekindergarten Program (UPP), a collaboration between two state agencies, the Department of Education and the Department of Human Services. This program is described by its originators as providing a "comprehensive, coordinated array of services. . . ."[4] One of its more innovative features is interagency management:[5]

> *To give guidance to the cooperative, coordinated approach represented in this initiative, the departments will enter into a formal interagency agreement and establish a management team to resolve issues which cross traditional agency responsibilities and jurisdictions.*

Grant funds are to be awarded equally to two eligible providers: local boards of education and local Head Start agencies. New Jersey's initiative represents collaboration in two important areas: administration and financing. First, two state agencies with quite different primary goals agree to work together to administer funds and to oversee the implementation of a jointly sponsored program. Second, local agencies eligible to receive these funds mirror the state agencies' shared task; equal amounts of funding are available to school boards and to Head Start agencies, and school locations are designated as a preferable location for the programs, thus increasing the potential for coordination at the local school building level.

Another function of coordination in the planning stage is to gather data on the need for certain services and on the existing supply of services. Such information, rarely gathered systematically at either the state or local level, may be used for further planning. For example, the Massachusetts Early Childhood Initiative of the state's Education Reform Bill (Chapter 188) requires a yearly needs assessment to be conducted by the Department of Education and local education agencies, in conjunction with local advisory committees composed of day care providers, resource and referral agencies, parents, school personnel, and others.

Nongovernment groups have also taken a leading role in working toward coordination in some states. The Kansas Association for the Education of Young Children (AEYC) collected data statewide in order to make recommendations on both state prekindergarten programs and state-subsidized day care. The Kansas AEYC meets monthly, has a lobbyist on staff, and takes an active policymaking role in the state. A university-based group in Montana was awarded a foundation grant to conduct a child care needs assessment and coordinate a network of early childhood programs. And in Texas, the United Way has organized the Child Care Working Group with over one hundred members from state agencies, child care providers, and the Texas AEYC to address the child care crisis in the state by stimulating local involvement in expanding and improving child care in Texas.

If a representative planning group is put together at the beginning of the legislative process, and if the public is assured of participation through hearings and a comment period, a state early childhood proposal can be firmly grounded on input from the many sectors that have an interest in its successful implementation. Coordination at this early stage can make an important difference when the bill or new program reaches the implementation stage.

Coordination in Implementation

To achieve continuity of care for children requires not only coordination in planning but also coordination in implementation. Real continuity in the child's day-to-day experience requires communication among providers, transportation between program sites, and, ideally, compatibility of educational philosophy among programs. Some state agencies charged with implementation of programs are developing interagency councils, task forces, committees, and commissions similar to those created for planning. These groups, which may be mandated by law, usually consist of heads of state agencies or their designees. Interagency groups deal with cross-cutting issues, including special education, licensing, teacher certification, and child care. Increasingly, states are establishing these mechanisms within governors' offices to coordinate services across all early childhood program areas or within departments of human services.

New York created the Council on Children and Families to coordinate services to children and families across service areas. The council, part of the governor's office, recently studied early childhood services in New York and made recommendations to the governor for coordination and expansion of prekindergarten and child care services. Members have formed the Interagency Work Group to look at integrating the state prekindergarten program with subsidized child care.

Alaska's Tri-Department (Health and Human Services, Education, and Community and Regional Affairs) Committee on Young
Children meets quarterly and holds an annual conference. The
committee coordinates services and discusses ongoing issues such
as training, regulatory changes, and services to low-income families. It also publishes a newsletter and a monthly list of licensed
providers. Similarly, the Arizona Office for Children formed a
group of representatives from the Departments of Education,
Health, Economic Security, and Commerce, the governor's office,
private corporations, and the United Way that meets regularly to
work on improving coordination of children's services.

Ideally, such coordination should be mandated in the program
legislation itself. However, in some instances informal coordination
is officially suggested. For example, in the absence of a formal
statewide coordinating policy, Texas has encouraged an informal
sharing of resources between public schools and other agencies:
The governor, in a letter to providers, urged cooperation at the
local level in support of the state's position encouraging contracting
between public schools and Title XX/SSBG child care providers.

Efforts at the Local Level

Coordination is particularly critical at the local level—where the
child is, in the community where services are actually made
available. Coordination can take a variety of forms. For example,
different sources of funds can be combined and allocated under
the auspice of a single organization. Or resources such as space,
funding, and personnel from different sectors or auspices can be
combined in a cooperative approach. Such cooperation will prove
especially useful in meeting families' child care demands if the
trend toward more part-day programs in public schools continues.

When coordination does occur at the local level, it is likely to be
a direct result of state mandates. The degree to which coordination
is mandated varies greatly from state to state. Most commonly,
local school districts and other agencies applying for state prekindergarten grants must show evidence of unmet local need. Some
grantees, including those in Illinois, Oregon, Vermont, and Massachusetts, must also demonstrate that cooperative efforts are in
place to prevent duplication of services and to enhance use of local
resources. But generally, there are few assurances that the full
range of early childhood programs and service providers are represented on the local coordinating committee or have been considered in the local proposals submitted to the state for selection; nor

are there provisions for redressing exclusionary practices in regard to the composition of local coordinating bodies.

Examples of Linked State and Local-Level Coordination Efforts

A few states have quite detailed and specific requirements for coordination at both the state and the local level. Several examples of such required coordination follow.

South Carolina In 1980 the governor of South Carolina created the Interagency Coordinating Council on Early Childhood Development and Education and an Interagency Advisory Committee to the council. The council includes the governor and state agency heads and the committee chair; the committee includes 27 members, who are broadly representative of state agencies, higher education, professional groups concerned with programs and services for young children, day care and Head Start, legislators, parents, and citizens. The committee is responsible for identifying issues, establishing priorities, and making policy recommendations. The council guides policy and coordinates resources and funding across agencies. The council and committee engaged in a four-year planning process that resulted in the inclusion of a prekindergarten program in the Educational Improvement Act of 1984.

The prekindergarten program in South Carolina is administered through the Department of Education. Only school districts may apply, although subcontracts are allowed. In applying for funds, the school district must consult with a local early childhood development and education committee, *if one exists,* for planning, maximizing resources, and avoiding duplication. If such a committee does not exist, the district is required to review the local resources itself and to avoid duplication.

Florida In Florida coordination between the Department of Public Instruction and the Department of Social and Rehabilitation Services, which oversees child care, has been mandated by law since 1974. The Child Care Coordination Council, created as a result of that law, was the basis for a state task force that also included advocates, early childhood education professionals, the Head Start community, and the child care provider community. The task force was a major force in the passage of the Prekindergarten Early Intervention Program in 1986.

The 1986 legislation created both state and local-level coordination mechanisms. An 11-member State Advisory Council is appointed to advise the superintendent of Public Instruction on implementing the pilot program, assessing the need for expansion, and planning for expansion. The 11 include 3 appointed by the governor to represent Head Start, subsidized child care providers and nonsubsidized providers; 4 appointed by the superintendent of Public Instruction representing elementary school principals, the state Bureau of Special Education, public school teachers certified in early childhood education, and early childhood advocacy groups; and 2 appointed by the secretary of the Department of Social and Rehabilitation Services, representing health services and child welfare. Finally, the president of the senate and speaker of the house each appoint one member. Administratively, the council is part of the Department of Public Instruction; its activities are funded ($50,000 in FY 1988).

Local school districts (which may subcontract) must create a district interagency coordinating council that cooperates in the development, implementation, and evaluation of the prekindergarten program. The 11-member district councils are appointed by local school boards and must include a parent of a child in the program; the program director; a school board member; a representative of an agency serving handicapped children; 3 service providers (one each from Head Start, subsidized child care, and a private program); 1 local child advocate; and 2 members representing social, medical, dental, or transportation services; and 1 other member. The council must assist the district in developing the proposal and must sign off on the submitted proposal. It is also responsible for coordinating children's services in the county (educational, social, health, child care, and others). Beginning on July 1, 1988, each council is required to submit annual reports to the state council and the superintendent of Public Instruction on the district's progress in implementing the prekindergarten program, the results of the district council's evaluation identifying the most successful program components, and its recommendations to the state Advisory Council concerning local and statewide implementation of the prekindergarten program.

Washington In the state of Washington the business community, through the Washington Business Roundtable, and the superintendent of Public Instruction each commissioned reports on early childhood education. The governor identified early childhood education as one of his top priorities. Washington has contributed state funds to Head Start since 1968 and has a state Head Start Advisory Committee. From these various convergent interests, Washington created a new prekindergarten program that is essentially an expansion of Head Start: the Early Childhood Assistance Act of 1985. Even though other early childhood actors (beyond

Head Start) in the state played almost no role in developing the legislation, they are offered a role in developing guidelines for implementing these new programs through the 30-member state early childhood advisory committee.

Direct contracts are permitted with school districts, Head Start programs, nonsectarian day care centers and preschools, and newly formed, community-based collaborations. Evidence of linkages with other services is recommended. All applicants are required to develop transition plans for children moving from the prekindergarten program into kindergarten. A joint planning committee for the transition effort must be established that includes all the public schools in the area the program serves. These schools must acknowledge in writing that the transition plan is in place.

Illinois　The prekindergarten program in Illinois sprang from education reform; it was proposed in the report of the state's Commission on Improving Elementary and Secondary Education and was legislated in an education reform package in 1985. There was very little involvement of the early childhood community in the development or passage of the bill until the last minute; as a consequence of that involvement, a provision was inserted that allowed districts to hire as teachers not only those credentialed in early childhood education but also those qualified under the licensing code as administrators of day care centers. Although it is somewhat illogical given that administrative qualifications are not necessarily related to teaching ability, this compromise does provide a route for certain experienced day care staff (without traditional teaching credentials) to access the higher salaries of the public schools.

Evidence of local coordination with other providers of early childhood services is required in proposals from school districts. Linkages with Head Start are specifically mentioned. School districts are permitted to subcontract with local agencies for part or all of the program. Most subcontracts are for the required screening or for transportation. In a very few cases (10 programs in small school districts), the educational component was subcontracted to a Head Start program.

Massachusetts　Early childhood advocates (including day care and Head Start) are credited with a strong behind-the-scenes role in the passage of Massachusetts' Early Childhood Initiative. In addition to the creation of a state Advisory Council on Early Childhood Education that advises the Department of Education on all aspects of implementation, it has subcommittees on specific issues, such as that on Staff Requirements and Staffing Patterns, which has proposed new teacher credentials for Nursery-3 and for

Young Children with Special Needs ages 3–7. The program is administered within the Department of Education by a newly created Office of Early Childhood Education. Three kinds of efforts are funded: programs for three- and four-year-olds, enhanced kindergarten and transitional first grades, and programs using creative approaches to combine early childhood education and child care.

Although only school districts may apply for funds (with subcontracts allowed), very specific local coordination is required. A local advisory council must be convened that includes a teacher, a parent, a representative of the local resource and referral organization, and others concerned with the care and education of children in the community. The local advisory council must develop and sign off on the proposal submitted by the school district. Applications must detail local needs, agreements with other service providers, how the program will serve children with special needs, how families will be involved, and how the program will coordinate with local elementary schools to ensure continuity through kindergarten and the primary grades.

Oregon   In Oregon the Department of Education organized the Early Childhood Initiative Committee, which has broad representation from the preschool, day care, and Head Start community and from the legislature. The committee developed legislation for prekindergartens for four-year-olds and a parent education program that was widely supported by education and early childhood groups. It was passed in 1987. The legislation creates an Advisory Committee to the Department of Education that includes state agency staff (the Department of Education's Early Childhood unit and Human Services Children's Services Division), Head Start, school districts, community colleges, and others interested in young children. The Advisory Committee develops program regulations.

School districts may apply for funds; subcontracts with other agencies are permitted. Head Start grantees and other nonsectarian organizations may also apply directly. The legislation specifies that funds may be used for establishing or expanding programs but may not be used for programs that supplant any existing Head Start programs. To avoid duplication and maximize local resources, applicants are required to coordinate their services with existing Head Start programs and other services to young children.

District-Level Coordination

Whether state-mandated or not, local-level coordination efforts necessarily start at the community level with personnel who are knowledgeable about resources in the community and who are connected with local experts. In California county child care councils or resource and referral agencies provide local-level coordination and, through their state networks, present local issues for state-level policy consideration. As noted earlier, in Massachusetts local advisory councils are mandated in that state's prekindergarten legislation. These councils, composed of representatives from all sectors concerned with young children, are charged with conducting community-wide needs assessments. Such local advisory councils are a beginning step in developing a process for rational decision making at the local level, before new or expanded services are proposed for state authorization and funding.

In some school districts coordination efforts deal only with funding, and then only in certain programs. In Greenville County, South Carolina, the district offers a full-working-day program that is partly funded by Social Service Block Grant Funds (Title XX/SSBG) and partly by local school district funds. But, although the program sits side by side with a half-day state-funded preschool program, no organized attempt is made to ascertain the employment status of parents whose children are in the prekindergarten program or to assist them with child care arrangements, beyond advising parents of the existence of the two full-working-day child development centers. This is a clear example of a lack of coherence in policy: The district partially coordinates funding (only for its full-working-day program), but information and substantive help for parents is not yet coordinated within the district's own programs. However, good relationships exist among some district personnel and the early childhood community outside the public schools. The principal who supervises the full-working-day program is very involved with the early childhood community through participation in a local training advisory group and in a local planning group developing a child care resource and referral capacity.

Other districts provide "one-stop shopping" for parents by providing a wide variety of services for young children. The Pomona (California) Unified School District offers a number of early childhood programs and parent support services, including half-day state preschool programs, children's centers (full-working-day and some evening and weekend child care), Head Start, school-age child care supported by state funds and parent fees, comprehensive programs for teen parents and their infants, respite care for children at risk of abuse or neglect, resource and referral, and the Alternative Payment Program (a publicly funded child care vendor voucher system that uses private child care providers). District counselors conduct service intake centrally and attempt to match family needs to program openings among the district's programs. Some programs are handled by the resource and referral agency, Child Care Information Service (CCIS). Pomona's CCIS director is a member of the local AEYC and maintains a healthy relationship with all nonpublic school providers.

The Palm Beach (Florida) County School Board offers another example of coordination of both funding and services. The district operates full-working-day programs for children of migrant agricultural and fishing industry workers, using various federal funds (Chapter I/migrant) and state migrant funds. The district also serves as one of three county agencies designated to administer Title XX/SSBG subsidized child care funds, operates three full-working-day programs itself, and contracts with a number of community agencies to provide child care services. This brings the district into a cooperative relationship with community programs and helps build bridges between the schools and private providers.

Community-Wide Coordination Efforts

Public schools can also be part of larger, community-wide planning and implementation efforts that are not necessarily stimulated by the passage of prekindergarten legislation, as in the following examples we found in study sites around the country.

In Dallas, Texas, the Child Care Partnership brought together business groups, religious leaders, and private and public schools—all those representing institutions with an interest in young children's care and education—to plan and coordinate the funding for child care at the local level. This group evolved from a mayor's task force on child care.

In 1986 a $5 million dollar tax levy proposed by the Seattle Public Schools to build 14 child care centers in elementary schools throughout the city was approved by over 70 percent of the voters. These centers are to be operated by community agencies and are designed for about 50 children, infant through school age. The ages of children to be served in each site will be determined by the local community, and public child care subsidies are to be an integral part of the programs so as to ensure access to families from all income levels.

The Palm Beach County (Florida) Children's Services Council was created and funded by referendum in 1986–1987. Funding was provided by a countywide property tax levy. The first year, this levy made more than $8 million available for coordinating and expanding the funding base for all children's services in the county. Membership on the council includes the county's public schools.

Conclusion

In summary, coordination is necessary because of the proliferation of programs and funding streams and because children and their families have multiple needs. Coordination can facilitate administrative efficiency and reduce service duplication. Coordination helps head off competition among service providers by establishing mechanisms for dialogue on some of the issues that are sticking points, such as teacher credentials and salaries. Shared resources may result in increased services to greater numbers of children. Formal coordination has the potential to facilitate the provision of comprehensive services for children and families. Most importantly, coordination in planning can integrate new programs and funding streams into the existing system.

The preceding examples of coordination from the states and some of the case study sites share certain important characteristics:

- They attempt to build bridges among different domains because services needed by young children and families cut across many domains.
- They recognize that children and families may be eligible for more than one program or service.
- They establish a context for local coordination at the level of the individual program, and they use local resources to achieve continuity of care in order to make the most of the educational opportunities provided to children.

Unfortunately, such examples are more the exception than the rule. In many, if not most, instances, coordination remains "pro forma," rather than a process that leads to joint action and shared resources. In general, truly collaborative resource sharing occurs rarely among state early childhood programs and the agencies charged with managing them. However, important links have been established in some states across agencies, including those in the child care and education communities. The Massachusetts experience, while not free of problems in implementation, illustrates the important role of local-level advisory groups in the coordination process.

Coordination is more common between state agencies that must work with the same client, because it facilitates their serving the client more effectively. Interagency collaboration between WIN and AFDC is an example of this "interdependence." Similarly, Head Start programs, schools, and health departments often work together under both state and local agreements. The Head Start programs receive screening and remedial services from schools and health departments; in turn, the programs provide at least 15 to 20 percent of the states' high-risk preschool population with comprehensive early childhood programs and also provide free services to handicapped children (in some cases, to a significant number of them).

Mandating coordination and providing financial incentives can play an important role in getting various players to work together. The federal government sometimes mandates coordination as a requirement for states to receive federal funds, as in the case of special education. Whether or not coordination is mandated, managing an array of programs in a coordinated delivery system requires leadership at the top of the administrative ladder. Governors, key legislators, and heads of state boards of education can play a major role in shaping legislation to build coordination between and among the various agencies concerned with early childhood, so that services provided are based on the child care and other needs of children eligible for state programs.

The Human Factor

While the mechanisms of coordination are structures (councils, committees, task forces), the goals of coordination affect human beings—children and families. A critical human factor that greatly contributes to the success or failure of coordination efforts is the actors who do the coordinating within the structures. Coordination at any level (state or local) requires respect and trust and other cooperative attitudes. Respect cannot be mandated. State interagency coordination efforts are more likely to succeed when the human beings who attempt them develop a sense of trust and mutual respect—when the collaborators have known each other for some time (or spend the time necessary to get to know each other). When they expect to continue in their roles they are more likely to have a stake in the success of both the process and its outcome.

The ultimate goal of coordination efforts is to make the most appropriate services easily available to all children and families who need them. One can imagine, in an ideal world:

- A wide variety of early childhood services existing all over the state.

- A transportation system in place, so that families can get to those services.
- A system of referral centers that actively seek out families, help them determine their own needs, and then match those needs with available services.
- An integrated funding system that supports reasonable program quality and family choice.

This ideal is a vision of what the early childhood system could and should be. As the importance of coordination is more widely recognized, and as states and localities have more experience in the processes of coordination, the early childhood system could gradually move toward becoming more like the scenario we postulate as ideal.

Recommendations

- Require both state- and local-level coordination and tie them together. Apparently the best way to make coordination occur at the state level among agencies and programs is to require it. Translating this to the local level can be done by mandating that it occur, by offering a working model, by providing technical assistance and funding, and by monitoring compliance. The more successful efforts are those where the state coordinating mechanism is clearly spelled out and the local one must mirror the state's.
- Ensure broad representation in the planning process. Day care providers, Head Start staff, and other early childhood professionals, legislators, the business and charitable sectors, academicians, child advocates, and parents should be among those constituencies invited to serve on state and local planning bodies.
- Specify and define exactly what is expected at both the state and local level at every stage of the process. Who appoints? What constituencies are represented? What authority does the coordinating body have over what areas?
- At the local level, provisions should be made for communities to assess their resources and needs as an initial step in the state's planning process. The state's plans will be more likely to address appropriately the needs of its many communities if local groups participate in planning. Local participation may prevent duplication and head off competition among local service providers.

- Clearly delineate administration and management of coordination on the local level. Responsibility for administration, which would include managing multiple funding streams and making maximum use of local resources, could be assumed by school districts, local child care resource and referral agencies, or other community agencies, either jointly or separately with built-in collaborative requirements.
- Make funding contingent on evidence of coordination. Clearly, the state's most effective instrument for shaping local practice is funding. Award or withhold funding based on evidence of collaboration. This is the time-honored approach of the federal government when it seeks to ensure certain practices in states.
- Distribute state prekindergarten funds to a range of community organizations. This will increase the supply of good-quality early childhood programs across service domains, in those settings where many children will already be enrolled who are eligible for state funding. It will also help equalize the status of the various groups participating in the coordination process.
- Fund the coordination effort itself. At the federal, state, and local level, coordination requires an investment of time and ongoing effort by coordinators which should be recognized and financially supported, as it is in Florida, New Jersey, and Massachusetts.
- To promote community-wide collaboration, the sharing and joint use of resources should be encouraged. For example, a school district could open its training sessions to all early childhood providers in the district or co-sponsor local conferences with other early childhood organizations.

Endnotes

1. Committee for Economic Development (1987). *Children in need*. New York: Author.
2. Porter, T. (1988). *Lives on hold*. New York: Child Care, Inc.
3. Bayh urging creation of office to coordinate child care services. *Indiana Star*, July 11, 1988.
4. Cooperman, S., and D. Altman (October 5, 1988). Personal communication. New Jersey Department of Education.
5. Cooperman, S., and D. Altman (May 1988). Excerpted and adapted from *Prekindergarten for urban children: A pilot program in New Jersey* (PTM 700.61). Trenton, N.J.: New Jersey State Department of Education.

Chapter 8

THE TEACHERS

Only high-quality programs, not mediocre ones, deliver the positive long-term gains for children suggested by the various longitudinal studies of early childhood programs for disadvantaged young children.[1] The quality of daily life for children who attend early childhood programs is determined in large part by the teachers in those programs. Teachers are the key to quality in any program for children.

The simplest definition of quality in an early childhood program is a small number of children with enough teachers who know what they are doing. A more thorough description is offered by Deborah Phillips and Carolee Howes in their excellent review of research on quality in child care:[2]

> *The research evidence is quite clear. Smaller groups appear to facilitate constructive caregiver behavior and positive developmental outcomes for children. . . . There is ample evidence that specialized [child-related] training is associated with good quality care. . . . Other evidence suggests that more education is better than less and that the amount and nature of a caregiver's preparation may augment each other such that more highly educated adults who have also received specialized training may be the most proficient.*

In this chapter the term *teacher* rather than *caregiver* will be used to refer to all staff members who work with young children. The terms *head teacher* and *paraprofessional* (or *aide*) will be used to designate these more specific roles. The head teacher is responsible for the whole classroom. Sometimes two teachers work together equally as a team; both are referred to here as *head teachers*. Paraprofessionals are the assistant teachers or teaching

---

Note: This chapter was authored principally by Kathy Modigliani.

aides who work with children under the supervision of head teachers.

To understand the crucial contribution that teachers make to the quality of public school-operated early childhood programs, a number of questions need to be answered: What qualifications are held by the teachers who work with the children in public early childhood programs? How do qualifications vary among the different states and different types of programs? How do teachers respond to their jobs? What can school districts do to attract and keep good teachers and to support them in doing their best? This chapter will answer these questions.

Teacher Qualifications and Program Quality

As noted, research about early childhood program quality suggests that the most proficient teachers of young children are those with a college degree which includes specific child-related training, for example, early childhood education and/or child development. Previous teaching experience is widely believed by early childhood professionals to be an important qualification for teachers. Some studies have proven teaching experience to be important, but more complex analysis is needed to understand the precise contribution of previous experience to quality; for example, what kinds of experience are most useful for which staff positions.[3]

The research on program quality shows clearly that teachers of young children need to understand child development and education in relation to the specific ages of children in their class. Teachers with coursework and student teaching related only to older elementary-aged children are *not* adequately prepared to be the head teacher in a prekindergarten classroom. Further, infant or toddler head teachers should have specialized training for that age group. States and school district policymakers set hiring standards for teachers to support program quality. Typically, teacher certification requirements include educational degrees, specific coursework, and supervised student-teaching experience.

Education and Certification

States and districts use certification in early childhood to ensure that teachers have specified coursework and supervised student teaching experience. But the exact requirements for such certification vary greatly among the states. In some an early childhood certificate signifies specific prekindergarten training; in others it signifies kindergarten and early elementary training with no specific prekindergarten work.

There is a good deal of activity among the states in revising and expanding teacher qualifications for those working with young children. Much variety exists among state standards. Usually, the agency regulating child care centers and private preschools has separate teacher qualifications from the department of education standards. A number of states have revised or are revising their teacher certification requirements for public school teachers working with preschool-aged children. Some education departments have developed a separate early childhood education certificate; others have added an early childhood endorsement or specialization to their elementary teaching certificate. Still other states have developed special requirements for teachers in their publicly funded early childhood programs by combining department of education teacher qualifications with child care staff qualifications. Sometimes an entirely new set of standards is developed, based on specialized early childhood education and child development coursework and experience conducive to the types of early childhood programs the state develops.

When major differences exist between DOE certification and child care licensing requirements for teachers, and there is no alternative way for child care staff to meet DOE standards, it is difficult for the state to contract with community organizations to provide early childhood programs. South Carolina, for example, mandates no education or experience requirements for child care teachers; directors may have either coursework or experience. In contrast, teachers in state-funded prekindergarten programs must have DOE teacher certification. This may explain why there are no subcontracted state-funded prekindergarten programs even though it is permitted in the legislation.

Teacher Certification Requirements in State-Funded Prekindergarten Programs Most of the states funding prekindergarten programs have established qualifications for their head teachers.[4] These requirements range from general (such as a bachelor's degree in any field) to specific (such as extensive coursework in early childhood education accompanied by student teaching with children younger than eight). Two states do not require head teachers in their prekindergarten programs to have state teacher certification. In Kentucky the state Department of Public Instruction has appointed a committee to develop certification standards. In Vermont prekindergarten programs (which are not limited to public school operation) are required to be licensed as child care centers and must meet those education and training requirements;

state teacher certification is not generally required, although the public school-operated prekindergarten programs may require it.

Teacher qualification requirements for state-funded prekindergarten programs tend to reflect the regulations governing teacher qualifications in the various eligible delivery systems. States which limit their prekindergarten programs to public schools (do not permit subcontracts or direct contracts with other agencies) are very likely to require bachelor's degrees and teaching certificates for their head teachers. States which *do* permit schools to subcontract, and/or allow direct contracts with other community agencies, are more likely to have devised alternative methods of meeting teacher education and certification requirements that share some similarities with the regulations governing teacher qualification in the eligible programs (Head Start or child care licensing standards). However, many states accept teaching certificates with concentrations in areas other than early childhood. Typically, specific early childhood certification is required only if this type of certification was available in the state prior to the enactment of the prekindergarten program. Few states have modified teacher credentialing to include early childhood certificates as a result of establishing a prekindergarten program. One exception is Massachusetts, which in developing program standards for its prekindergarten program, created a Nursery–Grade 3 Certificate that revised the former Kindergarten–Grade 3 Certificate. The new N–3 certificate also incorporates the requirements of Teacher of Young Children (ages 3–7) with Special Needs.

States rarely establish certification requirements for paraprofessionals working in prekindergarten programs. Maryland has unusually high requirements for aides in its prekindergarten program: a high school diploma or GED and prior work experience with children from birth to age nine, and 64 hours of early childhood education coursework (completed or in process). These requirements for aides in prekindergarten programs are equivalent to the requirements under day care licensing for child care directors of centers enrolling up to 20 children.

States with prekindergarten programs that extend beyond public schools (those that allow subcontracting and/or direct contracting) have usually developed alternative teacher qualifications in addition to DOE credentialing. States which permit Head Start agencies to operate state-funded prekindergarten programs generally require that teachers either meet Head Start qualifications or possess a state teaching credential. For example, Michigan allowed public schools to subcontract only to Head Start programs run by the public schools until 1988, when eligibility was broadened to include other nonprofit community agencies. One of the ways to qualify to be a head teacher in Michigan's prekindergarten program is to meet the Head Start staff qualification requirement: a Child Development Associate credential (CDA).

These alternative routes to teacher qualification are somewhat similar to staff qualifications under day care licensing. In most states one of many options to qualify as a teacher under day care licensing is to possess a valid teaching certificate, but much lower qualification levels are allowable. Typically, the qualification options include credentials ranging from a high school diploma (or GED) to a bachelor's degree. There is more similarity between prekindergarten teacher qualifications and center director or administrator qualifications under day care licensing.

Florida funds two prekindergarten programs and requires different teacher qualifications in each. The migrant program, which does not usually subcontract, requires Board of Education certification (either early childhood education or elementary). The Chapter 228 prekindergartens, in which subcontracting is encouraged, permit supervisors and teachers to meet child care licensing requirements.

Illinois permits teachers to meet either school code qualifications for an early childhood teacher certificate (a bachelor's degree with early childhood education coursework and supervised teaching in prekindergarten) or child care licensing requirements for supervisory personnel. A child care director (supervisor) must be at least 21 years old, have a high school diploma (or GED), and meet any one of the following requirements: (1) two years of college with 18 semester hours in child development; (2) one year of college with 10 semester hours in child development, be working toward the second year of college and the additional 8 hours of credit, and have two years of experience in nursery school, kindergarten, or licensed child care center; (3) a CDA credential and two years experience; or (4) a bachelor's degree in early childhood education or child development.

California is unusual in requiring uniform staff qualifications for all state-contracted programs through the DOE's Office of Child Development, whether in the public schools or in other agencies. All teaching staff in state-funded prekindergarten programs and subsidized child care are required to hold a permanent or provisional Children's Center Permit.

State-funded prekindergarten programs which permit community agencies to operate programs usually offer an alternative other than a teaching credential. The alternative route for teacher qualification is similar to that of Head Start and/or supervisor (director) qualifications under child care licensing. Even so, public school districts operating state-funded prekindergartens are very likely to require bachelor's degrees and teaching certificates.

District Requirements   Nearly three-quarters of all school districts surveyed required their early childhood head teachers (in prekindergarten programs of all types including state-funded prekindergartens) to hold bachelor's degrees. Even when bachelor's degrees were not required, many teachers had them; in fact, many held master's degrees. Half the districts reported that their head teachers were required to hold early childhood certification, with the most early childhood certified teachers in subsidized child care programs (72 percent) and the least in high school nursery schools (13 percent). In 77 percent of districts the only qualification required for aides or paraprofessionals was a high school diploma. Aides were seldom required to have any certification.[5]

Case Study Observations   Our site observations added to the evidence that good training contributes to good teaching. Inappropriately prepared teachers tended to rely heavily on structured curriculum materials and appeared to have difficulty with classroom management. Untrained aides appeared able to do a good job when they were supervised by competent, well-trained head teachers and had effective in-service training.

In communities lacking enough qualified teachers to staff prekindergarten programs, some districts have been forced to meet only minimum standards in order to fill open positions—or even to lower their education and/or certification requirements. In two cases where standards had been lowered, experienced teachers commented on the resulting threat to program quality.

Previous Teaching Experience

Most state-funded prekindergarten programs do not require teachers to have any previous experience beyond a supervised student-teaching practicum. Child care licensing standards, on the other hand, are much more likely to recognize the value of experience as valid teacher preparation and require experience and experiential-based training (such as the CDA credential). Child care licensing is also far more likely to substitute specific years of work experience with young children for educational attainment. The District Survey confirms that only child care programs require previous teaching experience for head teachers or aides. Fortunately, previous experience was common in other program types even when it was not required. In fact, 52 percent of programs of all types reported that at least half their current staff, when they were hired, had *both* early childhood certification and at least one year of experience with children under five.

As noted above, we do not yet understand the exact contribution of particular types of previous experience for different teaching roles, and the relationship between education and various types of previous experience. Based on the Case Studies, it appears that one consequence of inappropriate experience is inappropriate methods; that is, it is hard for teachers who have taught older children to "unlearn" methods that are developmentally inappropriate for younger children. Notwithstanding inconclusive research evidence, the Case Studies reinforce the wisdom of practice which strongly suggests that quality teachers are those with both child-related education and direct experience with young children.

The challenge for states and districts at this time is to develop teacher hiring requirements that recognize the value of both child-related education and previous experience so that the quality of teaching in prekindergarten programs will be good enough to benefit the children enrolled in them.

Policies Related to Recruitment and Retention

The ability to attract and keep good teachers is critical to any school's capacity to provide high-quality programs. Young children need good teachers who are committed to their work, as do children of any age. Administrators need a stable, competent work force that they can count on, so as not to waste hiring and training resources on employees who quickly resign. Parents need teachers they come to know and trust. And teachers need jobs that offer them a viable career where they can teach to their satisfaction.

The field of early childhood education is now experiencing severe teacher shortages in some communities. Do public schools face a shortage of qualified teachers? The answer varies by community and by program type. Some programs have numerous qualified applicants for every teaching job, as well as contented teachers who stay in their jobs for years. Other programs face a constant exodus of teachers. Some programs were forced to reduce their hiring qualifications or to offer unusually high salaries and otherwise accommodate a tight labor market.

What attracts good teachers and builds their commitment to perform at their best? This study found that salaries and benefits were important predictors of success in recruitment and retention. Besides compensation, other related factors were those which promote the teacher's ability to perform well: autonomy, class size and ratio, work schedules, and other working conditions.

Salaries

Even though 93 percent of all public school prekindergarten teachers, across all program types in the District Survey, were district employees, only 75 percent were paid on the same scale as other teachers in their districts. Occasionally when salaries were lower, the education and certification requirements were correspondingly lower than for other district teachers, but more often they were comparable or identical. The frequency of differential pay varied significantly by program type. Across all types of programs, those which tended to pay all teachers on the same scale were Chapter I prekindergartens, state-funded prekindergarten, parent education programs, and high school nursery schools. Special education teachers are often paid higher salaries.

Just over two-thirds of the locally funded prekindergartens paid standard district salaries, but only about one-third of the parent-fee programs and only one-quarter of the subsidized child care programs paid district-level salaries. Although some public school early childhood teachers are paid less than other teachers employed by their districts, they are usually paid more than teachers in other early childhood programs in their communities. In general, because of higher salaries, public school early childhood programs have correspondingly fewer problems in hiring and keeping qualified staff than other early childhood programs.

A clear relationship between pay level and funding source emerged from the District Survey. Programs funded by tax revenues were more likely to pay salaries close to or equal to those for K–12 and to require similarly qualified teachers. Head Start salaries and hiring requirements tended to be lower than those in other publicly funded programs. Programs funded by parents' fees paid the lowest salaries.

Average annual salaries for beginning teachers with bachelor's degrees in 10-month programs ranged from $12,480 for parent-fee programs to over $16,000 for state-funded and Chapter I prekindergartens. Teachers with master's degrees and five years experience were paid about $3,000 to 5,000 more, depending on program type. Teachers in 12-month programs were paid little more than the 10-month teachers, usually less than $2,000 more.

Aides or paraprofessionals in public school early childhood programs were paid low hourly wages. The highest annual wages for paraprofessionals were paid by the subsidized child care programs—an average of $7,055 for 28 hours per week, 48 weeks per year. Annual wages in other program types ranged from $2,793 (for 15 hours per week, 33 weeks) to $5,742 (for 28 hours per week, 44 weeks). While it should be noted that most of these jobs were part time and part year, most aides receive wages below poverty level.[6]

The Case Studies, which looked at the public school programs in their community contexts, showed that even when public school prekindergarten salaries were significantly lower than those of other district teachers, they were at the high end of those in the rest of the early childhood community. Although the relatively high public school salaries usually assure that a district has few problems attracting or keeping prekindergarten teachers, recruitment and retention of teachers is influenced by local conditions—for example, the supply of qualified (usually credentialed) teachers, the unemployment rate in the community, and the reputation of the district's programs.

One community offered this dramatic illustration of how relative these differences can be:

> The child care salaries in the district are about 10 percent lower than the K–12 pay scale, even though the child care teachers work 11 months instead of 10. In turn, the district's Head Start and state prekindergarten salaries for nine months were 20 percent lower than the public school child care salaries, but "they still make more than twice what other nonpublic preschool teachers earn."

The wage expectations of these teachers have been influenced by the traditionally low wages paid to early childhood teachers.[7] Sometimes prekindergarten teachers were satisfied with their pay, even though it was less than the K–12 pay, because they compared themselves with early childhood teachers in the community rather than the other teachers in their school systems. Twice in the Case Studies, we heard administrators justify lower early childhood salaries in terms of their "easier working conditions"—specifically, the fewer children and higher staff ratios. We also heard early childhood teachers take their lower salaries for granted; they implied that they did not deserve as much as the teachers in the higher grades or that equitable pay was simply impossible. One teacher mentioned, in complaining about her salary, "the union [for K–12 teachers] has not been in touch with us." She had not approached the union either. These teachers have internalized society's low regard for early childhood teaching to the extent that they neither advocate on their own behalf nor expect anyone else to.

In the Case Studies, programs funded by parents had usually set their fees to approximate "the market rate" in their community for the various services they offered (child care, nursery school). That is to say, they tried to remain similar in cost to the community programs providing the same service—and they suffered similar recruitment and retention problems. Turnover rates were notably high in these programs. Clearly, the market rate in a community is usually not high enough to support a good program.[8]

In some cases, the district's commitment to a parent-funded program was less than to its tax-funded, mandated programs. It appeared that pressure to bring the child care teachers into the district's standard pay scale might cause administrators to close the program rather than subsidize parents' fees.

Even in middle-income communities, administrators assumed that they had to keep parents' fees low. Some parents in these programs would support higher fees if they understood the negative impact on quality from keeping fees so low. Consider the following two cases, where fees were set in line with nearby community programs:

> When parents in one program were informed at a parents meeting about the teachers' salaries and benefits, they were appalled. They vowed to do some serious fund-raising and also clearly realized that this alone would not solve the problem. Some volunteered to pay higher fees, others wanted to advocate for more public support, but all agreed that wages should be increased.

> The director of another parent-fee funded program regretted teachers' low salaries and lack of benefits but assumed that additional "dollars could not be taken away from education [K–12 education]" and that parents' fee levels were already "overwhelming."

But the fees were not overwhelming. Cost was *not* cited as a problem by these parents; in fact, they were satisfied with the fees (which were average for the community), even though a number of them were blue-collar workers and/or single mothers. One parent volunteered that the program was a "bargain." Another felt that it was "far better" than other programs that cost more.

The consequences of the low compensation in this program were costly in their own way. The director reported that "hiring staff is a kind of a nightmare." Teachers were fairly upset about their lack of benefits and very upset about their salaries ($5.00/hour base pay), which were half those of the K–12 teachers. Another mentioned that she was hoping to get married so that she could afford to continue working at a job that paid no benefits. Many of the teachers agreed that they worked to "get out of the house," not out of economic necessity. Such salaries do not attract teachers whose economic necessity is greater.

In both these cases, fees were kept low because of the unquestioned assumption that parents could not pay more, when, in fact, middle- and upper-income parents may have been willing to pay higher fees to ensure that teachers were equitably paid. Higher wages allow a program to recruit qualified staff members who will tend to stay in their jobs.

Benefits

As with salaries, fringe benefits are generally better in public schools than in other early childhood programs, but 15 percent of the districts did not provide their early childhood teachers with benefits comparable to those of their other teachers. Benefit levels corresponded to salary levels; programs which pay relatively high salaries usually provide good benefits. Programs with low salaries tend to offer fewer benefits or sometimes none at all.

In the Case Studies, we found great variety in the benefits offered. Aides in the public schools were considerably less likely than head teachers to receive any benefits. Sometimes full-time teachers had benefits when part-time teachers in the same programs had none. In one program teachers got full benefits even when they taught only half time; in another, teachers who worked 30 hours per week were not eligible for any paid vacation, unlike full-time teachers. At one case study site, which ran a year-round program to accommodate the needs of working parents, the teachers had only two weeks paid vacation per year. They felt they needed more time away from the classroom to avoid burnout. One popular benefit offered in some programs is reduced fees for teachers' own children who attended the program or another in the school system. This benefit probably works as a recruitment incentive.

Unions

The District Survey did not ask whether prekindergarten teachers belonged to a collective bargaining unit. Nearly every possible union arrangement was found in the Case Studies. Some prekindergarten teachers belonged to the same bargaining unit as the K–12 teachers. Other prekindergarten teachers had their own contracts, with inevitably lower salaries, except for prekindergarten special education teachers. These districts took precautions to justify the differentiation between the early childhood positions and those in the rest of the district. In one, for instance, the early childhood positions were called "Head Instructors" and "Lead Aides" rather than teachers. Some teachers belonged to no collective bargaining unit, which may or may not have been true for the K–12 teachers in that district. Some lived in states which do not allow collective bargaining for public school employees (Texas, Florida).

Teachers believe that unions are one force responsible for the relatively high salaries and benefits of public school early childhood programs. One of the child care teachers commented that it was "because of the union that we are paid $20,000–$23,000 instead of $7,000–$9,000." Other working conditions appeared to be protected by unions as well, such as approximately 40-hour work weeks.

However, concerns about union contracts were noted in the Case Studies. In three different districts, administrators mentioned that they were reluctantly working with inadequate teachers because the unions made it difficult to fire a staff member. In another system, two teachers who were themselves union representatives complained that the union did not understand early childhood concerns. For instance, union members question why, if teachers of older children have to work with 25 to 30 children, prekindergarten teachers should get so few children. The teachers noted that they spent a lot of time explaining to their fellow union members that they were "not just babysitters." (This attitude comes as no surprise to early childhood advocates, who have encountered the same problem in many different groups.) One administrator observed that the early childhood teachers in his program were "not aggressive individuals" and did not get much support from their union, which was more focused on K–12 concerns.

In summary, ease of recruitment and retention is highly correlated with compensation. Most programs that offered district-level salaries and benefits had little problem attracting and keeping teachers; programs with low salaries tended to have significant problems in these areas. But some other factors influence recruitment and retention, factors related to teacher job satisfaction and commitment: autonomy, class size and staff ratio, work schedules, staff relations, and other working conditions.

Autonomy

When case study teachers discussed their satisfaction or dissatisfaction with their salaries and benefits, it is remarkable how often they introduced the issue of classroom autonomy. It appears that the satisfaction which comes from autonomy can counteract mild dissatisfaction with compensation. As a result, teachers who are able to make important decisions about their work tend to feel committed to their programs and their supervisors, thus contributing to lower turnover rates.

The teachers we observed and interviewed who were most excited about their work had the freedom to determine the daily activities of their classrooms. If they worked from a prescribed curriculum, it specified only broad general goals, allowing them to develop their own plans for implementation. In one district a committee of teachers was given the task of designing a developmentally appropriate program for full-day kindergarten. They appreciated this as the kind of truly creative challenge not available to many public school teachers. In another district two teachers developed an excellent and innovative series of curriculum units integrating the study of art and science. Each unit was of intrinsic interest to four-year-olds, who actively participated in exploring materials and solving problems about them. These teachers made creative use of their understanding of how children of this age learn and how to capture their interest and extend their thinking. It was obvious, as we watched the teacher carry out the exciting unit on clay, that she loved her work and felt highly rewarded by it.

In contrast, at another site the teachers were given a recipe-format curriculum with a minute-by-minute schedule designating each lesson for the entire day. Children were given pre- and post-tests on "the material," so teachers felt that they had to stick to the prescribed lessons. One teacher recalled the past, when there had been time for activities like cooking and sewing. Now discipline problems were the main activity that interfered with "time-on-task." It should be noted that most teachers in this program were not trained in early childhood education and development; the district had dropped its hiring requirement for early childhood certification. Although these teachers no doubt needed help in planning their programs, the "help" provided by their prescribed curriculum was developmentally inappropriate—the information was not "meaningful to the child in the context of the child's experience and development."[9] These teachers showed little enthusiasm for their work.

Usually, programs that gave teachers autonomy in their classrooms allowed them meaningful roles in administrative decision making as well. For instance, one district sponsored several centers which functioned autonomously. Teachers at each site met weekly to determine how their center should be run. They had district-wide monthly meetings to contribute to long-range planning. Teachers felt that they could count on the administration to listen to their suggestions. When hiring new teachers, the director looked for candidates who matched the specific nature of the staff they would join. Each center genuinely believed that it was the best one in the district. We were struck by the intense commitment these teachers felt toward their work.

Class Size and Staff Ratio

Research evidence indicates that both small class size and small number of children per adult are important factors in early childhood program quality.[10] From the teacher's point of view, there are clear reasons why small groups and favorable ratios are conducive to high-quality education. When teachers are responsible for a relatively small number of children, they can be more involved with each child as an individual. But when teachers are responsible for a large number of children, they tend to relate to them as undifferentiated groups. One advantage of relating to children as individuals rather than as a mass is that teachers can customize their teaching for each child. Another advantage is that they can observe each child growing and learning, a reward which in turn enhances their satisfaction and commitment.

In the District Survey, classes for four-year-olds were most common. Of those, 91 percent enrolled 20 children or fewer; 51 percent had 14 or fewer. There were an average of 16 to 18 children across all program types, except for smaller classes in special education, parent education, and high school nursery schools. Classes for younger children were correspondingly smaller.

Staff ratios for four-year-old classes tended to be nine or ten children per staff member in parent-fee funded programs and in state- or locally funded prekindergartens. Head Start averaged 7 or 8 four-year-olds per staff member; special education and high school nursery schools averaged four children per staff member. In the Case Studies, both small groups and favorable ratios were associated with individualized teaching and a smoothness of operation that was conducive to young children attending to their activities. In conclusion, our research shows that public schools are generally meeting acceptable group size and staff ratio guidelines in their early childhood programs.

Work Schedules

In the teacher interviews, work schedules were mentioned among
the reasons why teachers either liked their jobs or were thinking
about quitting them. Public schools have developed a range of
work schedules to meet various program requirements for classroom coverage. In some a majority of teachers and aides work part
time; in others, everybody works full time. In the District Survey,
most of the programs were operated for three hours or less per
day, five days per week for the school year—although in many of
them, teachers taught double sessions. Program types operating
during the summer as well were subsidized child care programs
(85 percent) and parent-fee child care (60 percent).

A special benefit of most public school teaching jobs is "summers
off!" Teachers in school-year programs mentioned this benefit as
an important reason for liking their jobs. The opportunity to be
with their own school-aged children was the most frequent reason
given for appreciating summers off. Summers are also a time to
restore oneself so as to avoid "burnout."

Unusual work schedules were sometimes the best arrangement
for both teachers and children. In one program that is open for 10
hours a day to accommodate working parents, teachers in two
classrooms work four 10-hour days per week. This schedule allowed
them to cover the entire day for children, from arrival through
departure. Five teachers were required; two teachers for each of
the classrooms and a fifth to cover for whichever teacher was off
each day.

In programs where some children attended only two or three
days a week while others attended five days, the teachers mentioned several disadvantages to the children and to the quality of
their experience, as well as ways their teaching was hindered. Key
activities must be repeated for those children who attend fewer
days and may be repetitious for children who attend for the full
week.

Part-time jobs involve a trade-off between time and income.
Some teachers preferred half-day schedules. One said, "I feel that
I have found the ideal career for having a child, because I'm
getting out in the mornings and I'm doing something for myself,
but I am still spending all afternoon with my child." This teacher
was married to someone with a good income. Unmarried teachers,
especially if they were parents, usually needed the income of full-
time work.

In evaluating teachers' working conditions, it is important to
consider the actual number of hours worked. In one program the

full-time teachers taught children in the morning and were paid for planning and administration in the afternoon. In another program the teachers worked with children for a full day and did the rest of their work in unpaid overtime. Their planning suffered not only from a lack of time but also from a lack of legitimacy and importance.

Thus, there is an unusually diverse range of work schedules in these programs. Each has its trade-offs; no one seems clearly best. But as in community-based programs, full-day full-year programs should be staffed so that teachers have enough breaks, planning time, and vacations to prevent them from burning out.

Staff Relations

Another variable in working conditions which we observed to be related to recruitment and retention is the quality of interpersonal relations among the staff. Good relations among the teaching staff, and between teachers and administrators, attract and keep teachers. One teacher, when asked why she chose to work in her program, reported that she had substituted in all the area school districts and found this one to be the most friendly. In another system where the teachers had worked together for years, one of them spoke of staff camaraderie. Another said they were "like family." At another site the teachers were not at all like family. In a highly bureaucratic system, they were isolated in self-sufficient classrooms with very little adult interaction of any kind. The absence of cooperation and support eroded the quality of their program.

Several programs located within elementary schools suffered from isolation and lack of respect from the rest of the school. Administrative leadership that communicates the special differences of early childhood programs helps to integrate the early childhood teachers into the whole school. It is important for building-level administrators to facilitate pleasant working relations among teachers, not only to attract and keep teachers but also to support and maintain good programs for children.

Other Working Conditions

The Physical Space and Materials Unfortunately, some public school early childhood programs are located in drab, older school buildings. Others have cheery rooms in old buildings, creatively transformed into inviting spaces. A few are in attractive new buildings designed specially for young children. One teacher volunteered that her program had an easy, noninstitutional atmosphere that "did not feel like it was in a public school." Another said that her school building was "a lovely place to work."

Some underfunded programs were poorly equipped. Teaching was made difficult because there was not enough for the children to do. Learning was made difficult because young children learn best through "hands on" experiences. Teachers whose classrooms included a rich variety of inviting, age-appropriate materials in good condition obviously found their jobs more pleasant and rewarding than did those who had to make do with a minimum of materials. A sufficient supply of materials and equipment certainly contributes to the quality of the child's experience as well.

Opportunities for Promotion Opportunities for staff members to take on increasing responsibilities, and earn increasing salaries, varied greatly in the case study sites. In one site almost every head teacher began as an assistant; some had first come to the program as parents. In other sites there were no opportunities for promotion within the district; head teachers were hired from the outside. In still others, where prekindergarten teacher salaries were lower than K–12 salaries, the early childhood jobs were seen as a route into the public school—a stepping stone to a "real teaching job." Mobility into K–12 jobs was perceived by some as a good opportunity for teachers, and by others as a loss to the district's prekindergarten programs.

Because high turnover is such a problem in other sectors of early childhood education, it is easy to forget that some turnover is a healthy aspect of any program. A good career ladder results in some staff turnover—employees leave their jobs to move to better ones. A moderate degree of such movement is better for a system than one in which teachers feel "stuck in dead-end jobs." In the Case Studies, some teachers did feel that they would have to give up teaching to improve their career level. Clearly, moderate mobility within a program is good for all concerned.

Because of their generally higher resource levels (higher salaries, better benefits), the public schools tend to have little problem recruiting early childhood teachers from the community. The degree to which this recruitment is seen as unhealthy and unfair competition is related to local market variations in the supply of teachers qualified to teach in the public school prekindergarten—which is related, in turn, to the range of acceptable teacher qualifications—and to the relative size of the public school's program compared to the rest of the community. The size and rate of growth of public school prekindergartens in a community strongly influence whether they are seen as competition or a career ladder—when a large number of qualified teachers are hired in a short time period, it can leave the rest of the community with no qualified applicants for their less well paid teaching jobs. In contrast, if there are only a few public school jobs, these prekindergarten jobs are usually seen as welcome career ladder opportunities.

Ideally, teachers see the school system as having built-in career ladders. As they gain experience and expertise, they can take on new responsibilities (mentor teaching, staff development, administration) and be promoted accordingly. Their work does not get stale because it is not stagnant.

Status and Respect   In most communities, simply being part of the public school system brings extra credibility and prestige to a program. Early childhood professionals in other programs are sometimes perceived as "just babysitters," but a public school teacher is rarely viewed as a babysitter. For instance, one father in a parent interview said he assumed that the public school is far better equipped to do child care than the private sector. (In fact, although his parent-fee child care program was run by the school, it received little in the way of public resources.) He perceived private child care as "watching TV."

Because a large part of job status in this culture is determined by salary level, the fact that public schools usually pay their early childhood teachers more than community programs do is another reason that public school teachers gain extra respect. But public school prekindergarten teachers who are paid less than the K–12 teachers may chafe under their lower status within the school, especially if their qualifications are similar. Sometimes this status differential is perceived even when the salaries are identical. In one program the teachers kept referring to their hopes of getting "public school" positions, even though their jobs were not only public school jobs but also on the district pay scale.

Throughout the field of early childhood education, the status differential between "educational programs" and "child care" is a problem. Even though the historic roots of this dichotomy are clear, the distinction is no longer appropriate. Any good early childhood program educates children *and* cares for their needs. Any preschool which teaches but does not meet the whole child's needs, or any child care program which meets basic needs but does not offer rewarding, stimulating, and growth-producing activities, is not a good program. Further, the need for balance between care and education is not very different from one time of day to another, even though the pace of activities may change.

This dichotomy was dramatized by one district which had two

programs: an "educational preschool" in the morning and "day care" in the afternoon. Even though all children in full-child care attended both programs, the teachers had never visited each other's classes. The preschool teachers were sent to the local AEYC conference; the child care teachers were not. The child care teachers were paid significantly less than the preschool teachers, in fact less than the aides in K–12 classrooms. The child care teachers claimed that they had started to teach the alphabet and counting, not because they thought it would be good for the children, but because they thought it would bring increased job status.

Other Policies to Promote Good Teaching

What other kinds of district policies concerning teachers promote child learning and development? Research suggests that a critical function of such policies is to facilitate teachers' positive, stimulating interactions with young children.[11] In addition to staff ratio and class size, teacher qualifications, and factors related to recruitment and retention which have already been discussed, three additional factors which promote good teaching were identified by the study. They are the curriculum, staff development, and evaluation.

Teachers and the Curriculum

In most public school prekindergarten programs, some form of curriculum is prescribed by the school district. As seen in the next chapter, "The Program for Children," a wide variety of curricula are employed, ranging from appropriate to inappropriate and flexible to rigid. As noted earlier, most knowledgeable teachers want and need to make at least some of their own decisions about the details of their teaching. The best curriculum specifies broad, general goals, allowing teachers to create their own plans for implementation. But the case study teachers who had no early childhood training seemed to appreciate being given activity ideas for their age group. For them, a specific curriculum gave needed direction. A further advantage of a *good* specific curriculum is that it can supplement the teachers' own ideas, thus reducing planning and preparation time. Ideally, then, the mandated curriculum should be broad, and additional specific curricular activities should be recommended and made available so teachers can use them as needed.

One of our most frequent observations was that the individual teacher makes a substantial difference in the quality of a class, regardless of the curriculum. In multigroup programs we saw a great deal of variation in quality from one room to another, even when the curriculum was highly specified. We saw good teachers who were nearly able to make up for a weak curriculum; we did not see a single case in which a good curriculum made up for a teacher who did not like young children or who had lost interest in teaching.

Teachers with no early childhood background often had problems with discipline. The problems seemed attributable in part to their lack of positive ways to guide behavior and in part to their more boring classes. Unfortunately it was often the case that the same programs in which teachers had no early childhood training also had administrators with no early childhood background. While either may have sensed that there was a problem, they did not know effective ways to improve the situation.

Staff Development

In the District Survey 98 percent of all programs reported that they offered some form of staff development, but the Case Studies showed that wide variability exists in what is called staff development. The best programs offered teachers continuing inservice education, even though they already performed at high levels. Other programs gave minimal attention to ongoing training. In one case, for instance, the only training consisted of head teachers' supervising their classroom staffs. A high turnover rate in this large district made some form of centralized training advisable, but no systematic response to the problem had been developed. In another case, outside experts were brought in to make occasional presentations, but there was no consistent follow-up. The District Survey showed that reimbursement for attending professional conferences and visiting other programs was offered by most districts.

While many states do not require specific forms of staff development in their prekindergarten programs, some states have made major commitments to in-service training. Maryland is unique in the extent to which it supports staff development in its Extended Elementary Education Program (EEEP). The Department of Education staff provide resources and assist with local curriculum development as well as conduct inservice training upon request for EEEP staff and other early childhood providers invited by the district. The DOE holds statewide conferences annually to which each participating school system sends a teacher. At least every three years, EEEP school principals and teachers are urged to attend national early childhood education conferences.

A unique feature of the Maryland program is the identification of certain schools as early learning support centers where teachers can receive training in specific problem areas. The Department of Education provides funds for substitute teachers and stipends for support teachers as well as to the support center school for housing the program. In another effort to improve the quality of programs, the state provides support for public schools interested in going through the NAEYC accreditation and validation process. DOE state staff provide an introduction and orientation for these schools as well as funds for all materials and a small stipend to each participating school. Twelve school districts have identified interested schools.

Another state which gives particular attention to staff training in its prekindergarten program is South Carolina. Its DOE holds a one-day, statewide conference annually for district personnel to discuss regulations and implementation strategies of their Education Improvement Act (EIA). Local district meetings are conducted by state-level personnel to acquaint principals with the curriculum approach specified for the prekindergartens. New teachers and aides are required to complete a minimum of 20 hours of preservice orientation. The Center for Excellence in Early Childhood Education, established by the Winthrop College School of Education, helps DOE staff in training personnel in the EIA program. State DOE early childhood education staff visit each program once a year. They provide on-site fiscal and program monitoring and technical assistance to each classroom teacher and aide team. Inservice training is also available from state staff for administrators, teachers, specialists, aides/paraprofessionals, and private agency personnel.

The District of Columbia offers a promising staff development opportunity for teachers in its prekindergarten program. The Early Childhood Mentor Program assigns new teachers without prior teaching experience to an experienced teacher/mentor for a two-year period. Similarly, Florida's Chapter 228 Prekindergarten programs must provide a staff development component, which includes a method for career development and a career ladder.

Some state teaching credentials require a number of hours of continuing education each year; sometimes the continuing education is required only for teachers with minimal educational qualifications. In the Case Studies we identified two major sources of continuing education: local colleges, including community colleges, and the local and state affiliates of the National Association for the Education of Young Children.

We observed that the quality of staff development tended to reflect the overall quality of administration. Some districts had helpful program coordinators who provided knowledgeable assistance to individual teachers as well as useful workshops and other group development activities. However, one district had a program coordinator in name only, who was able to do little more than "order supplies." Some districts provided effective staff development for the head teachers but, unfortunately, not for the aides, usually because aides' wages were paid for classroom time only. Several programs were troubled by a lack of trained substitute teachers, but none of the Case Studies revealed any attempt to train a pool of substitutes.

Evaluation

In the Case Studies the districts which offered little in the way of staff development tended to follow evaluation procedures which were perfunctory or worse. Sometimes teachers were evaluated by the central administration, who knew almost nothing about their work, while supervisors in their own buildings made no input into teacher evaluation. In one case study site, located in an elementary school, the principal came into each classroom for one scheduled and one unscheduled half-hour visit per year to evaluate the teacher and his or her lesson plans for those periods. The teachers were generally negative about this approach and did not seem to gain anything constructive from it. One said, "They are a waste of time. They make my blood pressure go up." In contrast, teachers at another site had three unscheduled observations a year, but they felt the evaluations were two-way, reflective discussions where administrators and teachers showed deep, mutual respect. These teachers spoke highly of seeing their own performances improve. Unfortunately, the development of paraprofessionals is not often included in these evaluation systems. In most districts, the aides or paraprofessionals were evaluated only by their own head teachers.

In the best cases teachers perceived official evaluation conferences as exploratory and interesting. Personal goals for improvement were derived from the evaluations, and teachers were helped to grow and develop new strengths. When on-site supervisors were knowledgeable and respected by the teachers, they could also function as important resources for ongoing, informal feedback and help.

Ideally, staff development and evaluation are interactional and continuing. Areas for a teacher's improvement are identified through evaluation, and opportunities for related growth and learning are specified. The teacher's progress is assessed periodically, leading to further development.

Conclusion

Early childhood programs must be sufficiently high in quality to be beneficial to children—in terms of the here and now of their daily lives and in terms of the eventual positive effects on their later schooling and adult lives. Young children who are in small groups, caringly taught by well-trained teachers, are experiencing quality. All children in early childhood programs everywhere deserve to experience quality.

If early childhood programs operated by public schools are to be high quality, they cannot be the poor relatives of the rest of the school when it comes to the budget. Prekindergarten classes need resources, and it is clear that their most important resource is their teachers. The assumption that "anyone can teach young children" is a myth. Young children need qualified teachers as much as children of any age do. They need trained head teachers who know about early childhood development and education.

Any good early childhood program has a solid core of well-trained teachers who have made a long-term commitment to the program and the children in it. Teachers must stay in their jobs long enough so that children, administrators, and other teachers can count on them. To attract and keep competent well-trained teachers, salaries, benefits, and working conditions must be improved in all types of programs in the early childhood ecosystem. In particular, public school-operated programs must pay prekindergarten teachers salaries and benefits equal to those of other teachers working for the district.

Very few good early childhood programs can be supported by parents' fees alone. Public school prekindergarten programs cannot be financed primarily by parent fees when those fees are set at the market rate in the community; the market rate is not high enough to support equitable salaries and acceptable staff–child ratios. While a partial solution might be to charge upper-income parents higher fees, the result would be socioeconomic segregation—only those children whose families could afford the price would benefit from the program. Those children who would benefit most would be denied entry. To ensure equal access for all children, early childhood programs that charge fees to parents should seek public funding to supplement fees paid by lower-income parents and to fully support those children whose families cannot afford any fee.

Good teachers help create good programs. When good teachers have the autonomy to create their own programs, they are challenged intellectually. They gain a sense of achievement as they watch children grow and learn in response to their teaching. They invest themselves in their work and feel a strong commitment to the program and to the administrators who help it all happen. These teachers tend to be satisfied with their jobs and do not usually leave them except for compelling financial or personal reasons.

Children deserve good teachers. Favorable staffing ratios and small classes are conducive to good teaching. Administrators in the best programs set a standard of excellence, hire staff members carefully, and provide effective curricula, staff development, and evaluation, all of which are necessary, especially for teachers untrained in early childhood education. Programs with a reputation for creating excellent teaching and learning environments, both for children and teachers, attract numerous qualified job applicants and find parents eager to enroll their children.

The entire early childhood ecosystem would benefit from having more such good programs within it. Public schools should become leaders in the early childhood community, developing high-quality early childhood programs with well-trained teachers, rather than perpetuating the system of underfunding and second-class status which is all too common today.

Recommendations

- Hiring requirements for head teachers throughout the early childhood ecosystem should reflect the combined wisdom of practitioners and researchers: More education is better than less; the amount and nature of teacher preparation interact— more highly educated adults who have also received specialized child-related training are probably the most proficient teachers; and previous experience working with young children is helpful.
- State teacher certification regulations, prekindergarten program guidelines, and child care licensing standards for early childhood teachers should all require child-related course-

work, student teaching, and other direct experience specific to prekindergarten-aged children.

- To encourage nonpublic school agencies to provide state-funded prekindergarten programs, early childhood certification for public school teachers and child care licensing standards for staff of nonpublic school programs should overlap significantly in terms of education and experience requirements.
- Preservice training, appropriate to the level of education and previous experience, should be offered to all teachers in the early childhood ecosystem.
- The amount and quality of preservice and inservice training available for early childhood teachers should be increased. Special assistance should be given to help untrained and inexperienced teachers improve their knowledge and practice.
- Staff development opportunities should be offered that support improved performance of staff on a particular rung of the career ladder *and* encourage movement up the ladder.
- In public school-operated prekindergarten programs, salaries and benefits of early childhood personnel should be equitable with those of other district administrators, teachers, and aides, to reflect their equivalent qualifications, to promote equal status, and to provide a qualified, stable work force.
- In programs funded by parent fees, public funding (federal, state, and/or local) should supplement or replace the fees paid by lower-income parents, while upper-income parents should pay their share of the true costs of good programs.
- To promote teacher autonomy and creativity, the curriculum should set forth broad, general goals and objectives of the program, while allowing individual teachers to use their own interests and ingenuity to plan daily activities. Specific curricular activities should be recommended for teachers who need more help.
- Administrators responsible for prekindergarten programs should be well grounded in early childhood development and education.

Endnotes

1. Lazar, I., and R.B. Darlington (1979). *Lasting effects after preschool: A report of the Consortium for Longitudinal Studies* (DHEW Publication No. [(OHDS)] 79-30178). Washington, D.C.: U.S. Government Printing Office.
2. Phillips, D.A., and C. Howes (1987). Indicators of quality child care: Review

of research. In D.A. Phillips (Ed.), _Quality in child care: What does research tell us?_ Washington, D.C.: National Association for the Education of Young Children.

3. Phillips, D.A. (Ed.) (1987). _Quality in child care: What does research tell us?_ Washington, D.C.: National Association for the Education of Young Children.
    Schweinhart, L.J. (1987). When the buck stops here: What it takes to run a good early childhood program. _High/Scope Resources_ 1, 9–13.

4. See _The State Survey_ for state-by-state details of teacher education and certification requirements. Marx, F., and M. Seligson (1988). _The Public School Early Childhood Study: The State Survey._ New York: Bank Street College.

5. See _The District Survey_, pp. 23–28, for additional information. Mitchell, A. (1988). _The Public School Early Childhood Study: The District Survey._ New York: Bank Street College.

6. A more detailed analysis of differences in salaries associated with the different program types and funding sources can be found in _The District Survey_, pp. 28–32.

7. Modigliani, K. (1988). Twelve reasons for the low wages in child care. _Young Children_ 43 (3), 14–15.

8. For a discussion of competition among providers in the early childhood community, see Mitchell, A. (1988). _The Public School Early Childhood Study: The Case Studies_, pp. 28–29.

9. National Association for the Education of Young Children (1986). _Good teaching practices for 4- and 5-year-olds._ Washington, D.C.: Author.

10. Phillips and Howe (1987). Ruopp, R., W.L. Bache, C. O'Neil, and J. Singer (1979). _Children at the center:_ Final results of the National Day Care Study. Cambridge, Mass.: Abt Associates.

11. Phillips, D.A. (1987).

Chapter 9

THE PROGRAM FOR CHILDREN

What do prekindergarten programs in public schools look like? In many ways the fears and concerns about prekindergarten programs under the auspices of public schools today mirror the concerns about public schools and kindergarten earlier in this century: the rigidity and structure of elementary school environments; the downward extension of primary curricula; unrealistic expectations of children; overemphasis on math and reading readiness and on skills acquisition; and overly large classes with only one teacher.

The classrooms we visited during the course of our 13 site visits were remarkably diverse just as any other type of educational setting for young children, whether it be a child care center, nursery school, or playgroup. They reflected a range of implicit assumptions about young children and how they learn. In their diversity, they expressed the subtle interaction of an individual teacher's personality, background, and training with the program's basic philosophy and goals. Even within a given school with a particular approach to the education of young children, shades of difference could be seen between one classroom and another down the hall.

One way to conceptualize the place of individual classroom activities within the larger scheme of educational practice in the public schools is by thinking of the classroom as the smallest of a series of concentric circles. Working outward from the innermost circle (the classroom), influences on what occurs there include the principal/program director, the district (superintendent, early childhood supervisor, school board), in the cases of many state-funded programs, the state (usually through the form of state guidelines, as promulgated by the state department of education)

Note: This chapter was authored principally by Janice Molnar.

and last, the federal government for progams such as Head Start and Chapter I. However, in all cases, the teacher is the final interpreter of the philosophies and guidelines that are generated at higher levels of authority.

Thus the one thing we are able to say without qualification about the classrooms we visited is that it is impossible to generalize. It is impossible to make a broad enough statement to fully encompass the richness and complexities of program implementation. Public school programs are neither all one thing nor another. Even in sites which had a clearly articulated philosophy and set of guidelines, the way the program was translated by the teacher in the daily rhythm of classroom activities and social exchange varied considerably. In this respect, at least, they are like early childhood programs everywhere.

Quality Programs for Children

Just as an actual classroom is affected by the teacher's personal experience and background, so too is our interpretation of what we saw influenced by our particular perspective. In our case, the lens through which we looked at classrooms was quality. Over the past 10 years research has identified the elements of good educational programming for young children. The criteria are the same whatever the setting.

Guided by research and best practice, the National Association for the Education of Young Children (NAEYC) took on the task of operationalizing the features of a high-quality, developmentally appropriate early childhood experience for children ages birth through eight and produced what is generally agreed to be the most comprehensive articulation of "quality" as it applies to the full range of classroom experiences. At the core of NAEYC's standards for early childhood programming is the definition of "developmentally appropriate." What this concept means is that a curriculum, if developmentally appropriate, is guided both by "knowledge of typical development of children within the age span served by the program" and by a responsivity to individual differences in "patterns and timing of growth, as well as individual personality, learning style, and family background."[1] NAEYC's specific guidelines for curriculum include ten features. Because of their importance, we highlight them here.[2]

- Developmentally appropriate curriculum provides for all areas of a child's development: physical, emotional, social, and cognitive through an integrated approach.

- Curriculum goals and plans are based on regular assessment of individual needs, strengths, and interests.
- Curriculum planning emphasizes learning as an interactive process.
- Learning activities and materials should be concrete, real, and relevant to the lives of young children.
- Programs provide for a wider range of developmental interests and abilities than the chronological age range of the group would suggest.
- Teachers provide a variety of activities and materials.
- Adults provide opportunities for children to choose from among a variety of activities, materials, and equipment, as well as time to explore through active engagement.
- Multicultural and nonsexist experiences, materials, and equipment should be provided for children of all ages.
- Adults provide a balance of rest and active movement for children throughout the program day.
- Outdoor experiences should be provided for children of all ages.

Key to these elements is understanding how young children develop. Thus a teacher's selection of specific activities and materials needs to be rooted in the knowledge that the young child's primary modes of learning are language and play, which are, respectively, the symbolic representation and reconstruction of the world the child experiences. A fundamental part of the teacher's role is to introduce experiences and materials which extend and differentiate this world. As we visited public school early childhood classrooms, we used the same criteria for evaluating the quality of the program that we would use in any other early childhood setting.

Data Collection Method: The Site Visits

Data for this chapter are drawn primarily from the Case Studies. The District Survey did not probe for program information, and the State Survey yielded program-specific information primarily for state-funded prekindergarten programs. And, in fact, a "paper review" alone would be inadequate for capturing the dynamic translation of a curriculum model into a program for children. Data on classroom programs were collected in the course of conducting the case studies through review of written materials, classroom observations (using the *Early Childhood Environment Rating Scale* and the *Stanford Research Institute (SRI) Classroom Observation System*), and individual and group interviews. During the five-day site visits, observations averaging 30 minutes each were made in every one of the prekindergarten classrooms in the designated site. In districts having multisite programs and/or more than one program type, efforts were made to observe briefly in a few other program sites. To assess continuity of curriculum approach between prekindergarten and kindergarten, observations were also done in at least one kindergarten class. Finally, teachers, parents, and administrators (both school-based and district-level) were interviewed about the classroom program as well as other issues. (For a more complete description of the method and instrumentation, see *The Case Studies*.)

A Profile of the Classrooms

The Physical Environment and Materials

Contrary to the negative stereotype many people have of public school early childhood programs, most of the classrooms we visited had the kinds of materials traditionally considered to be elements of any early childhood environment. Basic classroom equipment such as child-sized tables and chairs and appropriate shelving and storage space were present in almost every observed classroom. Large numbers of rooms had child-sized sinks (61 percent) and storage space for children's personal belongings (75 percent), indicating that many of the prekindergartens were housed in space designed for young children. The vast majority (80 percent or more) of the 76 classrooms on which we had the most complete information had creative play equipment: small toys, construction toys, puzzles, blocks, art and crafts materials, and housekeeping furniture and accessories. Record players and records were observed in these classrooms (over 80 percent), and over half had additional audio equipment such as tape recorders.

Young children learn best through active engagement with open-ended materials that allow them to explore at their own pace, in their own way, and to the extent of their interest. Unfortunately, however, 30 percent of the observed classrooms did not have painting easels (in a couple of cases, they were present but used as small bulletin boards). Just over half had sand/water tables (though for health reasons state regulations forbade them in a few of the sites). Not even half the classrooms had pets or other nature/science materials (43 percent and 45 percent, respectively). Not quite one-third of the classrooms had musical instruments; only 10 percent had a piano.

An intellectually stimulating setting for young children also requires challenging materials that promote children's sense of mastery over their environment. Some materials are designed to focus attention on a particular concept or set of skills. In the observed classrooms 55 percent had math manipulatives (cuisinaire rods, unifix cubes, number puzzles); 38 percent had language games (picture lotto, story sequence cards, letter puzzles). These kinds of materials extend children's language, reasoning, and conceptual abilities in a focused way when used in combination with open-ended materials. In contrast, 22 percent had commercial textbooks and/or workbooks; closed-ended paper-and-pencil activities are inappropriate for young children. Not only can they be a frustrating waste of children's time, but in many cases may permanently blunt children's curiosity and desire to learn.

Of course, it is important to acknowledge that it is not the presence or absence of particular materials per se that matters but how they are used. Our classroom observations provided illustration of both ends of the continuum. For example, we visited one relatively new and attractively designed open-classroom environment that, at first glance, was quite impressive. The classroom space was colorful and well organized. Materials were new and plentiful. But a second glance revealed that this "materials catalogue come to life" (to quote one of our observers) lacked life. There was little evidence to suggest that this was a space used by children. Children's work was not displayed. Teachers did not interact freely with children. By the end of our visit, the newness had worn off to reveal a sterile, uncreative environment. At the other end of the continuum was a dark, almost windowless classroom in a 60-year-old, rather worn building. A newly created prekindergarten, it was short of commercially produced toys, games, or other educational materials. But it had a highly skilled teacher with many years of Head Start experience, who filled the room with teacher- and parent-made materials and created a language-rich environment full of challenge and stimulation.

Multicultural Materials Particularly striking was the fact that across *all* classrooms, very little children's work was displayed. Neither were there many teacher-made materials present. In general, classroom displays were commercially produced. And in keeping with a general absence of culturally diverse materials, when the commercial displays depicted a personal character, it was usually an animal or cartoon personality (a Thanksgiving display that we saw in one classroom featured Walt Disney characters dressed as Pilgrims and Indians).

The lack of attention to cultural diversity was particularly disturbing in classrooms in which the children and teaching staff were themselves of diverse backgrounds. In a southern classroom of young black children that was devoid of culturally relevant materials (with the exception of a single picture of an Asian family hung on the wall), the teacher told the observer, "We celebrate Black History Month and Martin Luther King, Jr.'s birthday. You should be here then." In a northern classroom of black, white, Hispanic, Asian, and Native American three-year-olds, there was no recognition, through materials, bulletin board displays, storybooks, snacks, or songs, of the cultural heritage the room embraced within its four walls. In this particular classroom of predominantly non-English-speaking children, there were also no language games, no communication arts materials, only white dolls in the dramatic play areas, and no cultural or child art displays (the January bulletin board displayed penguins frolicking in a winter scene).

Learning Centers Learning centers help organize classroom space to facilitate small-group instruction and independent learning. They allow for the individualization of the classroom program through the encouragement of self-selected, child-centered activities.

In terms of the organization of space into learning centers, usually the "standard" centers—housekeeping, blocks, library, and art—were present in the observed classrooms. Rarer were the math, nature/science, and enriched dramatic play areas. Dramatic play areas should encourage children to explore well beyond the traditional housekeeping roles, for example, with costumes, real-world objects (firehats, suitcases, steering wheels) and other props that support a wide range of fantasy play. In fact, there were fewer learning centers present than one would suspect, given the materials at hand. For example, although almost every classroom (92 percent) had blocks, only 17 percent had block areas. In the remaining classrooms, there was insufficient space set aside for the blocks, so that the space more resembled a storage area (several shelves of blocks) than a center designed for concentrated creative activity. Further, although over half (58 percent) of the classrooms we visited had math manipulatives, not even a quarter (22 percent) had them arranged in a math center to facilitate their use. This lack of organization of the classroom environment does not encourage children's independent use of materials but instead pushes teachers to direct children's use of materials. In busy and stimulating environments, it is important for children to have private spaces where they "can get away from it all." Very few classrooms, even the very best, had planned quiet or cozy areas for children.

Space and Time for Gross-Motor Activity Given the importance of gross-motor play in the psychomotor development of young children, the lack of provision for gross-motor activity was especially salient. The majority of programs evidenced inadequate space, equipment, and time for appropriate attention to this domain of development. In many programs large-motor play was a token part of the schedule or used solely when the children "needed to let off some steam." In one daily half-day program, only 40 minutes of gross-motor activity *per week* was scheduled. This particular program happened to be a very academically structured program. The rationale for the lack of emphasis on gross-motor activity was based on limited time: "We only have an hour of structured [academic] time and we don't want to take away from it."

This situation was in stark contrast to the half-day schedule of another site, which gave a very high priority to gross-motor activity. In this three-hour program, there were two daily periods of large-motor play. The day opened with 30 minutes in one of the program's two "gross-motor rooms." These were open areas around which several classrooms were clustered. The spaces were carpeted and equipped with climbing equipment, large blocks, and other materials supportive of indoor large muscle activity. Later in the day, a 40-minute outdoor play period was scheduled. In inclement weather, children had the use of an indoor gymnasium, which was equipped to allow for the full-scale gross-motor activity generally only possible outdoors: tricycling, running, rope climbing, tumbling, swinging, jumping. We observed the teacher, aide, and children together playing number-based tag games; creating imaginary worlds comprised of block towers and tunnels and other stimulating activities. These periods offered far more than just "letting off steam." In this program physical activity is viewed as a creative learning opportunity.

Variation by Program Type

Program type, for example, Chapter I, state-funded prekindergarten, subsidized child care, or parent tuition supported child care, is the unique combination of funding source, purpose, and clientele. We expected that classroom profiles would vary in certain predictable ways according to overall program type. They didn't. This may have been because the relatively small number of classrooms in each group (or program type) meant that any aggregated look was overly influenced by strong "outlier" classrooms, that is, classrooms that were particularly high quality or particularly low quality. Or it may be that, regardless of sample size, there is more variability among classrooms within a program type than between classrooms of different program types. Based on the information that follows, we think that the latter is true. Public school early childhood programs simply defy easy generalizations.

Curriculum

Curriculum structures the experience of the learner. In its most narrow sense, it applies to the planning tools used in a classroom environment: lessons plans, activity guides, workbook series. Many people erroneously define "curriculum" as synonymous with "publisher" (as in "workbook publisher"). But its meaning extends far beyond that. We define curriculum as the underlying theory or set of principles that determines the design of the classroom environment, the materials used, and the articulated goals and objectives.

We encountered a range of curriculum types, and a corresponding range of educational philosophies, represented in the 13 sites. The most frequently reported curriculum was the High/Scope Cognitively Oriented Curriculum which five programs said they used, although it was not always easily recognized by observers as High/Scope. Four programs defined their approach as "developmental." The remaining programs lacked an overall label for their approach to educating young children, but they incorporated one or more standardized curricula (for example, Distar Language program, the Peabody Language program) into their daily program of activities.

The Cognitively Oriented Curriculum

Developed by the High/Scope Educational Research Foundation, the Cognitively Oriented Curriculum is based on the developmental theories of Jean Piaget as they apply to children three and four years of age. As described by David Weikart and his colleagues, it is concerned primarily with the development of symbolic functioning during the period of preoperational thought. In its earliest conceptualizations,[3] the curriculum stressed the concepts to be incorporated into daily activities (classification, seriation, spatial relations, temporal relations). More recently, classroom processes have also been emphasized (room arrangement, class groupings, structuring the daily routine through plan-do-review).[4]

What has probably given High/Scope's Cognitively Oriented Curriculum the most visibility are, first, findings from the ongoing study of their Perry Preschool Project and, second, their nationwide training project, which has reached a large number of public school early childhood supervisors. High/Scope's longitudinal study has demonstrated dramatic long-term effects among a population of disadvantaged youngsters from Ypsilanti, Michigan, who were enrolled in a High/Scope program as preschoolers. By age 19, a group of High/Scope graduates were less likely to have been referred to special education during their school years, more likely to have graduated from high school and to have enrolled in postsecondary education, more likely to be employed, and less likely to be arrested or be on welfare than a comparable group who had not attended such a program.[5]

These findings have had no small effect on educational policymakers. The South Carolina state prekindergarten program, for example, mandates the use of the High/Scope curriculum statewide. In another state, in a district which has been using the High/Scope curriculum for the past six years, a district administrator expressed her pleasure with it on the grounds that there is so much research available on it "which convinces parents that it is successful and will, in fact, improve their children's academic performance." Another administrator, in a different site, described its explanatory value for teachers as well as parents. "It helps us communicate to parents that there is a serious intent here." It also gives parents a way of following what their children are doing. "It is not mysterious. There are guidelines, and things are not left to the whims of one teacher." For teachers, it provides a unifying philosophy, a framework in which to work, a common language to use when talking about their work with each other, not just with parents.

However, in spite of its communicative value, the implementation of the High/Scope curriculum, as we observed it, was of uneven quality. In one classroom, for example, children were given assigned seats, admonished to "stay in your place," and generally addressed in a condescending rather than respectful manner. In another classroom the only feature that made it identifiable as High/Scope was the plan-do-review process of organizing the day. However, the children did not seem to attend to or engage in the activities they chose. It was the observer's perception that the child's act of choosing (planning) was more important to the teacher than the activity chosen. This was also a very teacher-directed classroom (notwithstanding child choice), perhaps because the scheduling was very tight and the teacher seemed to be continually redirecting the children.

The centrality of child choice in the High/Scope curriculum is at odds with some districts' official philosophy and goals. For example, one district that used High/Scope had as its goals for four-year-olds that "all four-year-olds would have access to a half-day preschool program," and "by 7/1/89, the percentage of students with formal preschool experience meeting the readiness standard on the [district's first grade test] will increase by 7 points over the 1984 level." In another site the official program objectives, as articulated by the district office, also seemed somewhat at odds with the assumptions about child development that underlie the High/Scope curriculum. In this district one of the key objectives is that "Given at least the average number of days instruction . . . at age four, at least 80 percent of the children tested will exhibit mastery of at least 90 percent of the items included in the [district's assessment kit]." Both districts' goals are statements of behavioral learning objectives that are consistent with neither Piaget nor High/Scope. Of course, there were also some examples of High/Scope as it was intended to be. As described by an obviously well-trained teacher in one of those sites, the High/Scope curriculum offered a clear structure "in which to do what a good teacher has always done."

The Developmental Approach

The language of developmentally appropriate curricula is well used in print and in verbal descriptions, but in practice it is *not* well understood. Four sites described their programs as "developmental." However, to borrow the words of a teacher trainer we spoke to, "There is far more talk about developmental philosophy than there is actual developmental education."

Perhaps our biggest shock came in a district whose written philosophy was a well-articulated treatise on developmentally appropriate education which stressed the uniqueness of individual children's trajectory of development and the importance of self-selected, experiential activities. We were, therefore, unprepared to see unit-based classroom instruction for four-year-olds. Each teacher followed approximately the same sequence of lessons. Pre- and post-tests were included with each unit, and criterion mastery tests were administered after each series of five units. Children were divided into ability groups based on their scores on the pre-tests. Lessons were presented according to difficulty "beginning with the lowest order of skills competencies and proceeding systematically to higher level tasks." In a six and one-quarter hour day, only 30 minutes were scheduled for independent activity in one of the classrooms we visited in this site. In another classroom in this site, the "Classroom Rules" were posted on the bulletin board. They read as follows: "Please obey all rules/Listen, teacher is talking/Pay attention/Follow directions/Be quiet when guests are present/Stay in line (hands behind)/Be quiet when resting and testing." In this classroom, we saw the enactment of a philosophy of education that was in direct opposition to the program's stated philosophy. This classroom was the opposite of a child-centered environment, which is supportive of child-initiated activity and characterized by warm adult-child interactions encouraging expressive language and individuality.

This complete misperception of the meaning of "developmentally appropriate" most commonly resulted in an excessive "academic" orientation. However, we observed one site in which a "play-based" curriculum almost completely excluded materials with an explicitly cognitive orientation. Overall, the classrooms in this site ranged from good to excellent in terms of materials, room arrangement, and activities observed. We would have been hard pressed to find fault were it not for the virtual absence of math manipulatives, language games, and science materials.

Considered together, these two extremes of misunderstanding reflect a more serious misconception of early childhood curricula. Too often, the choices are conceived on an either-or dimension: either a "traditional" laissez-faire, play-based program, or a formal, academic one. This is a false choice. Borrowing Lilian Katz' useful distinction between *academic* and *intellectual* rigor helps explain the mistake made by the latter district:[6]

> *Academic* rigor refers to strong emphasis on completion of school-like tasks, exercises, grade level achievement, grades and test scores, following instructions and meeting requirements, conforming to procedures and conduct necessary to succeed in academy and to fulfill its institutional requirements. *Academic* also suggests being out-of-touch and abstract. In contrast, *intellectual* rigor refers to characteristics of the life of the mind and its earnest quest for understanding, insight, knowledge, truth, solving intellectual puzzles, and the like.

Thus an early childhood program that is developmentally appropriate goes beyond "just" play to intellectually challenge children through the use of problem-solving materials.

Between these two points on the continuum, we saw a mix of challenging, age-appropriate, developmentally based curricula. An especially good example is Changes, an integrated art and science curriculum jointly developed by two teachers in St. Louis. On the day of our observation, the teacher passed around a bowl of clay powder and encouraged the ten children to use their senses and talk about how it felt, smelled, and the like. Next, a wet squishy ball of clay and a dry ball were passed around. Children were asked to compare how they were the same or different. Each child had a chance to hold the two pieces. The next step was to compare clay that was fired in a "special oven" with a piece that had been air-dried. She asked the children, "What would happen if you put these two pieces in water?" After taking time to discuss and generate ideas about this, they tried it out, first placing the fired piece, then the air-dried piece, into a dish of water. The children were encouraged to watch, to use their eyes to see what happened. The teacher explained that they would leave the pieces in the water and return to their experiment later.

Then the group moved to another part of the room and worked with clay set up on tables. They busily kneaded it with their hands, using rolling pins, clay bricks with designs on them, and other tools. The teacher asked the children about what they were doing without disrupting or directing their activity. The group returned to look at the two pieces of clay in water, to see what had happened to them over time. The teacher made a point of talking to each of the children, encouraged them to express themselves, and showed great respect for their ideas. The clay was taken out of the water and passed around and again the children were asked to see how they could change it.

In another site, a harvest theme was expressed throughout one classroom. Books and displays on gardening, farming, soil, and similar topics were featured prominently. In the middle of the room a large dirtbox (actually, a child's wading pool) was filled with large, root vegetables—rutabagas, potatoes, yams, carrots—which the children repeatedly dug up and reburied with great enthusiasm. In the classroom down the hall, children strung clay beads, painted at the easel with crushed blueberries, made pottery out of salt dough, and played with different types of houses (log houses, tipis, and hogans), in conjunction with a Native American theme. In yet another site, a "storekeeper" rang up groceries on an adding machine in the dramatic play area, while in another part of the room a small group of children predicted what would happen to their "pigs-in-a-blanket" after they went into the toaster oven.

According to teachers in these programs, however, it was not easy to convince parents that their children were really learning and not "just" playing. When teachers build on children's actual experiences, they often cannot easily point to the specific learning objectives reinforced by the activity; there are usually many. Yet without clear explanations, some parents cannot understand how experiential activities can be more valuable than structured, paper-and-pencil-based "prereading" and "premath" activities.

Other Curriculum Approaches

Several districts used locally developed or nationally standardized unit-based materials but did not hide behind the "developmental" label. They tended to be urban districts serving largely minority populations. We observed a district that used the Distar program in its double session half-day prekindergarten program. Distar is a structured, direct-instruction approach to teaching language. We observed an afternoon session that began with lunch. Lunch was followed by group time: the children counted to 30, sang the ABC song, did attendance (the teacher called out each name, and each child responded, "I am here, I am present" while placing his or her name card on the attendance chart), and discussed the clothes children were wearing (stripes, plaids, colors). The class then began a series of three 10-minute rotations. The teacher conducted the Distar group. This day's session included three unrelated lessons: one on vehicles, one on the days of the week, and one on the concepts wet-dry. While the teacher worked with the first group of four boys (the children were grouped by ability), a second group of six children worked with the aide, who conducted a lesson on shapes. Each child, in turn, copied the aide's drawings of a circle, triangle, square, and rectangle. (The children were pleased when they successfully copied the shapes, jumping up and down and clapping their hands.) The third group worked independently on puzzles. Each group moved in successive rotation, so that each child participated in each of the three activities. Following the structured learning period, the class, as a group, went to music, followed by a group art activity. Fortunately, it was then time for the children to go home.

Another district used three National Diffusion Network programs: (1) Early Prevention of School Failure, (2) Project STAMM, and (3) Talents Unlimited. The Early Prevention of School Failure Program, called the "Early Intervention Program" in this district, follows a diagnostic and prescriptive approach to the following areas: gross motor, fine motor, auditory skills, visual skills, and language skills. A pupil profile is constructed for each child on the basis of an initial screening done during the first three weeks of school, supplemented by observational data from parents. On the basis of the screening results, children are grouped by ability into one of three groups in each classroom. Throughout the year, it is the role of teachers to introduce new skills and develop reinforcement activities for a prescribed set of concepts. The teacher aides work to reinforce the skills through activities selected by the teacher. Thus, using a process of rotating small groups (similar to that described above), the teacher introduces a new skill in a small group lesson while the aide does a reinforcement activity with a second group and a third group has free play/center time. The individual student profiles are maintained throughout the year; teachers monitor the children using checklists in the different modality areas. For the purpose of instructional continuity, at the end of the school year each child's profile is passed to the child's next grade-level teacher.

Project STAMM (Systematic Teaching and Measuring Mathematics) is a sequential math program for grades K–2. It encourages the use of concrete materials in mathematical problem solving and is accompanied by a teacher management system by which children's performance can be easily observed and recorded. Talents Unlimited is a systematic program to enhance recognition and use of thinking skills. It provides children the opportunity to develop thinking skills through the "talent" areas of productive thinking, communication, forecasting, planning, and decision making. The three programs were chosen by a district-level steering committee as best meeting the learning objectives of the district.

Close monitoring of student progress in discrete skill areas, ability grouping based on the results of an initial screening test, limited teacher autonomy, and limited opportunity for child choice and initiative characterized these and several other curriculum approaches we observed in the course of our site visits. Even those districts that eschewed ability grouping but depended on standardized curriculum packages considerably limited the possibility of naturally occurring opportunities for creativity, spontaneity, and individualization.

Nonetheless, standardized curricula were generally well received. Overall, parents of children in these programs seemed to be pleased with the quality of the classroom program. "We have statistics on parent satisfaction. They're more than 90 percent satisfied in all categories," said a district administrator. One parent liked the prekindergarten program "because it's pushing my child to learn more and be prepared for the academic rigor of kindergarten." "Children excelling. That's the bottom line," said another parent. Teachers were not surprised by positive parent response.

They claimed that parents liked pencil-and-paper activities because it proved that their children "were really learning."

Many of the teachers also expressed satisfaction with the curriculum. However, it must be noted that the more enthusiastic opinions were voiced by teachers with little to no prior experience teaching preschool-aged children. Rather, they tended to be individuals who came to early childhood education with an elementary background and who appreciated a standardized curriculum primarily because it "told them what to do." Moreover, it more closely resembled the kind of teaching they were used to prior to being assigned to a prekindergarten classroom.

Continuity

Curriculum is one element of the child's experience in an early childhood program. Another aspect of that experience, which is closely related to curriculum, is continuity. Continuity refers to two things: the number and ease of transitions made by children in a given day and the compatibility of philosophical approaches and curriculum among the different programs that a child is engaged in over time. More simply, if the child is in a stable group of children, with the same staff for most or all of the day in the same location, a high degree of continuity is demonstrated. If the child experiences smooth and understandable changes from year to year, continuity is high. If changes are abrupt and disturbing, continuity is low. The following examples illustrate different degrees of continuity.

Daily Continuity

In one program the child and parent arrive together at 7:00 a.m. and have breakfast. The child then greets her teacher and goes off to play with one of the 15 other children in the room. After the teacher and mother converse, the mother leaves for work. When the child's father arrives at 4:30 p.m. to pick up his daughter, she is happily playing with the same children, and the same teacher, in the same room where her mother left her in the morning. The father is able to talk to the teacher about his daughter's day.

In another program the child is dropped off at 8:30 a.m. and stays with an aide in a group of 20 "early birds" until 9:00 a.m., when the teacher arrives. The child and a few others go to another room to join the rest of their preschool class (24 children in all). They spend the next three hours there. Then some children go home and the rest go to a large cafeteria to eat lunch with the kindergartners and first graders (about 150 children). After lunch the prekindergarten children go to the child care room for a nap until 3:00 p.m. After they wake up, they move to another room with other children who have just arrived from their all-day kindergarten class and remain there until 5:00 p.m., when they move into another room with the late pick-up group. The child encounters six different groups.

Being part of a relatively stable group of children and adults is commonly believed to be a more beneficial educational experience for young children than being part of an ever-changing (unstable) group.[7] Available research has focused primarily on infants and toddlers. It is clear that the continuity or stability of caregivers is key to infants' and toddlers' sense of security in child care. Researchers don't really know the extent to which findings about infants and toddlers can be generalized to slightly older children. However, it is sensible to assume that older children are affected in somewhat similar ways. We know that children who form secure relationships with teachers are not only better able to make a smooth transition between home and school but are also able to use the teacher as a source of security during the day. The essential elements of a secure relationship are the availability and predictability of the teacher. The child who has many different teachers during a day may not develop a secure relationship with any of them. Losing the teacher with whom a child has developed a secure relationship can be very painful to a young child. Children who lose a series of teachers with whom they have secure relationships may be so hurt that they decide human relationships are to be avoided because they cause pain.[8] These issues are therefore important:[9]

> *In reality, childrearing has become a collaborative endeavor with children moving back and forth—many on a daily basis—between their homes and child care. The effects of these two environments may be additive; they may compensate for each other; or some aspects of one may override aspects of the other in positive or negative ways. A full understanding of child development thus requires that both environments be examined.*

Long-Term Continuity

One goal of a good early childhood program is to ensure a smooth transition from prekindergarten to kindergarten. Continuity to kindergarten is frequently assessed by attending to the similarity of the program for children: Is the kindergarten experience an extension of the prekindergarten experience? Is there a similarity of focus and intent between prekindergarten and kindergarten classroom environments and activities? In the case of the transition to kindergarten, it is not enough to answer the above questions in the affirmative. Unfortunately, strong continuity *alone* does not assure an appropriate learning experience for children.

The reason is that kindergarten is frequently becoming "what first grade once was." It has become the expected point of entry for children into the schools; perhaps because of that, it has become the point at which to begin academic instruction. We saw that clearly in the kindergartens we visited. Almost without exception, the kindergarten consisted of a highly structured, academically oriented experience. Time was rigidly scheduled and divided into nonintegrated learning periods (reading time, math time, music time, large group time). The majority of the day's activities were teacher directed. Independent activity guided by child choice was generally limited to brief play times—as short as 15 minutes in half-day kindergartens. Learning materials, especially for language arts and math activities, were heavily reliant on workbooks and worksheets that supplemented standardized reading and math series. (Earlier we noted with concern that 22 percent of the observed prekindergarten classrooms used workbooks; in comparison, 78 percent of the kindergartens observed in those same sites used workbooks.) Even open-ended activities like art tended toward rigidity by emphasizing total-group art "projects," in which each child is directed to make the same thing (identical turkeys for Thanksgiving or hearts for Valentine's Day).

Given the nature of the receiving kindergarten environment, continuity between prekindergarten and kindergarten, considered alone, is not necessarily a good thing. This is not to say that we did not see continuity. We did. However, it was in those districts in which we saw a downward extension of the kindergarten and early elementary curriculum in the prekindergarten (in short, a developmentally inappropriate program for children) that we saw the smoothest continuity. Ironically, in those sites in which continuity was poorest, it was because the prekindergarten program *was* developmentally appropriate and the kindergarten program was not.

This pattern should be viewed with alarm. Both prekindergarten and kindergarten should focus on an upward extension of earlier development rather than a downward extension of schooling. Child development research shows that young children learn best through direct, concrete experience of the world rather than through symbolic manipulation of the type more often associated with formal instruction, particularly reading. There is no evidence that greater long-term gains result from those programs with heavy concentration on academic instruction.[10]

In fact, perhaps the opposite may be true. The consequence of an increasingly academic kindergarten program is a growing number of children who are unable to successfully negotiate the kindergarten curriculum. Across the country, parents can be heard complaining that their children are in danger of flunking kindergarten. Indeed many children are made to repeat the kindergarten year. At present, there are four solutions to this problem, three of which essentially rely on changing the child, the fourth on changing the kindergarten.

The first "solution" is to make the prekindergarten program more academic, and thus resemble more closely the kindergarten curriculum. We observed this strategy in practice in several districts. These were districts in which standardized curricula were in use in prekindergarten classrooms, in which teacher-directed academic activities were the norm rather than the exception, in which play was seen as a reward for learning, not as a medium for learning. Practices in these districts reinforce the negative stereotype about public schools' involvement in early childhood programs.

A second solution is the growing popularity of "developmental kindergartens," which essentially add a second year of kindergarten. These transitional classes—an extra grade between prekindergarten and kindergarten (usually called "developmental" kindergarten or "readiness" kindergarten), or between kindergarten and first grade (called "pre-firsts" or "transitional firsts")—are a new phenomenon across the country. They are generally a well-intentioned response to the fact that many children are not capable of meeting the demands of kindergarten and first grade and so are in danger of being held back or referred to special education.[11] Although "developmental" does not always refer to the nature of the curriculum of this "postprekindergarten" year, it did in the two developmental kindergartens observed in two of our sites. They were clearly appropriate to the developmental needs of kindergarten-aged children in terms of materials, activities, and equipment. We speculate that this was so because they existed in two sites that had strong, coherent philosophies of early childhood education. It is not a coincidence that in each of these districts a common philosophy about children and education was shared by the superintendents, early childhood supervisors, and teachers.

A third solution to the problem of an overly rigorous kindergarten program is to adjust the entrance age for eligibility to kindergarten. In the past 30 years, the average age of kindergartners has been gradually going up so that a child who might have been in the older half of the class in 1958 might now be one of the youngest children in the class.[12] Yet, no matter what the cut-off date for kindergarten entry, there will always be children born in the last three months of a 12-month year, the age-group of children frequently recommended for enrollment in developmental kindergartens.

The fourth, and we think the optimal, solution to the curricular mismatch between prekindergarten and kindergarten is to reconceptualize the kindergarten program as a developmental, age-appropriate program capable of meeting the needs of a diverse group of children. Such kindergartens existed 20 years ago, as described by Egertson:[13]

> *When kindergarten was for five-year-olds, no one worried whether children could sit still for long periods of time—the classroom was organized so that children could move around and select useful pursuits from a wide variety of materials and activities. No one worried whether children had long attention spans—they weren't expected to be able to sit and listen to lessons for the majority of the school day. Teacher-directed activities were then largely limited to music and story-telling. Twenty years ago, no one worried, either, whether children could count to 20, say their ABCs, or know their sounds. It was expected that the school would teach those things in good time. And no one worried about eye-hand coordination or auditory and visual memory. The materials and equipment were designed to help these capacities emerge.*

In several districts we saw efforts to improve the kindergarten through upward diffusion of the prekindergarten program—with varying degrees of formality. In all cases, it involved some degree of interaction between prekindergarten and kindergarten teachers. It ranged from informal communication between the prekindergarten and kindergarten teachers within a given school, to occasionally scheduled group meetings, to a concentrated, districtwide focus on developmental, age-appropriate practice across the grade levels. A districtwide, multiyear strategy was used in one district.

In this district a major objective of the director of elementary education and the early childhood supervisor is continuity of approach from prekindergarten through first grade. Their long-range plan is to institute a developmentally appropriate curriculum for all children from age three through age six. The district's prekindergarten program is a model of appropriate activities for three- and four-year-olds. A wide variety of materials and equipment are available, teachers are well-trained, and children have many choices. Their philosophy is expressed in the program's motto: learning through play.

This district employs many different strategies to introduce teachers to the "learning through play" approach and to encourage greater continuity. Grade level meetings are held jointly for pre-kindergarten and kindergarten teachers. Teachers are encouraged to visit classes in other schools in the district and in the levels below and above the one they teach. When full-day kindergarten was proposed, the committee of teachers that met with the early childhood supervisor to plan the curriculum included a few teachers from each level: prekindergarten, kindergarten, and first grade. This group learned together and from each other. The kindergarten curriculum they produced was so successful that it not only is used in the full-day kindergartens but was also proposed for adoption in all the district's part-day kindergartens. These methods (communication between teachers, teacher exploration of new curriculum approaches, and direct observations of early childhood classrooms) result in a more coherent curriculum across the pre-kindergarten, kindergarten, and early elementary levels and in greater continuity for children.

Conclusion

In a process paralleling the evolution of the last ten years of debate and research over child care,[14] the argument over the role of public schools in early childhood education is probably ready to move beyond the questions of *whether* the public schools should be in the early childhood business (such a question is clearly obsolete; they *are* in the business) or *in what ways* should they be, to the question, "How can we ensure the best possible experience for children?"

Good programs for children cannot be mandated, but the necessary conditions can be specified: small groups of children, caring and well-prepared teachers, a partnership of teachers and parents, effective and supportive administrators, and clearly stated philosophical principles. Good programs for children are based on principles of child development and theories of education. Teachers must have specific child-related training in early childhood education and child development, experience with young children, supervision from knowledgeable administrators, and the support of ongoing staff development. Curriculum guidelines should be clear and specific philosophically with broadly outlined goals, so that teachers can work creatively within, rather than be constrained and directed by, the curriculum. A particular kind of leadership is a critical element in the quality of any program for young children. Based on the case studies, we found that in public school-operated early childhood programs, effective leaders must have three characteristics: well prepared in early childhood education, well-known and respected by teachers (and building administrators) throughout the district, and respected by and influential with the district superintendent. This kind of leader can develop the necessary philosophy of early education and clearly and ably communicate it to teachers, parents, and district administrators and officials. For good appropriate continuous programs to be the norm in a public school district, the district must commit itself to appropriate practice throughout its prekindergartens, kindergartens, and early elementary grades. This requires a philosophical commitment to appropriate early childhood education and the commitment of financial and human resources for ongoing staff development and support to retrain teachers and administrators so the principles can be translated into practice.

Recommendations

- The guiding principles and philosophical base of the early childhood curriculum should be clearly articulated and communicated to all parents, teachers, and administrators.
- Staff development is essential to implementing a curriculum. Staff development opportunities that support the curriculum should be offered frequently and regularly for all staff (for example, to teachers, paraprofessionals, and principals in a school district).
- Curriculum goals should be clearly communicated to parents through discussions with their children's teachers, presentations by administrators, and written materials.
- As the direct supervisors of teachers, principals play a key role in the practice of early childhood education in a school district. Staff development should be directed toward increasing principals' knowledge of the theory, philosophy, and appropriate practice of early education.
- A sufficient supply of equipment and materials appropriate for young children should be available for every classroom and arranged in identifiable learning centers to encourage children's independent use. Available learning centers should include blocks, art, library, dramatic play, gross motor, sand/

water, manipulatives, math, science/nature, and writing/communication.

- Workbooks or other closed-ended, paper-and-pencil activities (such as ditto sheets) should not be used in programs for young children.
- Children's individual work—not teacher-made or commercial materials—should be prominently displayed at child's eye level throughout the classroom.
- Cultural diversity is a basic characteristic of our society. A wide variety of multiracial and nonsexist materials and activities should be available to children integrated throughout the curriculum. Multicultural materials and activities should encompass and extend beyond the cultures and ethnicities represented by the children (and adults) in the classroom and school.
- Physical activity using large muscles is essential for healthy development and should be an integral daily part of programs for young children. Such gross-motor activities require inviting indoor and outdoor spaces, varied and flexible equipment, regularly scheduled daily time, and engaged teachers who recognize and enhance children's learning opportunities.
- In all early childhood programs, developmentally appropriate practices, the child development principles that support them, and the learning they promote should be clearly communicated to parents in a wide variety of ways: in writing, verbally, by direct experience with materials and equipment.

Endnotes

1. Bredekamp, S. (Ed.) (1986). *Developmentally appropriate practice*. Washington, D.C.: National Association for the Education of Young Children, p. 20.
2. Bredekamp (1986), pp. 3–8.
3. Weikart, D.P., Rogers, L., Adcock, C., and McClelland, D. (1971). *The cognitively oriented curriculum*. Washington, D.C.: ERIC-National Association for the Education of Young Children.
4. Day, M. C., and R. K. Parker (Eds.) (1977). *The preschool in action: Exploring early childhood programs*. Boston, Mass.: Allyn and Bacon.
5. Berrueta-Clement, J.R., L.J. Schweinhart, W.S. Barnett, A.S. Epstein, and D.P. Weikart (1984). Changed lives: Effects of the Perry Preschool Program on youths through age 19. *Monographs of the High/Scope Educational Research Foundation 8*.
6. Katz, L.G., J.D. Raths, and R.D. Torres (1987). *A place called kindergarten*. Urbana, Ill.: Clearinghouse on Elementary and Early Childhood Education, p. 29.

7. There are practical considerations as well. The physical health of children in a stable group is likely to be better since contact with a smaller number of other children will reduce opportunities for transmission of common diseases such as colds and flu.

8. Howes, C. (1987). Quality indicators in infant and toddler child care: The Los Angeles Study. In D.A. Phillips (Ed.), *Quality in child care: What does research tell us?* Washington, D.C.: National Association for the Education of Young Children, p. 82.

9. Phillips, D.A. and C. Howes (1987). Indicators of quality child care: Review of research. In D.A. Phillips (Ed.), *Quality in child care: What does research tell us?* Washington, D.C.: National Association for the Education of Young Children, p. 11.

10. Spodek, B. (1982). The kindergarten: A retrospective and contemporary view. In L. G. Katz (Ed.), *Current topics in early childhood education*. Norwood, N.J.: Ablex Publishing Corporation.

11. Shepard, L.A. and Smith, M.L. (1986). Synthesis of research on school readiness and kindergarten retention. *Educational Leadership, 44* (3), 78–86. In fact, there is no evidence that an extra year of schooling solves the problems it was intended to solve. In what may be the only review of transitional classes, Lorrie Shepard and Mary Lee Smith conclude that "children in these programs show virtually no academic advantage over equally at-risk children who have not had the extra year. Furthermore, there is often an emotional cost associated with staying back." (p. 85).

12. Shepard and Smith (1986), p. 81.

13. Egertson, H.A. (1987). Recapturing kindergarten for five-year-olds. *Education Week*, pp. 19, 28.

14. Phillips and Howes (1987).

Chapter 10

BEING RESPONSIVE TO FAMILIES

What does it mean to be responsive to families? The concept of responsiveness to families has its roots in two issues: in concern about the changing nature of family life in America and in the widespread recognition that parent involvement is an essential component of successful programs for young children. As Heath and McLaughlin noted in a recent article in *Phi Delta Kappan*:[1]

> *Today's schools build on yesterday's notion of "family," both in form and function. Schools as social institutions have become outmoded, because the institutions on which they depend—particularly the family and the workplace—have changed dramatically.*

Families are changing rapidly. In many, if not most, two-parent households both parents are working to support the family, and the combined demands of work and family create real time pressures and stresses. Many poor families are under tremendous stress, whether parents work or not, because of deteriorating homes, neighborhoods, and communities. More children live in single-parent families, particularly children who are poor. Single parents obviously have even less time than dual parents and probably experience greater concern about their ability to support their family. Extended families living geographically close to one another are not common. All these facts must be acknowledged and taken into account when creating programs for young children.

Foundations of Family Responsiveness

Good early childhood programs have always recognized that the family is the primary influence in a child's life, and they view them

234

as partners who must be closely involved in the program for their children. Whether this program component is referred to as parent involvement (as in Head Start) or parent participation or parent support, it derives from the recognition that good programs for children *necessarily* serve families. Family-responsive early childhood programs are based on the premise that, while the primary service is provided to the child, it is the *family* that is the client.

Schools are commonly viewed, and often view themselves, primarily as educators of children, not as service providers for families. Or put another way, the school's client is the child rather than the family. Taking this perspective, the school views parents' role as supporting the school in educating the child—reinforcing at home what is taught at school, supporting the school through fund-raising efforts, or helping out in the classroom as a volunteer. This is a limited view of parents' role in schools. Parent involvement is a reciprocal relationship between home and school, not a one-way street. Given the current realities of family life and the wide range of possible parent participation, the traditional forms of parent involvement practiced in schools (the room mother, parent-teacher conferences during school hours, bake sales) are completely inadequate for today's families. In a recent nationwide poll by Lou Harris, 33 percent of parents said the most convenient time for meetings with teachers was in the evening, but only 9 percent of teachers said that time would be convenient for them.[2] Parent involvement practices must adapt to new realities and become responsive to families, particularly if schools are to have a larger role in providing early childhood programs.

Family responsive programs are based on three premises: a young child comes to a program or service from the context of a family, not only as an individual; any program or service offered to families for their young children will have an impact of some kind on that family as a whole; and family members may need support and services beyond the prekindergarten program for the child.

An Expanded View of Parent Participation

In its most complete form, parent participation includes at least five distinct components: fellowship with other parents, genuine opportunities to participate in governance of the program, opportunities to participate directly in the education of one's children, encouragement and support for parents *as* parents, and support for parents as adults with needs that may be only indirectly related to parenting but that are critical to the maintenance of the family.

Translating this broad and inclusive conception into the specifics of the parent involvement component in a good early childhood program might produce many—or even all—of the following services:

- Regularly scheduled social events for families.
- A room or area where parents can gather and relax.
- A governing council or board with the majority of its members parents of children in the program.
- An open invitation to observe or visit in the classroom, accompany children and staff on field trips, drop in for lunch, or volunteer in the classroom, as the parent's time permits.
- Parent support groups focusing on issues of parenting and child development.
- Help in securing social, health, and other services the family needs.
- Referral to adult education, GED programs, or employment training programs.
- A full-working-day, year-round program for children whose families need it.
- Active help for families in arranging the child care of their choice to supplement the program hours, by providing transportation and child care referral services and by including child care providers as partners in the education of children served.

Just as the good early childhood educator respects individual children's differences and knows that each child requires personalized attention, so must educators deal individually with families. No single form of parent participation will work for every family. Not all parents need or want to be involved in every aspect of their child's program. Not all parents have the same need for support, either as parents or as adults. And not all parents require child care. The good program must provide a "menu" of possibilities, from which parents are free to choose the forms and degrees of involvement that are most appropriate for their situation. No matter which, or how many items, each parent chooses from the menu, the program must actively encourage all parents to participate.

Comprehensive Services: Being Responsive to Families

The term *comprehensive services*, when used in relation to early childhood programs, means the array of services that complement the basic educational program for children. Early childhood educators assert that education cannot be meaningfully provided, to poor children or to any other children, without offering additional services. As a nation, we have long recognized that children who are hungry will have trouble learning, which is the basic reason the National School Lunch and Breakfast programs were originally enacted and continue to have widespread support. By the same logic, children who have poor (or no) health care services, or whose parents cannot support their children's education because they have not completed their own, also will have trouble learning.

The classic example of comprehensive services in early childhood programs is Head Start, which clearly defines what these services are and requires their provision to children and their families. All Head Start programs are required by the Head Start Performance Standards to provide an educational program for children *and* to provide social, health, and nutritional services, along with strong parent involvement. Head Start programs must have an identified staff person responsible for each component: education, health, social services, parent involvement. The level of services provided by Head Start provides a benchmark against which to measure other programs.

Comprehensive services include, at a minimum, *health services*, such as screening for developmental delays and physical examinations, or other direct health services provided by a doctor, nurse, dentist, and/or mental health professional; *social services*, usually provided directly by a social worker and by referral to community or government agencies and services, and including assistance with locating and obtaining services for which a family is eligible; *nutrition services*, which means serving meals and snacks so that children are receiving the major portion of their daily nutritional requirements during the program's hours; and services to parents so that they can be more effective supporters of their children and develop themselves as adults and as parents (usually called *parent involvement activities*, or *parent education*). Finally, *transportation* is a support service that may be critical to the child getting any program at all, let alone the comprehensive services that she or he may need.

District Practices: Head Start Versus Selected State-Funded Prekindergarten Programs

Comprehensive services are particularly critical for children who are at risk because of poverty, low educational attainment of their parents, and other disadvantageous circumstances. Head Start and some of the state prekindergarten programs we surveyed are designed to serve these children. Using District Survey data, it is possible to compare the reported provision of comprehensive services in public school-operated Head Start programs with public school-operated, state-funded prekindergarten programs. Five state prekindergarten programs were selected for comparison because they represent those that are operating on a large scale in states with large populations of poor children and are by design targeted to poor or at-risk young children (that is, they are serving a population of children similar to Head Start).

The California and New York state prekindergarten programs were created in the same era as Head Start (mid-1960s) and were clearly intended to provide levels of comprehensive service similar to Head Start. In both state programs comprehensive social, health, and nutrition services as well as parent involvement are required.

The prekindergarten programs in South Carolina (1983) and in Illinois (1985) are newer, but also clearly recommend that comprehensive services be offered, including health, social services, nutrition, and both parent participation and parent education. The Texas prekindergarten program is both new (1985) and extensive, serving more than 50,000 children and operating in over half of the state's local school districts. The Texas program requires few comprehensive services, only health screening and parent education.

Reported data from the District Survey that illustrate the services provided are displayed in Table 10–1.

Social and Health Services   One indication of the level of social and health services offered is the use of professionals other than teachers. Most Head Start programs frequently use nurses and social workers; many also frequently use dentists and psychologists. Nurses appear to be common in prekindergarten programs in all five states, but even in states with comprehensive requirements, social workers are rare except for a few programs in New York and Illinois. Psychologists and dentists are apparently not used.

Nutrition   Nearly all Head Start programs provide children with breakfast, a snack, and lunch. By contrast, only about half of the responding districts' prekindergarten programs in California, New York, and South Carolina provide a snack and one meal, either breakfast or lunch. About half the programs in Texas offer one meal only, either breakfast or lunch. Programs in Illinois do not appear to provide either breakfast or lunch, but about half do offer snacks.

Table 10-1 Comparison of Comprehensive Services in Selected State Prekindergarten and Public School-Operated Head Start Programs

Service	Head Start (N = 189)	Calif. (N = 51)	N.Y. (N = 43)	I.I. (N = 23)	S.C. (N = 19)	Tex. (N = 68)	La. (N = 15)
Professionals Used Frequently							
Nurse	☒	☒	☒	☒	●	☒	●
Dentist	●						
Psychologist	●			●			
Social worker	☒		☒	●			
Speech therapist	☒	☒	●	☒	☒	☒	●
Meals							
Breakfast	X	●	☒		☒	☒	☒
Snack	X	☒	☒	☒	X		☒
Lunch	X	X	X		☒	☒	X
Transportation							
None		☒	●			●	●
Home-school	☒	●	☒	X	X	☒	☒
To other child care setting	●			●			
Parent Participation							
T'cher conferences	X	X	X	X	X	X	X
Parent board	X	X	●	●	●		
Employed aides	☒		☒				

table continues

Table 10-1 *Continued*

Volunteers	X	X	X	X	•	☒	X
Fund raisers	☒	☒	•				
Advocates	☒	•	•				•
Parent Education							
Newsletter	X	☒	☒	X	☒	•	☒
Parent education workshops	X	X	X	X	☒		X
Parent-parent network encouraged	X	☒	X	•	•		•
Parent room			☒				

Key: **X** = at least 75%   ☒ = at least 50%   • = at least 25%.

Note: All data are from the District Survey (N = 1,681) and pertain to the 1985-1986 school year.

Parent Involvement   Parent involvement is a hallmark of Head Start. Nearly all Head Start programs have a parent board and use parent volunteers in the classroom. Many also employ parents as classroom aides and most use parents as fund-raisers and advocates. Overall, only California and New York prekindergarten programs come close to approximating Head Start in parent involvement. Illinois and South Carolina have some parent boards, and many Illinois programs report using parent volunteers. In Texas only a few programs report parent volunteers.

Parent Education   Most Head Start programs offer parent education workshops in addition to parent involvement in other forms, as do programs in New York, California, and Illinois. Some programs in South Carolina offer parent education workshops, while very few were reported in Texas, even though parent education is a specified element of service to be provided.

Transportation   Transportation appears to be provided about as much in state prekindergarten programs as in Head Start, but the destinations are sometimes different. Nearly all prekindergarten programs bus only between school and home, while some Head Start programs also bus between school and another child care setting.

Clearly, Head Start programs are providing better nutrition, social, and health services. Head Start programs, at least in terms of transportation services, address the fact that some children need longer hours of care. State prekindergarten programs present a mixed bag on parent involvement/parent education when compared to Head Start programs, with only those in New York and California similar to Head Start. The bottom line is that if a good early childhood education program must deliver comprehensive services, especially for poor (at-risk) children, then most state prekindergarten programs are not doing well enough and none appear to be doing as much as Head Start programs.

Findings from the Study

In the study, we were particularly interested in whether and how public school prekindergarten policies and programs included components responsive to families. The daily (and annual) schedules of public school programs are an indication of responsiveness to families with parent(s) who are working, in school, or in employment training programs. Transportation services are indicative of responsiveness both to working families and to those families with no access to transportation whose children are therefore effectively denied access to a prekindergarten program. Finally, comprehensive services, specifically including parent participation and parent education components, offer another indication of responsiveness to families.

Schedules

Part-day prekindergarten programs can best meet the child care needs of parents who work or attend school/training part time and whose work or school hours (including commuting time) coincide with the program's hours. Part-day programs also can be, and are used as, one part of a family's carefully constructed full-day child care package, which may also involve care by other family members, neighbors, and/or friends, or sometimes, in another part-day program.

The majority of states have developed prekindergarten programs that do not meet working parents' needs for full-working-day services. Programs are mainly part-day, although some states do permit full-school-day services (the District of Columbia, Kentucky, Louisiana, New York [only those that operated full school days before 1985], Ohio, Oklahoma, West Virginia), and five states' programs allow children to be served for the full working day. That so many of these programs are part-day contrasts with the widely used rationale that state prekindergarten programs are designed not only to enhance the development of young children but also to assist the growing number of mothers in the labor force.

The practices of local school districts, where many types of prekindergarten programs operate (including state-funded prekindergartens), mirror state policies. According to the District Survey, most public school-operated programs of all types are part-day (70 percent of all classes were reported to be three hours per day or less) and school-year only (80 percent of all programs).

Less than 10 percent of the 1,681 programs reported in the District Survey could be classified as child care programs (3.6 percent provided subsidized child care, 2.6 percent provided child care supported by parent tuition/fees, and 2.0 percent provided child care for teen student/parents). Both subsidized and parent-fee child care typically operate eight to nine hours daily, while child care for teen parents usually covers only the school day (six to seven hours). Child care for teen parents is a school-year program; subsidized child care is a year-round operation. Parent-fee child care programs are split, with 60 percent operating year-round and 40 percent during the school year only.

At the state level, attention to the needs of low- and moderate-income parents for full-working-day programs for the care and education of their prekindergarten children remains largely under the auspices of state social services departments through the Social Services Block Grant (Title XX) and/or state-subsidized child care programs. In states that have been able to make financial commitments to improving the quality and quantity of child care, significant attention is being focused on the quality of the education and care in these programs via improvements in regulations and in staff salaries (Massachusetts, Minnesota, and New York have made substantial efforts).

The states which permit full-working-day services in their state-funded prekindergarten programs are Massachusetts, New Jersey, Florida, Illinois, and Vermont, although few working-day services have yet been funded at the local level under these state programs. In 1987–1988 about one-third of the applicants funded in Vermont's new early education program were community agencies that offer full-working-day services, thus clearly making it easier for children who need these services to get them. About half the applications funded in Vermont that year noted that some of the funds would be used to pay for early education services in existing prekindergartens or child care centers. Because there was no indication in the applications of the actual length of day that children would be served or how the requested funds would complement other funds, it is hard to know if these providers actually were able to meet child care needs.

These findings indicate only modest attempts by states and school districts to support families in which parent(s) are working, participating in employment training, or completing their own educations on more than a part-time, school-year schedule.

Transportation

Providing transportation services makes it possible to reach children who cannot get themselves to a program (for example, children in families living in poverty in areas lacking public transportation) and to support the child care packages of working families. Transportation policies very among the states. Fewer than half the states with prekindergarten programs explicitly provide transportation; in those that do, it is often only to the child's home. Massachusetts and New York are exceptions, allowing transportation to licensed child care settings.

One-third of the local school district prekindergarten programs surveyed reported that they provided no transportation. Of the remainder, most reported providing transportation only to the child's home. Transportation to child care settings appears to be limited to two program types: About one-quarter of Head Start and special education programs reported providing transportation to child care settings.

Comprehensive Services

An array of comprehensive services (which generally include at least health, nutrition, and social services) is essential in programs that aim to serve at-risk children. If children deemed at-risk must be served in the context of their family and community, these essential services must be readily available to families as well as to children. A program that concentrates only on serving the child— no matter how comprehensive the services offered to that child— will not be as effective as a program that makes the family its client.[3] Families at risk have a variety of needs, ranging from basic ones such as housing and food and health care to higher-order needs such as adult education and employment training.

Some state prekindergarten programs are silent on the issue of comprehensiveness, while others address it only partially. However, states that explicitly use the Head Start model as the basis for their prekindergarten policies tend to use the language of comprehensiveness (parent participation, parent education, health, social services, nutrition) in their legislation. Table 2–5 lists, for all but the most recent state-funded prekindergarten programs, those states that mention, in their legislative and/or regulatory language, each of these five elements of comprehensive services. In contrast to those modeled after Head Start, state prekindergarten programs authorized by permissive statute make no explicit mention of comprehensive services; as with other aspects of these permissive programs, local district option is exercised regarding comprehensiveness.

Moving beyond state-funded prekindergarten programs into the general practices of districts in the variety of other prekindergarten programs they operate reveals a similar lack of comprehensiveness. One way to gauge whether districts are providing comprehensive services in their various programs for prekindergarten children is to examine these programs' employment of health and social service professionals (other than teachers) and their provision of meals and snacks to children.

District Survey data reveal that nurses are frequently used in all program types but that other health professionals (dentists and psychologists, for example) are common only in Head Start programs. Social workers were frequently employed in Head Start programs and, to a lesser degree, in special education, subsidized child care, and child care for teen/student parents. Social workers were rarely reported among all other program types. Children attending Head Start or child care programs are nearly always fed both breakfast and lunch as well as a snack during their program day. Children in other types of programs are likely to receive only a daily snack.

Parent Participation Practices

With the exception of six of the state-funded prekindergarten programs (Maine [both programs], New Jersey [only the permissive program], Pennsylvania, West Virginia, and Wisconsin) which require neither parent participation nor parent education, most state programs refer to both education for parents and their participation in their children's programs. Delaware and the migrant program in Florida mention only participation by parents; Texas mentions only parent education.

It is so widely accepted that parent involvement is a good thing that nearly every local school district prekindergarten program in the District Survey reported that some form of parent involvement was available in their early childhood programs. The most common form was parent-teacher conferences, a feature reported by 95 percent of programs of all types. Roughly half of all programs reported some other form of parent participation; the most common were distributing parent newsletters, having parents volunteer in classrooms, and offering parent education workshops. Nearly all Head Start programs and subsidized child care programs reported parent participation in governance via a parent advisory council or parent board. Many parent education, parent-fee child care, and Chapter I programs also reported having parent councils or boards. Such parent participation was rare in all other program types. Participation in governance is a particularly effective way to empower parents; it has been successfully used in all Head Start programs for decades. It is also a very common practice in not-for-profit child care programs which are governed by boards of directors, a majority of whom are parents.

Issues and Policies at the State Level Beyond State-Funded Prekindergartens

The State Survey examined the states' broader early childhood policy, that is, beyond the state prekindergarten initiatives.

Some Promising Indications

It is notable that during the same period the state prekindergarten programs were being developed, many of these same states (those with prekindergarten programs) were also paying more attention to other child care programs and to concerns reflecting a growing interest in family issues, especially those relating to work and family life. For example, school-age child care programs for children kindergarten age and older are now in place in many states and school districts, partly due to increased federal attention to the issue. The federal Dependent Care Block Grant enacted in 1986 has made modest amounts of funding available to the states for development and improvement of child care programs for school-aged children. In addition, a number of states have committed state funds specifically to school-age child care and many school districts have established these programs, often through parents' efforts and administered by parent groups. Contracting between the public schools and community-based school-age care providers is a commonly used mechanism to establish programs in schools.

Employer-related child care has received attention in a few states. Child care resource and referral agencies have been established in several states, linking parents with existing services and/ or working to develop new services. In some states, Head Start is able to extend its program day with the use of Social Service Block Grant/Title XX funds.

Unresolved Issues and Problems

In the State Survey interviews, many respondents (in almost every state) cited insufficient funding for child care and insufficient supply of early childhood services generally, and many mentioned a need for more comprehensive services, especially health care, for families. Some respondents noted the isolation of low-income families and children in the cities and in rural areas and noted bias against low-income families and public assistance clients. Expanded services for non-English-speaking populations are badly needed.

Others mentioned that many state-subsidized child care programs do not provide for a mix of children from all income groups; limited funding means that eligibility is limited to the poorest families or only to protective service cases. Some respondents also told us that public school programs for four-year-olds lack the necessary parental involvement and are inflexible regarding the needs of working parents. Also mentioned was the need for child care for sick children as well as for infants, children of teen parents, and children whose parents work night-shift jobs.

Finally, respondents also noted problems with funding and transportation policies. Local school districts which might seek to provide extended hours for a state-funded prekindergarten program are hampered by the fact that most states do not permit prekindergarten funds to support full-working-day services. As for transportation, until states revise transportation laws and raise transportation subsidies, children in many school districts will not be bused at all or will be bused only to their homes.

Levels of Commitment

While some states appear to be addressing family needs in a number of policy arenas at once (if not in a coordinated way) other states appear to have lower levels of commitment to these family issues. States without prekindergarten legislation also tend to have lower levels of commitment to other services for young children, such as child care. The disparity in commitment is partially a question of resources.

Like any other form of state spending, the commitment of funds to early childhood programs, whether those programs stem from a child care perspective or an educational one, is greatly influenced by the state's economic health. States with robust and expanding economies generally feel a strong present need for more workers; these states are likely to support expanded spending on child care when it is viewed as a strategy for recruiting more women into the labor force, and/or expanded funding for early education programs when they are viewed as improving the quality of the future work force. Massachusetts and Florida are the leading examples, with their extensive child care *and* prekindergarten programs. In contrast, those states with less healthy economies, little need to recruit more workers, and less funding to commit may still be convinced to spend state funds on early childhood programs by arguments that these programs will influence the quality and skill of the future work force. States like Washington, Oklahoma, and Michigan offer evidence of this.

Attitudinal, as well as financial, barriers to improving all services for prekindergartners continue to exist in some states. In some states, there are continuing difficulties with public acceptance of women working outside the home, thus affecting the ability of these states to enact legislation and appropriations that appear to encourage women to work. In some states there is general resistance to spending public money on poor people—even children. These attitudes impede the development of services for young children that meet the needs of their families.

States that legislate children's programs despite serious financial constraints have a history of strong commitment to public responsibility for disadvantaged citizens. We concluded that states actively engaged in prekindergarten legislation are also generally inclined to do more in other areas of children's services. Although this general commitment to a variety of children's services appears to be a pattern, each of the services is still considered separately—legislatively and fiscally. Additionally, the absence of mandated (or strongly encouraged and supported) coordination between child care programs and education programs at the state level continues to keep these early childhood streams separate. No state has yet initiated a comprehensive children's policy encompassing all types of services. Clearly, child care programs and other children's services that are in the process of being expanded and improved via increased state spending and regulatory reform can be seen as part of an overall approach to meeting the child care and education needs of children.

Family-Responsive Policies in State-Funded Prekindergarten Programs

The study found a number of examples of family-responsive state prekindergarten policies. In this rapidly changing arena of social policy, new programs and policies are being considered in legislative sessions across the country. In general, states have enacted three types of legislated prekindergarten programs that might be considered family-responsive: direct service programs to children that have comprehensive features and specifically include parent involvement (including state contributions to Head Start); direct service programs for prekindergarten children that include attention to issues of working families; and parent education programs. The following examples can be considered as forerunners of future progressive policy.

California is an example of a state that includes health, social, and nutrition services and parent education and participation (as well as staff development and evaluation) in its program, which was modeled after Head Start. The schools are encouraged to offer afternoon child care programs or to utilize existing child development programs, such as the children's centers, and contracted child care providers are encouraged to provide full-working-day, year-round programs. Parents serve on advisory boards, are provided with opportunities for parent education, and are encouraged to spend time in the classroom. A few programs have developed family child care home satellite networks for families requiring full-time care.

New York State's prekindergarten program mandates parental involvement, including parent education, participation in decision making, and opportunities for employment in the program. A few of the older (pre-1985) New York prekindergarten programs are full-school-day programs; a few others use funding from sources other than the state education department to extend to full-day programs. Transportation is a district option; if provided, transportation must be offered to any child care arrangement the family has made. Transportation is fully funded, 90 percent by the state and 10 percent by the district.

Grants from Washington's Early Childhood Education and Assistance Program (ECEAP) include funding for health, social, and nutritional services; transportation; parent education; home visits; and referral to other community services. ECEAP is administered by the state's Department of Community Development.

New Jersey began a new early childhood program in FY 1988 which gives priority to funding Head Start programs that expand to full-year, full-working-day services. However, public schools, private nonprofit agencies, and subsidized child care programs may also apply. The services provided must be comprehensive, including supplementary health and social services, transportation, and a strong parent participation component. New Jersey's program is administered by the Department of Human Services.

In Delaware, pilot programs for four-year-olds are now half-day, but future development will be based on an evaluation assessing the needs of working parents. In the District of Columbia, 3,444 children are served in programs that are now full-school-day programs; in 20 schools, parents pay fees for before- and after-school care for their four-year-olds. In Florida several programs are attempting to meet the needs of families: Head Start is extending its day in a few locations, using Title XX funds; schools are encouraged to offer child care by combining Department of Education and Department of Health and Rehabilitation funds; and funds have been made available to provide child care for special needs children. School boards in three counties administer state child care funds and contract for child care services with community agencies.

Two states have focused on improving child development through parent education. Minnesota has a statewide program administered through the community education departments of local school districts that provides information to parents of children under age five about child development and learning, health, and community resources. The program is delivered through weekly group meetings facilitated by a parent educator and through an ancillary program for children supervised by an early childhood educator.

Missouri's program funds local school districts to provide the Parents as First Teachers programs; all local school districts are required to offer it to all parents with children under the age of five. The Parents as Teachers program authorizes school districts to offer a minimum of four personal home visits by specially trained parent educators. Districts may also offer group education sessions for parents who are participating in the home-based program. The home visits are scheduled to allow participation of both father and mother; group meetings are designed to enable families to share common parenting concerns.

Kentucky's Parent and Child Education program (PACE), enacted in 1986, is an example of combining adult education with early childhood education. The PACE program, aimed at parents who have three- or four-year-old children and do not have high school diplomas, focuses on offering basic skills (literacy) and child development information to parents while simultaneously offering their children a good prekindergarten experience. Parents attend adult education classes and spend some time participating directly in the classroom with their children.

In 1987 Connecticut also emphasized parent education by funding five Parent Education and Support Centers under the Department of Children and Youth Services, with five more planned for 1988–1989. Vermont has funded community-based Parent-Child Centers, which provide an array of services to parents and their children under three as well as support to pregnant women and their families. Initially, five centers located throughout the state were funded; funds for expansion have also been appropriated.

These developments indicate the beginnings of a growing awareness of the need for more comprehensive programs that address both children's and parents' needs and the interconnections among them. A combination of factors and influences in each state appear to create the conditions that lead to these programs, including well-informed staff in the various agencies at the state level and in state legislatures who share a commitment to creating good programs for families; good working relationships among these individuals carefully built up over time; strong influence by a well-organized child/family advocacy community; a variety of good quality service delivery resources at the community level; public and business community support; and the economic strength to financially launch and sustain these programs.

Family-Responsive Policies and Practices in Local School Districts

The ability to operate family-responsive programs is not based solely on understanding facts about families and knowing what constitutes good early childhood practices regarding parent involvement. It is also a matter of attitude and the disposition to use the knowledge possessed. That most parents work may be a well-known fact, but it does not necessarily result in redesigning the parent involvement component of a program to accommodate working parents. That families living in poverty have multiple needs may be known, but the comprehensive array of services to address these needs is not offered. Notions about the proper role of school versus that of family affect not only the policies and practices of schools but also the expectations that parents have of schools.

Schooling *was* once responsive—if not exactly to families, then to the requirements of the agrarian economy of the nineteenth century. The typical school schedule—six hours a day, ten months of the year with summers off—supported the economic needs of families dependent on agriculture. School fit well with morning and evening farm chores; the entire family labor force was available during the peak work season; children were occupied with school during slow work seasons. Very few families now depend on an agricultural schedule for their economic livelihood. Ironically, although the school structure and the economic needs of families were once balanced, they are now badly mismatched. The nature of work has changed dramatically, while the structure of schooling has remained unchanged—held in place by the momentum inherent in such a vast and enduring system of traditions and habits. The weight of tradition is heavy; its consequences are difficult to question, let alone change. The power of tradition affects much more than school schedules, assigning a particular role for parents to play in their children's schooling. Based on old models of family structure (mothers at home) parents are to be supporters—homework helpers and cupcake bakers—of the educators who are assumed to know best how to educate. Generations of children have absorbed this model and then acted it out as they became parents (and teachers). School personnel operate with the same expectations of the parents' limited role, and the system endures. These common, limited expectations make partnerships between parents and schools difficult to achieve on a system-wide basis, although there are certainly examples on the school level. Successful partnerships, of course, depend on leadership.

Whereas teachers are those most often in direct communication with parents, the nature of these interactions—how supportive, responsive, respectful—is influenced by the school's leader. Just as the overall quality of the program for children is greatly affected by the program's leader, so are attitudes toward families and the responsiveness of practices. The leader shapes the philosophical approach that determines the goals, content, form, and degree of parent participation enacted in a given program, and his or her views can strongly affect how teachers and other direct service staff respond to families. One teacher in Fort Worth summed up her rather complacent and narrow view of the purpose of parent involvement: "At the beginning and the end of the day [when parents pick up their kids], they have a chance to learn from us." Another teacher required parents to wait in the hall to pick up their child each day. Sometimes, the leader's attitudes toward making parents welcome are expressed in small and subtle ways: In one school where we interviewed parents, the principal refused to allow refreshments to be served at the interview because refreshments were "never allowed" for parent meetings. However, in other sites, we found that the principal and teachers operated on an expanded concept of parent-teacher relationships; one parent told us, "[All the staff] here make you feel that being a family is important."

Through the direct observations and face-to-face interviews conducted during the site visits, we were able to examine the family-responsiveness of school districts from the perspective of administrators, teachers, and parents. Most programs espouse and incorporate at least one of the five components of parent participation noted earlier (fellowship with other parents, direct involvement in children's education, participation in governance, support for parenting, and adult education/development). However, very few embrace and act on all of them.

Child Care Programs Supported by Parent Fees

Perhaps because they are offering services for a fee (competing with other community child care providers) and in order to survive must be sure that the services meet what families are demanding in their communities, those school districts that operate parent fee-supported child care programs seem to be more family-responsive than districts with other types of programs. The following two school districts are both examples of fairly extensive parent participation across all five components, even including some involvement in governing the program.

Westside Community Schools in Omaha, Nebraska, has made a clear commitment to families in the district's Five Year Strategic Plan. One of the 15 strategies in the plan is "to respond to the special needs of the nontraditional family unit and working parents." Throughout the district all schools have instituted flexible scheduling of parent-teacher conferences; teacher in-service days have been consolidated; parent nights are held instead of mother or dad nights; breakfast programs operate in two schools; and prekindergarten and child care services are provided in six sites (more than half of all elementary schools). These six sites are collectively the Westside Early Childhood Centers.

Many parents who use the Westside Early Childhood Centers are active in the Parent Advisory Council (PAC), which deals with program-wide policy issues, organizes fund raising, and is the formal vehicle for parent input into the centers. The parent participation menu also includes parent education workshops organized via the PAC and some parent participation in classrooms and on field trips (mainly by nonworking mothers, although some are able to take time off work for it). To accommodate all parents, head teachers in each center stay in touch through newsletters (for each site) instead of relying only on meetings.

Parents reported that they felt encouraged to participate in a variety of ways of their choosing. There are no set requirements, and parents have felt very little pressure from staff (although some from other parents). Parents active in the PAC openly discussed their mutual respect for each other's choices about working or not working and their recognition that those choices dictate the degrees and kinds of parent participation.

Affton-Lindbergh Early Childhood Education in St. Louis, Missouri, is described by parents as an extremely responsive and supportive program. The director's sincere commitment to supporting families and her quiet insistence on translating that commitment into action appear to be the foundation of the staff's attitudes. Nearly every staff member expressed—in both words and actions—genuine support and respect for parents. As one parent said, "There's something for everyone here. The director and staff are willing to try to offer whatever parents want in terms of services, workshops, social events." Another said, "The staff work with you as a family." One mother shared her experience in recovering from a Caesarean birth: Her child's teacher would meet her at the car so the mother didn't have to walk up the stairs to the classroom. Another mother, whose child attended part-day and was cared for by a family child care provider for the rest of the day, related that her child's morning teacher involved the family child care provider by sending home program notices for her and offering to include her in parent conferences. This mother said she appreciated these efforts and noted that the staff had made no attempt to pressure her to change to full-time hours within Affton-Lindbergh's program, thus demonstrating their respect for her choice of child care.

The parent association is very strong, has well-attended meetings, and gave numerous examples of how the director listens to them and respects and acts on their ideas. For example, new schedules were offered in the part-day program to accommodate parents who wanted only two or three mornings a week; the hours of the full-working-day program (6:30 a.m. to 6:00 p.m.) were set in response to parent input. Parent involvement in classroom activities is generally very high. Parents reported that many variations are accepted; involvement can be active or passive, frequent or infrequent. Planning an event (a classroom party or whatever) is as good as attending it. No parent felt pressured to participate or felt looked down on as a working parent with less time to contribute.

A section of the building lobby is furnished like a comfortable living/dining room and is called Parents' Place. To encourage more informal parent-staff interaction, breakfast is available there every Friday from 7:00 to 8:30 a.m. for families to eat together with staff.

Teachers applied for and received grants (from the Missouri Department of Education) to support development of two innovative family-responsive programs. One, called "Frogs and Tadpoles," sponsors monthly activities for children and their fathers (or another important male in their lives). The other offers hands-on workshops, held on weekends, for parents and children to explore together the teacher-designed, integrated art/science curriculum.

Full-Working-Day Prekindergarten Programs

Generally, school district prekindergarten programs that operate for the full working day seem to be somewhat more responsive to parent concerns than part-day programs. Perhaps this is because one of the purposes of these programs—caring for children while their parents are otherwise engaged—inherently extends their focus beyond the child to the family.

The Chapter I/Migrant Early Childhood Program of the Palm Beach County, Florida, School Board provides full-working-day programs for migrant prekindergarten-aged children. Principals and district administrators believe firmly that parents are essential to children's success in school. Community resource staff assigned to each school are the primary liaison with parents. They offer workshops (on such topics as making toys from materials available in the home), and many go to the fields and fishing docks to make contact with parents. Some teachers also make a home visit to each child in their class. Agricultural and fishing industry parents work dawn to dusk, so parent meetings are held later at night, beginning at 9 p.m., after parents finish work.

Parents want their children to get an education and are grateful to the school for the migrant program and for the transportation. (All migrant children are bused to and from school.) The parents did not appear to believe it was their place to suggest changes in school programs, but rather to do their part in supporting their children to stay in school (as much as migrant life permits) and to do well there.

The Child Development Centers in the school district of Greenville County, South Carolina, offer full-working-day programs for three- to five-year-olds. These two centers, along with one other state-subsidized child development center operated by a black community agency, are the only sources of child care for low-income families in the county. All the families whose children are enrolled in the district's two centers have low incomes, and nearly all are black. Parents work in nonprofessional jobs, are in employment training programs, or are unemployed and receiving AFDC. A full-time social worker, shared between the two centers, makes frequent home visits, organizes parent meetings, refers families to community services, and helps straighten out problems with services or agencies.

These centers are not noticeably different in format from many other child care centers for low-income families anywhere. The difference in Greenville is human, not structural. The social worker is a lifelong member of Greenville's black community and has worked in the district's child development program since it began. She has carefully built up a strong base of trusting and mutually respectful relationships with the families whose children attend the centers. The principal who administers the centers exudes a deep but quiet sense of respect for the community generally and for these parents specifically along with high expectations for children. Parents said he was "easy to talk to" and well liked. These key personnel have helped to create a climate of respect for families and responsiveness to their needs that makes the difference between a good but unremarkable program and one that clearly is more.

There are no formal requirements for parent involvement, but teachers encourage parents to go on field trips, visit classrooms, and attend meetings. Monthly parent meetings are held during the day, are fairly well attended, and focus on topics such as discipline or handling stress.

Parents reported good relationships with their children's teachers and with the principal. They said, "Teachers really like us, they smile. They include us in this program." Some teachers regularly send home notes about children's activities; they were much appreciated by parents. Parents did wish that aides were more involved in parent-teacher conferences because they feel the aides know their children well. (Aides work the full calendar year; teachers work school year only. Some aides have been employed in the centers longer than the teachers.)

The school district of Greenville County also operates more than forty half-day classes for four-year-olds. Philosophically, these half-day classes appear to be more consistent with the district's stated policies and actions than are the full-working-day programs. The district superintendent noted that serving 40 children for a half day was, in his view, preferable to offering a full-day program for 20 or 30 children. The district rejected participating in a school-age child care venture with the local Y. However, the district has supported the two Child Development Centers (full-working-day programs) since 1971, with increasing financial commitments of local funds over the years. (The district has never directly competed for state child care funds with the one other community-based child development program in Greenville.) Based on statements from district administrators and on district actions, it appears that these centers continue to be supported not because they assist working parents per se, but primarily because they are a highly valued service in the black community. The centers stand as tangible evidence of the district's commitment to Greenville's black community.

Full-School-Day Prekindergarten Programs

Three programs, in New York and Texas, offer examples of parent participation with an emphasis on direct involvement in the child's education. In Buffalo, New York, prekindergarten classes are part of schools called Early Childhood Centers that span prekindergarten through grade 2. Parent involvement activities are seen as important throughout the Early Childhood Center as a whole, not only in the prekindergarten classes. Monthly *Homework Calendars* are sent home, offering a daily suggestion for making a common event in family life into an educational activity for parents and children to do together, such as having children find items in the grocery store while shopping or match socks while doing laundry. Children can telephone a story-on-tape that is recorded weekly. One school also offers a telephone recording of the week's special events for children and parents.

Parent teacher associations are very active in some schools, and parents are encouraged to visit their child's classroom and participate in field trips. Parents who had younger children noted that being able to bring them along while volunteering was very helpful. Working parents noted that teachers seemed to understand the limitations on their time and accept whatever involvement they could manage. These parents wished they could participate more but found it difficult because nearly all parent activities were scheduled during their work hours. Principals generally did not regard their schools as child care arrangements and made virtually no adjustments to accommodate working parents. One principal professed to have "no idea" which children had working parents. Nonetheless, working parents felt that the existence of the full-school-day program represented a tangible form of support for them. One mother explained that when she had been struggling financially to pay for her son's child care center, she felt that her stress was passed on to him. Having him in the (free) public school program helped them both relax.

The Chapter I prekindergarten program in the Fort Worth, Texas, independent school district aims to involve parents directly in the education of their children. *Home Helps* is a district-designed packet of home teaching ideas and suggestions that is given to each child's family. Monthly Chapter I parent council meetings are held, and prekindergarten parents are encouraged to join the school building PTA. Two parent-teacher conferences are scheduled during the year, at which attendance is required by a "parent or other representative of the child's family." Children can be dropped from the program if this requirement is not met.

Many children in this full-school-day program have working parents. (Teachers in one school estimated that more than half the children in the prekindergarten class had working parents.) These parents discussed the difficulty of participating in school activities primarily held in the daytime. Even night meetings were difficult (especially for single parents) because no child care was provided. Parents did not seem to expect the school to make parent participation easier for working parents, but they felt the school and the principal were receptive to parents if they wanted to come in to talk or visit a class during school hours.

Part-Day Prekindergarten Programs

The state-funded prekindergarten program operated in the Dallas independent school district does not explicitly require parent involvement. Generally, there is one group parent meeting in the beginning of the year to explain the program and answer parents' questions. Two parent-teacher conferences are held during the year; parents are encouraged to visit the classroom and accompany their child's class on field trips. Parents are required to take turns bringing the daily snack for their child's class.

Parents whose children attended the afternoon session said their best opportunity for informal parent-teacher communication was at the drop-off or pick-up times. Unfortunately, this informal opportunity is not available to parents of children in the morning session: Their children arrive for breakfast before the teacher arrives (they are supervised by an aide during breakfast), and teachers are on their lunch break at the end of the morning session.

In general, parents seemed eager for more information and involvement in the program, but they expressed some uncertainty about what they should expect the school to do and whether it was appropriate for parents to request more. Working parents whose children attended the prekindergarten relied on relatives and neighbors to care for their children during the rest of the day; they felt that a three-hour program was long enough and that children need to relax at home. These parents did not expect a school to offer an appropriate balance of activities for a young child for a full working day.

The Chapter I Child Parent Centers and the state-funded prekindergarten programs operated by the Chicago public schools offer an example of one district's use of two different approaches to parent involvement, especially in dealing with parents' needs as adults. In each program, certain aspects of parent involvement are mandatory. In both programs, parents are required to participate at least one-half day per week in parent education activities and/or in classroom volunteer work. If this requirement is not met, their child can be dropped from the program. Any family member can fulfill this requirement. Because younger children cannot be brought along, parents make arrangements to trade child care with another parent or friend in order to participate.

In the Child Parent Centers, a parent room is set up as both a gathering place and a classroom for parent education activities. A part-time parent resource teacher staffs the parent room and offers scheduled workshops. The state prekindergarten also includes parent education activities, using meeting areas in the school building rather than a specially designated parent room. In both programs the topics discussed in workshops are based on the district's parent education curriculum, which includes four components: child development, training for classroom volunteering, methods for reinforcing education at home, and family living. In addition to offering recreation and arts and crafts activities, the family living component covers areas such as money management, accessing social services, and nutrition. This component was immediately helpful to some parents. One remarked that she had learned how to keep her electricity on while paying off the overdue bill; others had enrolled in a GED program as a result of coming to the parent workshops.

Parent Education Programs

Programs explicitly designed to offer parent education are clearly responsive to parent needs for support as parents. These programs can also offer opportunities for fellowship, a role in governance, and direct participation in a program with their children. The Duluth Early Childhood Family Education Program is certainly responsive to this wider range of family needs. It serves 1,500 families at seven neighborhood sites, two hospitals, and three special program sites. Rather than simply presenting factual information about child growth and development, the parent education curriculum covers the complex interactions among family members in the context of society. High-quality programs for children are offered while their parents attend the sessions.

Specialized programs are offered for first-time parents, teen/student mothers, stepparents, multi-stressed families, parents whose children have handicaps, low-functioning mothers, and incarcerated parents. The Working Parent Resource Center, located in the business district, includes child care resource and referral. A drop-in program is offered at a low-income housing project. The first sessions are free, after which families are charged $30 per quarter or whatever they can afford. No family can be denied service in any program because of inability to pay.

Conclusion

Clearly, these examples show the multitude of operational definitions of parent participation, differences in attitudes toward parents, and variations in responsiveness to families that can occur in public school programs. The most common definition of parent participation is based on one element: reinforcing education at home. Fellowship with other parents is rarely a stated objective. Working parents are acknowledged in a few programs and offered appropriate alternative ways to participate in some. A few programs offer services and activities to parents, both as parents and as adults. A few offer genuine participation in governing the program. Fewer still offer a combination of these elements.

School policies and staff attitudes are not the only factors determining responsiveness to the needs of parents. Parental expectations enter into the equation, too. Many seem to have quite modest expectations of what a school ought to do to support and involve them. Most parents grew up with and are accustomed to a model of school as a strictly educational enterprise focused on children. Because their children are young, often this is the parents' first encounter with school as parents rather than as students. Given the limited view of most schools toward parent participation (as support at home for teachers' educational efforts), it is not surprising that parents have come to expect little. A few parents who have experienced genuine participation—for example, through a Head Start program's parent council—expect more and some have become empowered enough to demand more. All parents should expect to be respected as partners in the education of their children, not only as supporters. As partners, parents deserve a role in setting policy for their children's program. Working through the school building parents' association or creating a prekindergarten parents' council are both strategies that parents have successfully used to become more involved.

In a few programs, parents and staff have overcome the barriers on both sides and have been able to create supportive, family-responsive environments. We can learn much from their examples.

Although there is clearly a wide gap between the ideal of family-responsive programs and what now exists, the study found many examples of family-responsive programs and policies at both the state and local level. These examples provide models that are currently available to policymakers, school administrators, and elected officials for implementation. These models could be employed to enhance state-funded prekindergarten initiatives being enacted now, to inform those under consideration for the immediate future, or to form the basis for one strand of a comprehensive state children's policy.

Recommendations

- Define parent participation explicitly to include a menu of components such as direct participation in children's education, a role in program governance, employment training and job counseling, parent education, and other forms of participation that may be appropriate to the families whose children attend a specific program.
- Require broadly defined, multiple-option parent participation in all early childhood programs and require that all elements be addressed in the practices of local programs.
- Require that parents have a role in policymaking and governance of programs through parent councils specific to the prekindergarten program.
- As part of teacher and administrator preparation require coursework and practice-based training in developing healthy reciprocal home-school relationships based on a broad definition of parent participation.
- Require that all children be fed at least one meal and a snack

daily in all programs of three hours or less, and two meals and at least one snack in programs longer than three hours.
- Require that programs link families with additional health or social services through referral, or make those services available as part of a comprehensive program.
- Design programs for disadvantaged children (and their families) based on existing successful models of comprehensive services to families, such as Head Start.
- Permit transportation from school to other child care arrangements as an allowable cost in the operation of state prekindergarten programs.
- Make full-working-day child care a service eligible for state prekindergarten funding to accommodate the needs of working parents or parents in job training programs.
- Encourage community-based organizations that already provide comprehensive full-working-day services to operate state-funded prekindergarten programs.
- While services in one site for the full-working day may be preferable for children's sense of continuity, if service in a single site is not possible connections between child care and prekindergarten programs must be carefully coordinated (such as through information sharing, transportation) so that continuity is maintained.
- Mandate, at both the state and local levels, significant parent involvement in designing new programs and modifying existing ones.

Endnotes

1. Heath, S. B., and M. W. McLaughlin (1987). Child resource policy: Moving beyond dependence on school and family. *Phi Delta Kappan,* 68 (8).
2. Harris, L., and Associates (1987). *The Metropolitan Life Survey of the American Teacher: Strengthening links between home and school.* New York: Metropolitan Life Insurance Co.
3. Schorr, L. B. (1988). *Within Our Reach.* New York: Doubleday.

Chapter 11

THE FUTURE: WHERE DO WE GO FROM HERE?

Young children at risk have become a focus of concern throughout society. Demographic projections point toward a future society in which ethnic minorities, traditionally disadvantaged, will become the majority in some areas, as they already are in many urban schools. The educational needs of ever-increasing numbers of disadvantaged children and the growing need for child care, fueled by dramatic changes in family life, are trends that cannot be ignored.

In this decade, states have taken the lead in trying to change educational failure into success for disadvantaged children. A wave of new state-initiated prekindergarten programs, mainly for at-risk young children and generally in public schools, have been established. Future early childhood efforts in the states are likely to be driven by child care concerns—fueled in part by federal actions like passage of the Family Support Act of 1988 and the increasing likelihood that major federal child care legislation will be enacted.

The Present

Currently, 32 states fund a total of 48 early childhood efforts: 33 distinct prekindergarten programs, 1 pilot and 2 statewide parent education programs delivered via public schools, and 12 state contributions to Head Start. This book has presented a descriptive picture of these state efforts and the current role of public schools in providing early childhood programs for young children, within the existing ecosystem of the early childhood community. Schools are now clearly a player in that system.

The Early Childhood System

In contrast to the educational system for children five and over, early childhood services are delivered through a diverse array of public and private organizations operating programs financed by a mixture of public and private funds. The regulatory systems governing these programs differ by programs' auspices and funding sources, as do the criteria for determining children's eligibility. This diverse collection of services for children under five is the early childhood community or ecosystem as it is currently constituted. It is a multibillion dollar enterprise in which public school-operated programs represent roughly 3 percent of the whole. Public schools are a small but essential and growing element of the early childhood system.

Good Early Childhood Programs

All children deserve a minimum guarantee of a good early childhood program. The various longitudinal studies of early childhood programs for disadvantaged young children have proven the effectiveness of high-quality early childhood programs in producing positive long-term gains for children. High-quality programs must have well-trained, caring teachers working with small groups of children. Parent involvement is an essential component of successful programs for young children. School policies, staff attitudes, and parental expectations work together to determine how responsive a program can be. The changing nature of family life in America demands innovative approaches to involving parents and responding to their needs as well as to their children's.

The best early childhood programs (those that deliver higher-quality service to children, satisfy parents, and earn the respect of the overall early childhood community) are characterized by strong leadership. As in all effective education, the leader is a critical ingredient. Good teachers—working as partners with parents—supported by the leadership of effective administrators together create good programs for children.

Public Schools as Providers of Early Childhood Programs

Although there is much variation among state-funded prekindergarten programs, those that specify and fund a reasonably good quality program (favorable staff–child ratios, well-trained teachers, comprehensive services, an appropriate curriculum for children, local coordination mechanisms) represent a promising resource for extending the benefits of early childhood education to greater numbers of disadvantaged young children. About one-third of the state prekindergarten programs appear to offer this promise, notably the long-standing programs in New York and California and the newer programs in Washington, New Jersey, Massachusetts, South Carolina, and Illinois.

Local school districts, as operators of prekindergarten programs, are much like any other member of the early childhood ecosystem—responding to funding opportunities and to the expressed needs of their community. Local education agencies operate a wide variety of early childhood programs funded solely or from a combination of federal, state, and local sources including parent tuition. Basic aspects of program quality—the average class sizes and staff–child ratios—for all types of public school-operated programs were reasonable and within the boundaries of good practice set by the early childhood profession. However, our Case Studies suggest that the quality of some of these programs—as well as others outside public schools—is not sufficient (excessive cognitive focus of curricula, lack of choices for children, excessive teacher direction). The general lack of comprehensive services (no meals, little use of specialists, no transportation) except in Head Start programs is a continuing concern because at-risk children have many needs that must be met to ensure their educational success.

Universal Prekindergarten

Demand for prekindergarten programs for disadvantaged young children comes from many quarters: business, civic and government leaders concerned about the future of the work force and of society. Consumer demand for prekindergarten programs for all children comes from families at all income levels who are seeking to satisfy their needs for programs that offer good education and socialization for their children and child care while they work. The price tag of these programs, clearly, must be within the limits of families' resources. The call for universal prekindergarten is prompted by these demands.

Universal access to early childhood services is a reasonable policy goal *if* it is pursued within the context of the entire early childhood system *and* the public interest in funding such services. The most effective route toward universal prekindergarten is gradual expansion of public funding for programs for children under five, offered in a variety of settings with an assumption of shared financial responsibility among parents, the public, and the private sector.

Targeting

Until greater investments are made in early childhood programs, not all children will be able to participate. Clearly, the most disadvantaged children gain the greatest benefits from a high-quality prekindergarten experience. Given that tests of "educational disadvantage" or "at-risk" status are far from precise, poverty (low family income) is a sufficient criterion for selection of children. At the same time, policymakers and program operators must recognize that implicit eligibility criteria—recruitment and enrollment procedures, tuition, hours, location, and access to transportation—are powerful factors in determining which children will be enrolled in a particular program.

Universal access to prekindergarten services that are good for children and for parents can be achieved through a combination of supply building across the early childhood system and greater commitments of public funds—not only from education sources, but from social service sources and the income tax code—in order to support those families who cannot otherwise afford prekindergarten.

The Role of States

The early childhood community will continue to grow in response to demand—from parent-consumers concerned about their own children and the public at large who are concerned about children's future. Policymakers and influencers at all governmental levels have the potential to affect how the early childhood system grows. Given the strong role that states have assumed in this decade, it is likely that much of the action will be on a state-by-state basis.

Improving at-risk children's chances for educational success will remain as a focus. However, emphasis may broaden from current efforts to expand educational opportunities (such as creating new prekindergarten programs) to greater concern for child care needs and for coordination of the "dizzying array of multiple actors" in the early childhood community.[1] For example, Governor Cuomo of New York, in his recent state-of-the-state message to the legislature, noted:[2]

> *We will continue moving toward [the] goal [universal prekindergarten for all four-year-olds] by providing funds for the expansion of*

the existing prekindergarten program. Priority for funding will be given to those programs that offer or arrange for full-day care. In addition, I will direct the Department of Social Services to work with the State Education Department to develop mechanisms to assure that the full-day needs of parents are met in a coordinated manner.

State action will continue to be the driving force in responding to the combined need for better education and child care. However, the problem is national in scope, reflecting broad changes in society. As the *New York Times* noted in a recent editorial:[3]

In a nation that constitutionally protects the free movement of individuals and commerce, state-by-state solutions to a national social problem are rarely optimal.

Federal action—especially in regard to funding—is necessary. Governor Cuomo probably spoke for many states when he said:[4]

The need to increase the supply of child care has become an issue of national concern and debate. While recent federal welfare reform legislation calls for significant expansion of available child care, it is imperative that the federal government offer greater support to state efforts to meet this burgeoning need.

Driven by their differing individual economic and social conditions, states may create new programs or modify existing ones in response to idiosyncratic forces. The degree to which meeting the needs of children and families is seen as a public responsibility influences state action. Influential individuals—governors, in particular—have the ability to shape new initiatives. Developing the early childhood system state by state will reinforce the already wide differences among states in terms of the quality and availability of programs for young children. A federal role, beyond funding, may be necessary to ensure equal treatment for all of the nation's youngest citizens.

Federal Policies with Potential to Effect Change

While states are best able to design programs to meet the unique conditions and needs of their communities, a federal role in funding is widely advocated and is a powerful influence on states. Federal policy direction, although not as welcome as federal dollars, is also a strong (and often positive) influence on the action of states. At least three areas of recent and prospective federal policymaking will affect the early childhood community throughout the nation: special education, welfare reform, and child care.

Special Education

The federal special education law (PL99-457) significantly impacts the provision of early childhood special education. The law mandates service to three- through five-year-olds by 1990 and encourages expanding services to children from birth to age three and to their families. A basic premise of this extension of services to very young children is the primary importance of the family; an Individual Family Service Plan (IFSP) is required rather than the traditional Individual Education Plan (IEP). This legislation requires that a state agency be designated to coordinate services to these children and their families. Because the state education agency is not always designated—it may be the state health, or mental health department—the opportunity for collaboration across service domains is ripe.

Depending on the precise definition of disability adopted by a state, there is the potential for overlap among children defined as "at risk" for purposes of entry into prekindergarten programs and those with "developmental delays" as defined by the state under PL99-457. At present, about one-third of the states are seriously considering adopting a broad definition of disability which would encompass environmental risk. Environmental risk, in turn, would certainly include educational risk factors. Any potential overlap or conflict can, of course, also be seen as an opportunity for creative collaboration.

Welfare Reform

Passage of the Family Support Act of 1988 has defined federal policy direction in the area of welfare reform. The Family Support Act repeals the WIN program, replacing it with the Job Opportunities and Basic Skills Training (JOBS) program. States must require AFDC parents with young children (over age three), with limited exceptions, to participate in JOBS as a condition of receiving AFDC. The act directs that parents of children under six be required to participate part time only—20 or fewer hours per week. States must guarantee child care not only to AFDC recipients in the JOBS program but to *all* AFDC recipients who are working or in a state-approved employment training program. These federal funds for child care are not capped, and the federal share is greater than before (equal to each state's Medicaid matching rate—usually at least 50 percent and higher in poorer states). The effects of these changes will be felt in every state.

As states begin to implement the Family Support Act provisions, many will be faced with the fact that the mothers who are required to work (or participate in JOBS) under welfare reform are the very same mothers whose children are targets of state-funded prekindergarten efforts. The vast majority of such prekindergarten programs are part-day. It is impossible to estimate how many children from families receiving AFDC are in these (and other part-day) public school programs. From our case study interviews, it seems likely that some programs in some locations (such as certain neighborhoods in Chicago with Chapter I Child/Parent Centers or State Prekindergarten, and neighborhoods in NYC where either Project Giant Step or New York State Prekindergarten programs operate) are now populated almost entirely by children on AFDC. When their mothers are required to go to work or enter training programs—even on a part-time basis (since commuting time plus training time will exceed the three hours that programs are in session)—those program sites may well be empty as mothers encounter difficulties trying to arrange additional child care.

Although the conflicting demands on families are apparent, conflict carries the potential to create new approaches to serving children and families that will meet both sets of demands. The Family Support Act calls for states to "coordinate child care services with existing early childhood development and education programs, including Head Start, Chapter I, school and nonprofit child care including programs for handicapped children."[5] Unfortunately, beyond stating that coordination should occur, the act did not further define or specify coordination.

One approach to the conflicting demands of welfare reform and early education is to view welfare reform as a strategy for targeting early education efforts. Young children whose families will be affected by welfare reform are precisely those children who would most benefit from a quality prekindergarten program. Welfare reform could be the vehicle for reaching (at least part of) the population of children at risk, as well as a way to extend the benefits of good early childhood education to more poor children whose parents work. At a minimum, it is essential for policymakers concerned about young children who are at risk to ensure that any and all programs for children under welfare reform be good-quality, comprehensive, educational programs.

Child Care

Child care is a burning issue for families at all socioeconomic levels and, in recent years, has moved rapidly higher on the national public policy agenda. For example, in the 1988 session of Congress,

70-odd bills were introduced that addressed child care in one way or another. The more prominent of these bills differed markedly one from the other in their conception of the child care system, although public schools figured as a provider agency in all of them. One bill (Act for Better Child Care [ABC]) proposed to support and enhance the existing multiple delivery system, including public schools; another (Smart Start) would provide funding for full-working-day programs for four-year-olds in schools and other community agencies; a third (the New Schools Child Care Demonstration Act) envisioned the schools as the locus of a network of services for children starting at infancy. All three bills have been reintroduced in the 101st Congress along with the Child Development and Early Education Act. This act combines elements from the three other bills and was purposely introduced as a vehicle for compromise. The act has three titles; Title I resembles Smart Start, Title II focuses on public schools, and Title III is essentially ABC limited to children under three.

If enacted, the first two of these bills would expand the supply of full-working-day services under many auspices available in communities. In the resulting climate of increased attention and resources, public schools could expand their role as providers of child care. The third bill, which is smaller in scale and focuses primarily on public schools, would provide support to dramatically increase the child care role of schools in a small number of communities. Other recent legislation has proposed use of the tax code to provide modest funds to low-income families with children, whether working or not. This form of legislation only indirectly influences the role of schools as child care providers. Compromise legislation is likely to combine elements from the various child care bills and may incorporate tax credits as well. However, any federal policy shift, and certainly the combination of multiple federal policy changes, has the potential to dramatically affect the provision of early childhood services in communities.

The Dual Systems Perspective

To better understand how the future early childhood system might look (and how to influence its development), adopting a dual systems perspective is useful. First, we must stand firmly rooted in the early childhood ecosystem and analyze any new developments from that perspective. The objective is to improve quality and increase access across the ecosystem. Some children are already in good-quality early childhood programs, such as Head

Start, state-funded prekindergarten, or child care. But many are in poor-quality programs. Policies should be aimed at improving the poor programs and making more good programs available. Some programs offer good early childhood education, and some clearly don't. We must be concerned about improving poor-quality programs no matter where they occur in the ecosystem because all the parts of the ecosystem—not only those programs specially designed as educational interventions—will contribute to the later success or failure of children.

Second, we must take the perspective of the family, not only the child. Early childhood public policy is not an intervention seeking to save children from their families. Children are not at risk because of their families; they are at risk because of conditions that both they and their families suffer (poverty, deteriorated neighborhoods with crumbling social structures, poor housing). At-risk children are essentially poor children—poverty is the single most reliable predictor of school failure and at-risk status. Rather than only trying to ameliorate the *effects* of poverty by providing publicly funded prekindergarten programs for at-risk children, we should also be working to ensure that fewer children are poor and therefore at risk. This means helping families to move out of poverty. Nonworking poor parents need access to training and jobs, but they will not be able to take advantage of them without adequate child care. Adolescent parents need to finish school so that their children will have some chance of doing the same. Public policy for young children must support both children *and* their families.

In evaluating possible policy alternatives on the route to the future, public officials and concerned citizens must ask two sets of questions: First, is it good for children and their families? Does it meet parents' needs for involvement, for support as parents and as people, and for child care? Does the policy help parents support themselves and their children? That is, does it make *family sense?* Second, how does this policy (or new program or funding source) affect the early childhood ecosystem? Does it improve quality, expand access system-wide? Does it support or supplant existing successful programs (such as Head Start)? Is it *good for the ecosystem?*

Family-Responsive Early Childhood Policy

The task of responding to the multiple needs of young children and their families has grown well beyond what any one system or agency can handle. A one-dimensional response (a new program) is inadequate. The scope of the situation requires multiple resources and collaborative action guided by principles grounded in the family and in the early childhood ecosystem. Policy actions proceed from principles that are usually implicit rather than explicit. We believe the principles that inform actions in regard to young children and their families should be made explicit and clearly articulated.

We strongly believe the time has come for making comprehensive, cross-cutting, family-responsive early childhood policy. We can no longer afford to have welfare policy and education policy and employment policy and community development policy moving on different tracks. We must recognize that we are dealing in different arenas with the same families. What is required are policies and programs based on the understanding that service domains intersect—and must cooperate.

When policies and programs are designed, whether by public government units or private institutions, their architects must recognize that families—not cities, or counties, or states—are the basic unit of society. Children live in families, who live in neighborhoods, which together make up a community. Family-responsive early childhood policy must be built from the community up because different communities have different resources and different needs.

The ultimate goal is an integrated, unified policy that can guide action for the state's (or even the nation's) children and families. The establishment of broad principles for such a policy will ensure that any future actions that are necessary for whatever reasons (such as response to changing federal funds or mandates, or to changing circumstances in the state, or to new developments in a community) will flow from the values that have been established as a foundation.

Collaboration

Such an integrated policy must be constructed carefully and collaboratively. Each government level—federal, state, county, city, community—is essential to the process. Every "affected party" throughout the early childhood ecosystem has a stake and therefore must have a role in the process. The collaboration necessary to create and carry out family-responsive early childhood policy will require both "sticks and carrots" (mandates and incentives). At the state level the governor plays a critical role in setting the tone—clear and solid commitment from the top communicates the value of the exercise. Collaboration must be required (and supported) at the state level among agencies and, in turn, the same commitment (and support) must be required from their counterpart agencies at the local level. Collaboration must be practiced at all levels, from the federal government down to neighborhoods, both horizontally and vertically.

In practical terms, collaboration at the state level will require agency heads to work together to coordinate existing services, weed out duplication, enhance cooperative efforts, and plan for necessary new efforts based on the information coming from collaborative efforts in communities throughout the state. Successful collaboration requires a shared goal—or at least a real need for each other's resources or abilities in order to reach separate (but noncompeting) goals. It also requires a serious commitment of human and fiscal resources. Although the forces of competition among direct service providers in a community may be stronger, local collaboration rests on the same principles as state-level collaboration: shared goals, interdependence, and incentives. The awarding of state funding for state agencies and local providers of all early childhood services should be made contingent on evidence of collaboration.

Thoughtful and thorough analysis of the existing early childhood ecosystem is needed to identify the strengths that can be built upon and the weaknesses that need correction throughout the system. This analysis involves examination of the dimensions of the programs under various auspices to see if they are equivalent, and if they are not, how and to what extent they differ. Some dimensions to be considered are quality and comprehensiveness of services provided, child eligibility criteria, level of funding, and regulatory status, among others. Action at many levels will be required to address inequities discovered in this process. For example, differences in quality among programs may be related to differences in staffing, for example, preparation and on-going development of staff. Working toward equity might require revisions in class size regulations among the regulatory systems at the state level, changes in the scope and content of teacher preparation programs in higher education institutions in communities, and retraining of supervisors in program sites.

A Vision for the Future

No matter where we live, or at what level of government we operate (or hope to influence), the policy challenge facing us all is to create enough good programs to satisfy the combined needs for child care and education of all children and their families, regardless of income, focusing first on those families whose needs are greatest. These programs must be good for children, responsive to families, and respectful of the integrity of the existing ecosystem.

Good, family-responsive early childhood programs available to all families, in every community and under many auspices, is a desirable and ultimately achievable policy objective. We see public schools as a relatively new player in the field, with a definite role as one part of the solution. However, the whole solution will emerge across the entire early childhood community and throughout its multiple delivery system. Our vision for the future builds on the existing principles, programs, and funding sources and proposes a framework for moving among these and adding new dimensions to the system. We envision participation at federal, state, and local levels, working collaboratively first to develop a set of principles (call it early childhood policy, or a family policy, or children's policy, or comprehensive services policy) that will guide action, and then acting on those principles to create connected networks of programs and services for children and families in communities.

The State as Modulator and Mediator

Although comprehensive services for families must be designed to meet local community (even neighborhood) needs, they must be conceptualized, coordinated, and supported primarily at the state level. States should begin by developing a framework within which a variety of services can be made available at the local level, based on the particular needs of different communities. Conducting an assessment of both needs and resources on a systematic and regular basis—across the state and across domains—is a function that the state should assume. The assessment will identify and direct attention to gaps in services, gaps which will be filled by reorganizing existing resources or by allocating new resources.

States need to have a clear policy and a review process that allows them to evaluate their legislative and funding proposals against the set of specific goals articulated in the policy. Both existing and proposed policies, programs, and services should be evaluated in a way that produces the equivalent of an "environmental impact" statement for the early childhood system. The statement should answer such questions as: How does the policy, program, or service affect the early childhood ecosystem? How does it impact on the existing set of policies and programs in a state? Does it increase options and scope of service? Does it improve the quality of services (curriculum, continuity, and comprehensiveness)? Is it good for children? Does it make family sense?

This conception of future policymaking efforts implies more efficient and more family-responsive use of existing resources, as well as the commitment of new resources to support expanded action. Funding for this set of new and expanded activities can come, in part, from reallocation of, or more closely coordinated use of, currently existing sources. These include federal, state and local public sources, as well as private sources such as corporations, charitable organizations, and families. Federal categorical funding sources that exist can be expanded through higher appropriation levels (for example, increased funding for child care via the Social Service Block Grant) and by adding new categories of funding (such as proposed federal child care legislation) that mesh with existing ones. The various funding streams (from whatever sources) must be coordinated at the most efficient level, which is probably the state.

Precedents exist for coordination of planning and provision of services. One example of a cross-domain, comprehensive approach is the planning process mandated (and financially supported) by the extension of special education to infants and toddlers under federal law (PL99-457). The special education model is instructive in considering planning issues for the needs of *all* young children. Coordinated planning is encouraged by the federal government (with financial incentives and disincentives). It is family responsive and involves multiple service (and professional) domains. It recognizes that in order to provide education, a whole host of other issues must be addressed, such as the involvement of families in the education of their children and the need to coordinate the provision of services from many sources to a child. Although the PL99-457 planning process is not without problems such as turf-guarding and the difficulty of finding commonality across diverse domains, it offers some evidence that comprehensive planning is possible.

A second model—this one from the past—is the once-mandated State Title XX Plans, which were developed annually from 1975 to 1981 in each state that received funds under Title XX. The planning process cut across human services domains, although it didn't include education (except in California). The plan included citizen review, public hearings, agency sign-offs, and interagency agreements. There are also some lessons to be learned from Title XX's failures. The major flaw in Title XX planning was that no state had sufficient funds to do more than a fraction of what its needs assessments indicated—which led some states to severely scale back their needs to match their resources. Competition among services (for example, services for the elderly against services for children) also occurred within the state agency responsible for Title XX funds and among local providers in some states.

Involvement from the Federal Level

Currently, federal policy proceeds on the basis of categorical programs, each with its attached funding source. These separate programs could be made more coherent under a set of goals and principles that would direct the flow of funding to states and to communities. States (and local jurisdictions) can then add their own programs and funds to this stream. Imagine a river, with smaller rivers and streams flowing into it at different points along its way, becoming a vast river of support for families and children as it reaches communities. The federal tributaries would include Chapter I, Title XX/SSBG, Head Start, Education for the Handicapped, USDA Child Care Food Program, Dependent Care Block Grant, WIN (now replaced by JOBS), AFDC, the WIC Program, and various health programs. Each one of these programs represents an array of specialized services that meet certain specific needs; taken together, they become a comprehensive and responsive system of services for children and families. This system of converging funding streams can more efficiently collect existing sources of funds (categorical or otherwise) and can effectively incorporate funds from new sources, such as those created through welfare reform or the passage of a major (federal) child care bill.

So that this "river" can flow, the guiding federal principles should be developed collaboratively with states. Mixing and blending of programs and funds must not only be permitted but actively encouraged. Successful implementation, particularly with regard to existing categorical funding streams, will be greatly facilitated by federal encouragement of such options as waivers regarding child and family eligibility, uniform financial reporting across categorical programs, and simplified (and uniform) evaluation procedures. New federal programs and funds must merge smoothly with their predecessors.

Encouraging creative "mixing and matching" to produce good programs for families must continue down the river from the federal to the state and then to the local level. Blending of funds has to continue at the state level and, most important, be actively encouraged as the river of support reaches into communities.

Regulations must be made coherent among programs, and funding methods must be rationalized.

Action at the Local Level

At the local level, a variety of organizations and agencies should be eligible to receive state and federal funding, to complement and augment their current programs and services. For example, a day care center that wants to meet additional needs (beyond child care) of families whose children attend the program should be able to obtain funds to provide those services and/or be linked up with existing programs that offer them.

Neighborhoods include an array of possible providers of family-responsive early childhood programs, such as Head Start centers, community child care programs, neighborhood houses, and community health centers. Communities will need to perform a clearinghouse function, so that parents can find out where to go for which service or combination of services. The local early childhood system should support parental choice and offer a diversity of options. There are multiple entry points into such a comprehensive system. These entry points permit parents to pick those services they need from a wide array of choices. If a family goes to a family service association for information, it should be possible to refer that family to the appropriate sources for whatever services are needed. Some families may be most comfortable with a school; others with Head Start; others with a child care center. Families have different needs for, as well as different levels of comfort with, different systems. Parents must be able to choose where and how they want to receive services, in terms of location, cultural preference, and other preferences. Multiple services should be available through a variety of deliverers to ensure adequate choice for families. Clearly, not every service will need to be available in every site in every neighborhood, but a healthy array of services sufficient to satisfy the needs and preferences of a given community should be the goal.

The choice of which local agency delivers a particular service (a direct service provider, a child care resource and referral agency, a multiservice agency, a family service agency, a municipal agency, a public school) depends on the nature of the community and on the responsiveness of a particular agency to a range of community needs. An example from the past is the neighborhood settlement house, which offered everything from food, shelter, and clothing to employment for adults and kindergartens for their children—something for every member of the family. We envision modern-day versions of settlement houses in many neighborhoods, not just in those whose inhabitants are poor. These would be community centers, in the best sense, supporting and binding the community—across income and class lines.

Many organizations have the potential to serve as centers for family-responsive programs. Public schools, in many communities, are the hub of the community and would therefore be an appropriate setting for such programs. In other communities, other institutions—churches or neighborhood associations, for example—would serve this function well.

Probably every reader of this book knows of one (or more) enterprising local entrepreneur who is passionate about offering the best possible services to families. These dedicated individuals manage to draw funds from every available source, carefully constructing a menu of early childhood services tailored to their community, from which families can make the selection of their choice. Surviving multiple financial audits from every funder, defending their "unprecedented" mixing of Head Start funds with state child care funds for teen parents, they persevere. The state with child-focused, family-responsive, community-based policies (and practices to match) would actively work to support and simplify the efforts of such an entrepreneur.

What would it be like if a state (or even the nation) realized the vision we present here? What would it be like to live in such a state? The following story illustrates our vision of the future.

An Example of a Family

First, here is what happens in a state without family-responsive policies and programs.

The Johnsons are a married couple with two preschoolers: One is under the age of two and has special needs; the other is a four-year-old. Since her husband lost his job, Mrs. Johnson has gone back to work as a waitress. Mrs. Johnson works full-time, and Mr. Johnson is looking for work. The family is eligible for several government programs: partial state funding for sliding fee scale child care, the state preschool program, and services for their handicapped infant. Mr. Johnson's employment history has made him eligible for various federal and state job training programs. The family is currently receiving food stamps. There are no local child care resource and referral programs. In the Johnsons' state, the few services available are delivered categorically.

Now, for the first time since her children were born, Mrs. Johnson is looking for child care, preferably a place that will take both children. Her friend tells her about a program run by the school district; another friend tells her of a local child care program. She visits the child care center but is told that the program has no subsidies to help her pay for care; she calls the preschool program but learns that the nearest school-based program is three miles away, takes only four-year-olds, and provides no transportation. The younger child was already receiving some remediation on a part-time basis from the local handicapped children's center; staff there told Mrs. Johnson that no child care program in the area would accept her child. Finally, Mrs. Johnson found a neighbor to care for both children while she works. The arrangement is unstable, and because the younger child is often ill, one of the parents frequently has to stay home to care for him.

Now suppose that the Johnsons lived in a state that had created family-responsive policies and programs. The situation would be dramatically different.

On each of the children's birthdays, the Johnson family receives a packet of materials describing the array and location of services available in the community. The directory lists a community service center that provides resource and referral to child care and other services, such as employers who sponsor on-site child care, parent education programs, and the like. With one telephone call, Mrs. Johnson can enroll the four-year-old in the nearest of two prekindergarten programs; one is located in the public school and the other in a child care center that will accept her handicapped younger child. In addition, she finds that the public school will provide transportation for her older child in the afternoon (after the prekindergarten program ends) to the day care center where his younger sibling receives full-time, mainstreamed care with services specific to his handicapping condition.

The community service center referred Mrs. Johnson to services she and her husband needed as well. Mr. and Mrs. Johnson signed up for the parent education program offered by the local public school in the community center in their neighborhood. Mrs. Johnson received special education and employment counseling and Mr. Johnson was enrolled in a retraining program.

How was this made possible? The Johnson family lives in a state that enacted prekindergarten legislation in the mid-1980s. Mandatory coordination at the state and local level was one provision of the original legislation. Through their experience in carrying out the required coordination activities over the years, state agency heads had collaborated to encourage the governor and the legislature to improve and expand a number of the state's programs for young children. As a result, new initiatives were enacted, including a statewide parent education program and a variety of new child care funds. Over the same period, coordinating councils (set up by the prekindergarten law) were functioning in local communities all over the state. Many of these local councils had also become cooperative advocates for each other and had begun, on a community basis, to improve services for young children and families. At the annual conference of the local and state councils, the governor proposed that a statewide unified planning process be undertaken to create a blueprint for the state's commitment to children and families.

The Johnsons' needs could be adequately addressed because a number of specific changes had occurred over time. One of the first results of the coordination efforts required by the prekindergarten law was a revision of the Department of Education's transportation policy to allow schools to bus children from schools to community child care programs. This made it possible for the elder Johnson child to be transported, after the school-based prekindergarten program, to the child care center his brother attended all day.

As a result of the unified planning process, a commitment was made to merge funds contributed by four major state agencies (education, human services, community development, and economic security), creating a jointly managed, interdepartmental funding stream to support the state's new Community Service Center Act (which became the model for the federal act which followed it two years later). Existing community agencies of any type (local child care resource and referral agencies, neighborhood associations, libraries) were eligible to apply for these funds. In some communities the public schools became the Community Service Agency; in other communities, family service or other multiservice agencies applied. In those communities where no agency existed, the state provided technical assistance to community groups that organized to establish new agencies to provide these services. In addition to the monies from the four state agencies, the state was able to apply for additional federal funds to support its Community Service Centers because it had complied with the federal requirement to participate in a linked state-level and community-based planning process. It was the local community service center, with federal and interdepartmental state funding, that was able to give Mrs. Johnson the wealth of information she received in her one telephone call.

Another outcome of the unified planning process was the discovery, through the statewide needs assessment, that serious inequities existed in salary, status, and benefits in early childhood teacher salaries among different program types. Public schools had the best compensation packages, while parent cooperative child care centers had the worst. It was further noted that the inequities in compensation seemed to be related to differences in program quality for children. It was also found that the child care system, in order to raise the quality of the services provided, required additional resources to match those available to public schools.

Two principles of the state's unified plan for children and families guided state action in addressing these findings: ensuring uniform quality to all the state's young children and equalizing the resources available to the state's citizens across communities. To make the equity adjustment permanent, the legislature appropriated funds to equalize salaries across professional domains and then adjusted the reimbursement rates for different service types and different communities. This action supported a number of the legislature's earlier decisions: reform of teacher education curricula throughout the state and revision of the regulatory system. Funding had also been provided for joint training programs available to professionals across child and family service fields. Topics such as expanded roles for family participation in education, case management techniques, and knowledge of community resources were covered in the joint sessions. The earlier regulatory review had upgraded staff qualification requirements and created a uniform code of standards that applies to all child-serving agencies throughout the state. The impact of this set of events touched the Johnson family when they visited the two nearby prekindergarten programs to decide which to enroll their children in. Mr. and Mrs. Johnson were impressed with the quality of both programs.

These scenarios illustrate the real dilemmas families face every day, in every community. In the first, the Johnsons do not fare particularly well. In the second, the Johnsons have many more choices and can satisfy many of their needs with greater ease. The second scenario is both more family-responsive and more complicated to enact. The possibilities suggested by the second scenario are not impossible to achieve; throughout this book we have offered examples of programs that are good for children and of practices that are responsive to families. The examples are drawn from existing programs operating in the current imperfect system, often with insufficient resources. No one program we found was perfect, or even approached the ideal we envision, but each offers hope for the future.

Endnotes

1. Committee for Economic Development (1987). *Children in need*. New York: Author.

2. Cuomo, Mario M. (1989). *Message to the Legislature* (January 4, 1989). Albany, N.Y.: Office of the Governor.
3. From an editorial on financing universal health insurance coverage: Washington's Lesson for Washington. *The New York Times*, January 7, 1989.
4. Cuomo (1989).
5. American Public Welfare Association (1988). Welfare Reform Legislation enacted by the 100th Congress. *The W-Memo*. (W-12-14) Washington, D.C.: Author.

BIBLIOGRAPHY

Administration for Children, Youth and Families (1965–present). *Head Start program information report*. Washington, D.C.: Author.

American Federation of Teachers Task Force on Educational Issues (Winter 1976). *Putting early childhood and day care services into the public schools: The position of the American Federation of Teachers and an action plan for promoting it*. Washington, D.C.: Author.

American Public Welfare Association (November 19, 1988). Welfare reform legislation enacted by 100th Congress. *W-Memo* (ISSN 0163-8300). Washington, D.C.: Author.

Bayh urging creation of office to coordinate child care services. *Indiana Star* (July 11, 1988).

Berrueta-Clement, J. R., L. J. Schweinhart, W. S. Barnett, A. S. Epstein, & D. P. Weikart (1984). Changed lives: Effects of the Perry Preschool Program on youths through age 19. *Monographs of the High/Scope Educational Research Foundation 8*.

Blank, H., J. Savage, and A. Wilkins (1988). *State child care fact book 1988*. Washington, D.C.: Children's Defense Fund.

Blow, S. E. (1900). Kindergarten education. In N. M. Butler (Ed.), *Monographs on education in the United States* (pp. 35–76). Prepared for the United States Commission to the Paris Exposition of 1900.

Bredekamp, S. (Ed.) (1986). *Developmentally appropriate practice*. Washington, D.C.: National Association for the Education of Young Children.

Bruner, J. (1980). *Under five in Britain*. Ypsilanti, Mich.: High/Scope Educational Research Foundation.

The Children's Defense Fund (October 1988). *Summary of the Family Support Act of 1988, public law no. 100-485*. Washington, D.C.: Author.

Clarke-Stewart, A., and C. Gruber (1984). Daycare forms and features. In R. C. Ainslie (Ed.), *Quality variations in daycare*. New York: Praeger.

Committee for Economic Development (1987). *Children in need*. New York: Author.

Cooperman, S., and D. Altman (October 5, 1988). Personal Communication. New Jersey Department of Education.

Cooperman, S., and D. Altman (May 1988). Excerpted and adapted from *Prekindergarten for urban children: A pilot program in New Jersey* (PTM 700.61). Trenton, N.J.: New Jersey State Department of Education.

Council of Chief State School Officers (1987). *Elements of a model state statute to provide educational entitlements for at-risk students*. Washington, D.C.: Author.

Council of Chief State School Officers (1988). *A guide for state action: Early childhood and family education* (Preface). Washington, D.C.: Author.

Cuomo, M. M. (January 1989). *Message to the legislature*. Albany, N.Y.: office of the Governor.

Day, M. C., and R. K. Parker (Eds.) (1977). *The preschool in action: Exploring early childhood programs*. Boston, Mass.: Allyn and Bacon.

Educational Research Service, Inc. (1986). *Kindergarten programs and practices in public schools* (stock no. 219-21724). Arlington, Va.: Author.

Egertson, H. A. (May 20, 1987). Recapturing kindergarten for five-year-olds. *Education Week,* pp. 28, 19.

Fein, G. G., and A. Clarke-Stewart (1973). *Day care in context*. New York: John Wiley & Sons.

Gnezda, T. (in press). *Economic implications of child care: Early childhood education policy. A legislator's guide*. Denver, Colo.: National Conference of State Legislatures.

Grubb, W. N. (May 1987). *Young children face the states: Issues and options for early childhood programs*. Rutgers, N.J.: Center for Policy Research in Education.

Harms, T., and R. M. Clifford (1980). *Early Childhood Environment Rating Scale*. New York: Teachers College Press.

Harris, L., and Associates (1987). *The Metropolitan Life Survey of the American Teacher: Strengthening links between home and school*. New York: Metropolitan Life Insurance Co.

Heath, S. B., and M. W. McLaughlin (April 1987). Child resource policy: Moving beyond dependence on school and family. *Phi Delta Kappan,* 68 (8).

Henderson, A. (Ed.) (1987). *The evidence continues to grow: Parent involvement improves student achievement* (ISBN #0-934460-28-0). Columbia, Md.: National Committee for Citizens in Education.

Howes, C. (1987). Quality indicators in infant and toddler child care: The Los Angeles Study. In D. A. Phillips (Ed.), *Quality in child care: What does research tell us?* Washington, D.C.: National Association for the Education of Young Children.

Hubbell, R. (1983). *A review of Head Start research since 1970. Head Start Evaluation Synthesis and Utilization Project* (DHHS-OHDS-83-

31184). Washington, D.C.: U.S. Government Printing Office, Administration for Children, Youth and Families.

Illinois State Board of Education, Department of Planning, Research and Evaluation (January 1985). *The status of kindergarten: A survey of the states.* Springfield, Ill.: Author.

Kahn, A. J., and S. B. Kamerman (1987). *Child care: Facing the hard choices.* Dover, Mass.: Auburn House Publishing Company.

Katz, L. G., J. D. Raths, and R. D. Torres (1987). *A place called kindergarten.* Urbana, Ill.: Clearinghouse on Elementary and Early Childhood Education.

Kerr, V. (1973). One step forward—two steps back: Child care's long American history. In P. Roby (Ed.), *Child care—Who cares?* New York: Basic Books, Inc., pp. 85–89.

King James version of the Bible (I Timothy, Chapter 6, Verse 10).

Lazar, I., and R. B. Darlington (1978). *Lasting effects after preschool: A report of the Consortium for Longitudinal Studies* (DHEW Publication No. [(OHDS)] 79-30178). Washington, D.C.: U.S. Government Printing Office.

Lazerson, M. (1970). Social reform and early childhood education. *Urban Education* 5: 84–102.

Lazerson, M. (1971a). The historical antecedents of early childhood education. *National Social Studies Education Yearbook,* Part 2: 33–53.

Lazerson, M. (1971b). *Origins of the public school: Public education in Massachusetts 1870–1915.* Cambridge, Mass.: Harvard University Press.

Marx, F., and M. Seligson (1988). *The Public School Early Childhood Study: The State Survey.* New York: Bank Street College.

Marx, F. (n.d.). *Changing ideologies about child care services: 1800 to 1960.* Unpublished.

Marx, F. (n.d.). *Notes on history of early childhood education and day care.* Unpublished.

McKey, R. H., B. J. Barrett, L. Condelli, H. Ganson, C. McConkey and M. C. Plantz (1985). *The impact of Head Start on children, families and communities. Final report of the Head Start Evaluation, Synthesis and Utilization Project* (Stock No. 017-092-00098-7). Washington, D.C.: U.S. Government Printing Office.

Mitchell, A. W. (1988). *The Public School Early Childhood Study: The Case Studies.* New York: Bank Street College.

Mitchell, A. W. (1988). *The Public School Early Childhood Study: The District Survey.* New York: Bank Street College.

Modigliani, K. (1988). Twelve reasons for the low wages in child care. *Young Children* 43 (3): 14–15.

Morado, C. (1985). *Prekindergarten programs for four-year-olds: State education agencies initiatives.* Ann Arbor, Mich.: University of Michigan.

Morgan, G. (1987). *The national state of child care regulation 1986.* Watertown, Mass.: Work/Family Directions.

National Academy of Early Childhood Programs (1985). *Guide to accreditation.* Washington, D.C.: National Association for the Education of Young Children.

National Association for the Education of Young Children (1986). *Good teaching practices for 4- and 5-year-olds.* Washington, D.C.: Author.

National Association of State Boards of Education (1988). *Right from the start.* The report of the NASBE Task Force on Early Childhood Education. Alexandria, Va.: Author.

National Center for Education Statistics (1986). Preschool enrollment: Trends and implications. Report reprinted from *The condition of education* (065-000-00276-1). Washington, D.C.: U.S. Government Printing Office, Department of Education.

National Center for Education Statistics (1987). *Condition of education.* Washington, D.C.: U.S. Government Printing Office, Department of Education.

National Education Association (1969). *Kindergarten education in public schools, 1967–68* (Research report 1969-R6). Washington, D.C.: Author.

National Governors' Association (1986). *Focus on the first sixty months: Proceedings of the National Early Childhood Conference* (No. 3058). Washington, D.C.: Author.

National Governors' Association (1986). Report of the Task Force on Readiness. *Time for results: The Governors' 1991 Report on Education* (No. 3049). Washington, D.C.: Author.

Phillips, D. A. (Ed.) (1987). *Quality in child care: What does research tell us?* Washington, D.C.: National Association for the Education of Young Children.

Phillips, D. A., and C. Howe (1987). Indicators of quality child care: Review of research. In D. A. Phillips (Ed.), *Quality in child care: What does research tell us?* Washington, D.C.: National Association for the Education of Young Children.

Porter, T. (1988). *Lives on hold.* New York: Child Care, Inc.

Quality Education Data (1985). *QED education mailing lists 1985–86.* Denver, Colo.: Author.

Rauth, M. (1976). *A long road to an unresolved problem: Comprehensive child care in the U.S.* Washington, D.C.: American Federation of Teachers.

Ruopp, R., W. L. Bache, C. O'Neil, and J. Singer (1979). *Children at the center: Final results of the National Day Care Study.* Cambridge, Mass.: Abt Associates.

Schorr, L. B. (1988). *Within our reach.* New York: Doubleday.

Schweinhart, L. J. (1987). When the buck stops here: What it takes to run a good early childhood program. *High/Scope Resources* 1: 9–13.

Select Committee on Children, Youth, and Families (1987). *U.S. children and their families: Current conditions and recent trends*. Washington, D.C.: U.S. Government Printing Office.

Shapiro, M. S. (1983). *Child's garden: The kindergarten movement from Froebel to Dewey*. University Park, Pa.: The Pennsylvania State University Press.

Shepard, L. A., and M. L. Smith (1980). Synthesis of research on school readiness and kindergarten retention. *Education Leadership* 44 (3): 78–86.

Spodek, B. (1982). The kindergarten: A retrospective and contemporary view. In L. G. Katz (Ed.), *Current topics in early childhood education* (Vol 1, pp. 173–191). Norwood, N.J.: Ablex Publishing Corporation.

Stallings, J. A. (1977). *Learning to look: A handbook on classroom observation and teaching models*. Belmont, Calif.: Wadsworth.

Stern, J. D. and M. O. Chandler (Eds.) (1988). *The condition of education: Elementary and secondary education* (vol. 1, CS 88-623). Washington, D.C.: U.S. Government Printing Office, U.S. Department of Education, National Center for Education Statistics.

Stern, J. D., and M. O. Chandler (Eds.), (September 1988). *1988 Education Indicators* (CS88–624). Washington, D.C.: U.S. Government Printing Office, U.S. Department of Education, National Center for Education Statistics.

Steinfels, M. O. (1973). *Who's minding the children? The history and politics of day care in America*. New York: Simon and Schuster.

U.S. Bureau of the Census (1985). *Current population survey: School enrollment supplement*. Washington, D.C.: U.S. Government Printing Office.

U.S. Bureau of the Census (1987). *Who's minding the kids?: Child care arrangements, winter 1984–1985* (Series P-70, No. 9). Washington, D.C.: U.S. Government Printing Office.

U.S. Bureau of the Census (1988). *State population and household estimates with age, sex, and components of change: 1981–87* (Series P-25, No. 1024). Washington, D.C.: U.S. Government Printing Office.

U.S. Department of Education (1985). *Common core of data survey*. Washington, D.C.: U.S. Government Printing Office.

U.S. Department of Labor, Bureau of Labor Statistics (August 1988). *Labor force statistics derived from current population survey, 1948–1987*. Bulletin No. 2307. Washington, D.C.: U.S. Government Printing Office.

U.S. Office of Educational Research and Improvement (1987). *Public elementary & secondary school membership, graduates, and staff by state: School year 1987–88. Final tabulations* (DR-CCD-87/88-5.1p). Washington, D.C.: U.S. Department of Education.

U.S. Office of Special Education and Rehabilitative Services (1979–present). *Annual report to Congress on the implementation of the Education of the Handicapped Act*. Washington, D.C.: U.S. Department of Education, Office of Special Education.

The University of the State of New York (1982). *Final report: Evaluation of the New York State experimental prekindergarten program*. Albany, N.Y.: The University of the State of New York, The State Education Department, Division of ESC Education Planning and Development.

Washington's Lesson for Washington (editorial on financing universal health insurance coverage). *The New York Times*, January 7, 1989.

Weikart, D. P., Rogers, L. Adcock, C., and McClelland, D. (1971). *The cognitively oriented curriculum*. Washington, D.C.: ERIC-National Association for the Education of Young Children.

Weiss, H. (1987). Family support and education in early childhood programs. In S. L. Kagan, D. R. Powell, B. Weissbourd, and E. F. Zigler (Eds.), *America's family support programs*. New Haven: Yale University Press.

Westat, Inc. (1987). *Private schools and private school teachers: Final report of the 1985–86 Private School Study*. Washington, D.C.: U.S. Department of Education, Office of Educational Research & Improvement.

Wilson, M. (1984). *List briefs*. Los Angeles: Mike Wilson List Counsel, Inc.

Wilson, M. (1988). *A strategic overview of the early childhood market*. Los Angeles: Mike Wilson List Counsel, Inc.

INDEX